Advanced Ethernet/802.3 Network Management and Performance, Second Edition

Advanced Ethernet/802.3 Network Management and Performance, Second Edition

Bill Hancock

Digital Press
Boston Oxford Melbourne Singapore Toronto Munich New Delhi Tokyo

Digital Press™ is an imprint of Butterworth-Heinemann.
 A member of the Reed Elsevier group

Recognizing the importance of preserving what has been written, Butterworth-Heinemann prints its books on acid-free paper whenever possible.

Trademarked products mentioned in this book are listed on page 298.

Library of Congress Cataloging-in-Publication Data
Hancock, Bill, 1957–
    Advanced Ethernet/802.3 network management & performance / by Bill Hancock. — 2nd ed.
              p.   cm.
    Includes index.
    ISBN 1-55558-144-7 (pbk : alk. paper)
    1. Ethernet (Local area network system) I. Title.
TK5105.8.E83H26 1995
004.6'8—dc20   95-19761
                                                                          CIP

British Library Cataloguing-in-Publication Data
A catalogue record for this book is available from the British Library.

The publisher offers discounts on bulk orders of this book.
For information, please write:

Manager of Special Sales, Digital Press
Butterworth-Heinemann
313 Washington Street
Newton, MA 02158-1626

Order number: EY-T140E-DP

10 9 8 7 6 5 4 3 2 1

Printed in the United States of America

Contents

---

7 Switching Bridges   115

---

8 Using Protocol Analyzers   127

---

9 Understanding SQE/Heartbeat   137

Preface

This book consolidates in one volume the discussion of common, practical Ethernet/802.3 network management and performance issues that most sites will face at one time or another. It is not intended to be the ultimate compendium of network management and performance. It is, however, intended to point out the problems in managing a network and in providing adequate performance and response to users on the network. This book is suitable for those readers who are already somewhat familiar with the technologies and terminology associated with Ethernet/802.3 LANs and their components.

Although other books offer more technical details and different theories on Ethernet/802.3 network management and performance, few books are as comprehensive as this one. This book is an extension of my first book on Ethernet/802.3 networks, *Designing and Implementing Ethernet Networks,* and is not intended to cover common ground. Instead, I offer additional help in configuring, managing, and controlling Ethernet/802.3 networks for those users who have already installed them.

I hope you find this book enjoyable and useful. Drop me a line sometime at Network-1 and let me know how I can improve the next edition.

Acknowledgments

No book is possible without the help and ideas of a great many people.

To start with, there is my partner and friend Robert Russo. Bob, though he claims not to be what he calls a "technical weenie," understands computer and network management and performance much better than any other executive I know. He is a valuable asset to our company, an insightful and articulate executive, a gifted business and marketing manager, and a good friend. He has even become a Macintosh convert, so there is hope for him yet! Without Bob, this book would not be here.

Technical expertise, of course, is important. I have my share, but my partners in technology at Network-1—Ken Conquest, Brett Dolecheck, and Thomas Nelson—have spent many an hour discussing this book, its contents, and its examples and ruthlessly correcting typos, misspellings, grammatical errors, and in general anything that needed fixing. As the implementers of my bizarre notions on network products and as network experts themselves, they have provided inestimable ideas and comments. They are valuable assets in technology and good friends to work with—even if they do beat me in racquetball (although, truth is, I let them).

Bill Hancock
Hancock@Network-1.com

Advanced Ethernet/802.3 Network Management and Performance, Second Edition

The General Theory of Ethernet/802.3 Operation

By learning the general rules of configuration presented in this chapter, you will come to understand some of the problems and performance issues that arise as a network is populated. But before you can fully appreciate Ethernet/802.3, you need to learn a little about the history of Ethernet itself.

The History of Ethernet

Ethernet is a local area network (LAN), bus-oriented technology used to connect computers, printers, terminal concentrators (or servers), and many other devices. (See Figure 1.1.) Ethernet itself is a hardware technology consisting of a network medium—either cable or wireless—and connectors at each networked machine. Such an arrangement allows devices to "converse" with one another. Additionally, software that can access the Ethernet and cooperate with networked machines is necessary.

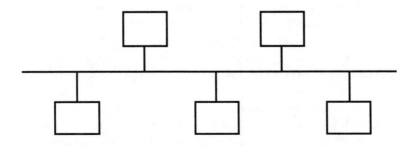

Figure 1.1
A Simple Bus-Oriented Ethernet/802.3 Configuration

Ethernet arose from a network developed at the University of Hawaii in the early 1970s. Called ALOHA, the network originally connected the main campus site on the island of Oahu to seven other campuses located on four Hawaiian islands. ALOHA was originally a ground radio-based terminal network; it worked very much like remote radio stations communicating to a central station. What made ALOHA revolutionary and, therefore, the "parent" of Ethernet was the way that stations transmitted data on the network and, because of the mechanism involved, its simple implementation and cost-effectiveness.

Norman Abramson, a professor at the University of Hawaii, published a series of papers (1969, 1970, 1973, 1977) on the theory and applications of ALOHA. His work demonstrated a mechanism by which multiple stations on a network could use the same channel for multiple-node communications. By using a technique called contention, nodes would transmit data to the central facility on Oahu whenever they had data to send. If the frequency was not busy, the central hub node would accept the transmission and send an acknowledgment (ACK) to the remote node. If the remote node did not receive an acknowledgment within a certain amount of time (200 to 1500 milliseconds), it would assume that its packet had collided with another and would automatically resend the data. Through this mechanism, multiple nodes could communicate over the exact same frequencies simply and expeditiously.

Some of the ramifications of such a setup are obvious. If there is no way for one station to detect another station's transmission, then there will likely be a good many collisions requiring retransmission. Another issue is the quality of the signal: radio signals are notoriously subject to interference from, among other things, weather, electrical fields, and other signals. Also, the more data to be sent and the more nodes trying to use one channel at the same time, the more retransmissions will occur, which can cause additional throughput delays.

Based on various tests of channel utilization vs. total resource availability, "pure" ALOHA effectively uses approximately 18% of the available resources. While this figure may seem inordinately inefficient, keep in mind that ALOHA allows any station to send at any time: if there is only one station transmitting at one time, 100% of the resources is used. This figure illustrates the main problem with contention networks: the more data and nodes on the network contending for a resource, the more variable is the performance of the entire network.

In 1972 ALOHA was enhanced to provide some synchronization of access (called "slotted ALOHA"), which increased the effective usage of the channel resource to about 37%, although the network was still plagued with collisions more than 26% of the time. Over time, ALOHA has changed dramatically and has served as a model for packet broadcast systems as it has expanded to satellite technology as well as LANs.

But what do packet radio broadcasts have to do with Ethernet? Quite a lot. Ethernet derives its basic functionality—contention—from ALOHA and shows how valuable one good idea can be.

The Xerox Connection

The concept of Ethernet was originally developed at the now famous Xerox Palo Alto Research Center (PARC) as a way to connect office devices in a network that would allow high-speed data transfer. The definitive paper on Ethernet was published in 1976 by R. M. Metcalf (now of 3COM fame) and D. R. Boggs. The original implementation of Ethernet functioned at 3 megabits per second (Mbps) and allowed 100 connections. Additionally, the network could use more than one device on the same cable transmission medium and could allow all devices on the cable to "contend" for the cable resource on a first-come, first-served basis.

Where Ethernet differs greatly from ALOHA is in collision detection. ALOHA allows any station to transmit at any time; Ethernet does not. An Ethernet station first "listens" to the network to see if it is free. If it is, the station can send. If the cable is busy—that is, if the station hears a transmission—the station waits and then tries again. If two stations happen to transmit at the same time, a collision occurs and both stations back off, wait a random amount of time, and try again. Because traffic arrival and retransmissions take place so randomly, tests have shown that Ethernets, under a full load, can utilize effectively 90 to 95% of available resources.

Following the initial testing of the Xerox 3-Mbps Ethernet, performance analysis was done to assess the viability of such a network in the office environment. Statistics on an Ethernet showed an interesting distribution of resource utilization that is unlike that of other types of networks. First, one must look at *when* data arrives. In a 24-hour period, data doesn't flow evenly, it arrives in spurts. Look at any business and you will see why. People do not work 24 hours a day, computers are not used continuously, and data transfers do not happen regularly. So, statistics on Ethernet performance have to be viewed with a calibrated eye.

Because the nature of most office traffic is "bursty," it is logical to assume that the Ethernet/802.3 network will also be bursty. With this in mind, consider studies which have shown that over a 24-hour period, the average load on test Ethernets (the 3-Mbps kind) was usually less than 1%. If loading factors were considered at the worst times of the day, the following statistics on a 100-node, 3-Mbps Ethernet surfaced:

Worst second of the day:	40% saturation of the cable
Worst minute of the day:	15–20% saturation of the cable
Worst hour of the day:	3–5% saturation of the cable

Ethernet performance is based directly on the arrival time of data and the amount of data being sent. Obviously, the nature of the data is relevant as well. File transfers, especially large ones, can tie up the resource and cause other file transfers to contend with one another. Lots of short, bursty traffic (such as control messages) causes a different kind of contention pattern to emerge. If very few nodes are communicating, fairly reasonable speeds can be expected and delivered. In short, the number of nodes, the amount of traffic, and the interarrival time distribution all factor into Ethernet performance.

Over time, Xerox developed the Ethernet technology into a viable LAN technology that began to provide the promised connectivity necessary to solve office networking problems. With a new network technology also came the need for new software to control the technology, so protocols such as the Xerox Network Services (XNS) protocol were developed to provide enhanced connectivity services beyond Ethernet's basic data transmission.

Ethernet's Limitations

Ethernet is not without shortcomings. Because of its contentious nature, Ethernet's creators had to make finite the number of nodes (or systems) to ensure that the resource would not be saturated. The creators imposed a minimum packet size (64 bytes) and a maximum cable-segment length, so that Ethernet stations could accurately detect collisions on the network. Ethernet's developers also set a maximum packet size, which allowed stations to know when a packet transmission should be complete, thereby helping detect errors on the network. Further, the Ethernet concept does not allow networks to guarantee data delivery: data delivered to a remote site is not subject to sequence checks (making sure the packets arrive in the right order), missing-packet retransmission requests, and other such necessities. To compensate for these shortcomings, on-system software (or hardware) facilities that cooperate with other nodes on a network are necessary.

Cable Issues

Different lengths and types of cable are allowed in the Ethernet V2.0 standard. The first, thickwire (RG-8) cable, is a large-diameter cable (0.365 to 0.395 inch in diameter) that may be configured in lengths of 23.4, 70.2, 117, or 500 meters (or combinations thereof). Cable length affects many network characteristics, such as harmonics, waveform alignment, noise, and electrical propagation time (for example, a 23.4-meter cable has a 0-microsecond (μs) delay, while a 500-meter cable has a 10-microsecond delay). Up to 100 connections (or taps) may be added to a 500-meter thickwire.

The second type of Ethernet V2.0 cable is called thinwire (RG-58A/U) or "cheapernet," due to the cable's low cost. Thinwire cable may be up to 185 meters long and may connect up to 30 BNC T-connections at its greatest length. Figure 1.2 shows one type of connector used with thinwire. Thinwire is less immune from noise and interference than thickwire, but it is still more than adequate for most networks in offices and in environments subject to low-to-moderate radio frequency and electromagnetic interference (RFI and EMI). Thinwire is especially useful for networking in laboratories and light industrial environments where RFI/EMI may be a problem.

IEEE 802.3, which is a different standard from Ethernet V2.0, has the same basic configuration requirements for thickwire (10BASE5) and thinwire (10BASE2), although the thickwire diameter in 802.3 is 0.405 inch. Additionally, however, 802.3 allows the use of a 1-Mbps version of thinwire (1BASE2) and unshielded twisted-pair (UTP) cable as a suitable medium for CSMA/CD access. UTP (10BASET) allows one connection at one end of the UTP run and a connection to a twisted-pair concentrator (repeater) unit at the other end. (Figure 1.3 shows one type of twisted-pair connector.) UTP concentrators allow various numbers of connections, depending on the vendor (the average is 12 UTP connections and one 15-pin connection to the backbone cable). Runs of UTP cable from the connection point to the concentrator cannot exceed 100 meters due to problems such as noise, jitter, distortion, and near-end crosstalk. Figure 1.4 is an example of a 10BASET topology.

A recently completed standard is 10BASEF, which allows the use of a fiber optic cable itself as the 802.3 transmission medium. The new section of the 802.3 standard provides for fiber optic cable *connections* between 802.3 networks and fiber as the network itself.

While not a participant in either the Ethernet V2.0 or the 802.3 series of standards, Motorola has developed and is marketing a wireless microwave

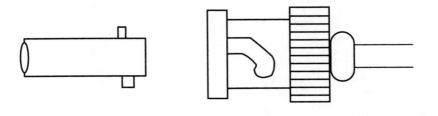

Figure 1.2
Thinwire BNC Connectors

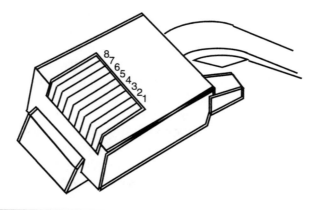

Figure 1.3
A Twisted-Pair RJ-45 Connector

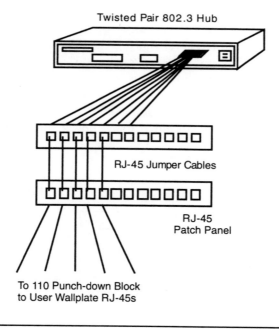

Figure 1.4
A Typical 10BASET Connection Topology

(omnidirectional) network called Altair. Altair replaces the traditional copper or fiber medium with a wireless microwave connection. Altair is currently more expensive than traditional cable plants, but it is also much more flexible, allowing connectivity in areas where cable may not be able to reach. One or more users can connect using a user connection device (or user module), which then connects to the network as a whole through a network control station (or control module) located within 120 feet of user relay devices. The control station is connected to other control devices or to a traditional copper cable. Figure 1.5 illustrates some of the basics of a wireless network.

Extending a network requires specialized hardware, such as bridges and repeaters, that can be costly and tricky to configure to stay within established guidelines. Figure 1.6 shows one bridge configuration. Ethernet, therefore, is a *local* area network, a network that is designed to provide communications inside a building or, possibly, across a campus. It was not designed to be used in a wide-area mode where leased lines and other types of connectivity (such as X.25 packet switching) have traditionally been used. Although many vendors do offer wide-area capabilities, traditional line speeds are substantially less than the maximum rate of performance typically seen on Ethernet/802.3 networks—with the exception of telecommunications speeds above T3 (about 44 Mbps).

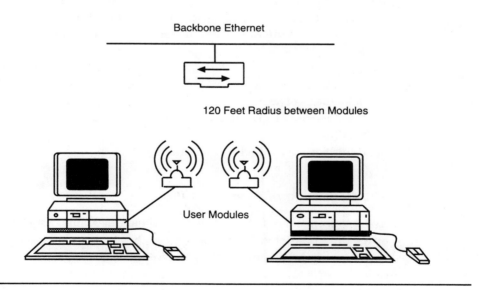

Figure 1.5
A Wireless Ethernet/802.3 Configuration

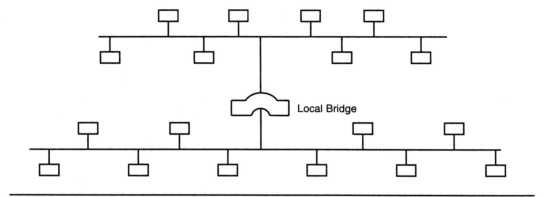

Figure 1.6
A Local Bridge Configuration

Vendor Consortiums

Like any good idea, Ethernet developed and spread. Unfortunately for Xerox, it has been one of the few companies not to profit heavily from Ethernet product offerings. Through a consortium organized in the early 1980s, Xerox, Intel, and Digital Equipment Corporation (DEC) published a vendor standard now known as the Ethernet Blue Book ("The Ethernet, Version 2.0," November 1982). This book prescribed the methods in which Ethernets would be developed and implemented, and how the Ethernet hardware and data-link services would work.

This consortium is particularly interesting in that it paired Xerox and Digital, companies that in many ways are competitive in the office environment. Through the pool of multicompany talent, however, the basic 3-Mbps Ethernet has been expanded, greatly, to the 10-Mbps version—and will soon appear in a 100-Mbps version—and many of the restrictions on the original Ethernet standards have been modified or enhanced.

The Beginning of Standardization

As the concept of LANs developed, many standardization organizations jumped on the proverbial bandwagon. Some began to organize standards for other types of network technologies that would serve the needs of various business applications. LANs for offices, factories, process-control environments, and many other applications began to appear. Such networks consisted of modified Ethernet concepts, token rings, token buses, twisted-pair wire, fiber optic cable, and many other techniques and technologies. At the time such LANs were being proposed and explored, there was no overwhelming demand from potential customers for such connectivity, so many networks and ideas simply faded away.

IEEE Committee 802.3

Through it all, however, a select number of types of LANs became popular for various applications. One standardization authority, the Institute of Electrical and Electronics Engineers (IEEE), formed a committee in February 1980 to promote and provide LAN standards for use by industry (particularly office environments, initially). Called IEEE Project 802 (vendors usually call it Committee 802), the committee was charged with providing LAN-oriented standards for consumers as well as related standards that would allow inter-connectivity between different Committee 802 standards. (The *802* is derived from the year 1980 and the month of February (2)).

IEEE Committee 802 generally develops standards that conform to the bottom three layers of the Open Systems Interconnection (OSI) model developed by the International Organization for Standardization (ISO) in 1978. The OSI model provided an architectural blueprint by which networks would be developed that would allow flexible enhancement and reconfiguration as well as interconnectivity with other compatible OSI-oriented networks. In the OSI model, layer 1 (the physical layer) and layer 2 (the data-link layer) are typically defined by the network technology being used. Ethernet, for example, since it is predominantly hardware, fulfills layers 1 and 2 of the OSI model quite nicely. Because the consortium of Xerox, Intel, and Digital had produced Ethernet but not an acceptable domestic or international standard for the LAN technology, the IEEE formed Subcommittee 802.3 and produced an IEEE standard for a technology very similar to the Ethernet specification. Due to the IEEE's influence over domestic (U.S.) and international standardization authorities, IEEE standard 802.3 eventually became an ISO standard (IS 8802/3). Technological details from Ethernet V2.0 (the Xerox/Intel/Digital standard) were used as a basis for the IEEE 802.3 standard, but the IEEE standard introduced some fairly serious technical differences that make the two standards somewhat incompatible. (Technically, 802.3 is *not* Ethernet, but most people call it Ethernet nonetheless.)

First, the physical characteristics of the prescribed cables are different. The Ethernet V2.0 standard calls for 50-ohm coaxial cable that is 0.375 or 0.395 inch in diameter (depending on whether the cable is PVC or Teflon). The IEEE specification retained 50-ohm cable, but increased the diameter 0.405 inch. On the surface, such a difference seems trivial. But the IEEE felt that the change was necessary for improving the electrical characteristics of the cable. Unfortunately, the difference means that transceivers (the devices that attach to the Ethernet cable) must have a conductive spine that is long enough to reach the center conductor on the 0.405-inch diameter cable. Since the Ethernet transceiver was designed to have a spine long enough to connect to the center conductor of the smaller-diameter coaxial cable, the spines of V2.0-compliant transceivers would be too short to reach the center conductor and make contact. In short, a V2.0 transceiver would, technically, be incompatible with an IEEE 802.3-compliant cable. In reality, many vendors have provided a workaround by supplying upper transceiver assemblies that can connect to both V2.0 cables and 802.3 cables.

Cable diameter is not the only difference between 802.3 and V2.0. When transceivers are connected to a cable, usually the only way to tell if the transceiver is working is to transmit data to the network. In the V2.0 specification, after each packet transmission from a system, the transceiver generates a signal known as signal quality error (SQE), which is read by the controller on the host system so that the controller knows that the transceiver is, at least, alive. Over the years, this SQE has become known as the transceiver "heartbeat." However, 802.3-compliant transceivers do not necessarily generate an SQE signal unless a real signal quality error has occurred on the connected medium. So if a V2.0-compliant controller is mated with a transceiver that is IEEE 802.3 compliant, the controller will think that the transceiver is dead. Again, many vendors have adapted to the problem by enabling most transceivers to be switch-selectable between 802.3 and V2.0: the installer sets either jumpers (wires) or a DIP switch in the transceiver. But since not all vendors have done so, you should be careful in your choice of transceiver for a particular controller.

In the case of 802.3-compliant controllers, the need for SQE as a heartbeat is common. Therefore, a V2.0 transceiver will usually work with most 802.3 controllers that plug into host computers. But in 802.3-compliant bridges and repeaters, the SQE as an actual error becomes a problem. V2.0-compliant bridges and repeaters connected to a network segment expect SQE as a heartbeat, but 802.3-compliant bridges and repeaters expect SQE to be an actual error. So 802.3-compliant bridges and repeaters must be used with transceivers that use SQE as an actual error signal. Again, exercise care when selecting and purchasing transceivers, making sure that your choice is compatible with the proper bridges and repeaters.

A Comparison of Ethernet V2.0 and 802.3 Frame Formats

A more important difference between the two standards is the issue of packet format. On Ethernet V2.0 networks, controllers generate a packet format as shown in Figure 1.7.

The General Theory of Ethernet/802.3 Operation

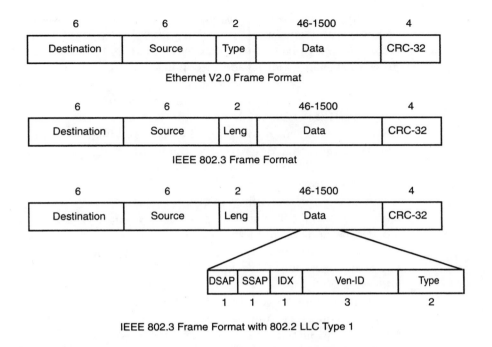

6	6	2	46-1500	4
Destination	Source	Type	Data	CRC-32

Ethernet V2.0 Frame Format

6	6	2	46-1500	4
Destination	Source	Leng	Data	CRC-32

IEEE 802.3 Frame Format

6	6	2	46-1500	4
Destination	Source	Leng	Data	CRC-32

DSAP	SSAP	IDX	Ven-ID	Type
1	1	1	3	2

IEEE 802.3 Frame Format with 802.2 LLC Type 1

Figure 1.7
A Comparison of Ethernet/802.3 Frame Formats

Prior to the destination address (48 bits), a 56-bit preamble and 8-bit start frame delimiter (SFD) are transmitted. The preamble's function in life is to allow the physical layer signaling (PLS) circuitry the opportunity to reach its steady state. The start frame delimiter is a bit sequence 10101011 that immediately follows the preamble and indicates that the frame (packet) being transmitted on the Ethernet is valid.

Destination is the 48-bit Ethernet destination address that is usually encoded in ROM on each and every controller on an Ethernet. In reality, all 48 bits cannot be used for a particular node. The 48-bit field is actually broken down into three elements of bits that, together, make up the 48-bit address. The first element is called the least significant bit (LSB) and will be set to either 0 if the address is an individual node address (singlecast message) or 1 if it is a group address (multicast or broadcast message). A group address is used on an Ethernet when a node wishes to send a message to more than one destination at a time. The individual nodes decide who is a member of a particular group: no one node tells other nodes what group they will be in. Each node must know its group independently. The second element of the destination consists of a second bit in the 48-bit address set to either 1 for a locally administered address or 0 for a globally administered address (UPC). Locally administered addresses designate Ethernet addresses that are set up and identified by the local network control facility or personnel.

Globally defined addresses are assigned by the current Ethernet address custodian, the IEEE. Global Ethernet addresses (UPCs) are assigned on a group basis to vendors who manufacture Ethernet products that will work on networks with more than one type of vendor hardware; UPCs are also assigned for situations where the vendor of the hardware/software does not know what kind of Ethernet environment its products will end up in. The final element of the destination is the remaining 46 bits, which are assigned on a node-by-node basis by the vendor of the product being used. These 46 bits usually designate a particular node or multicast address.

To help identify node addresses seen on the networks, Appendix B of this book contains a collection of known vendor address assignments for controller addresses.

Ethernet addresses are usually installed in ROM by the manufacturer of the Ethernet controller and are usually represented in hexadecimal in a 6-byte format, such as 08-00-A0-01-FA-03. The source address is the sending machine's 48-bit address. The type field is unique to V2.0 and stands for protocol type. Ethernet V2.0 allows multiple protocols to exist on an Ethernet at the same time. To facilitate the differentiation of protocols, Xerox, which functions as the custodian of protocol types, prescribes the usage of the TYPE field for packets of certain protocols. The data field is the section of the Ethernet packet that would carry the data being transferred from one machine to another (usually some higher-level protocol such as DECnet, local area transport (LAT), Xerox Network Services, Transmission Control Protocol/Internet Protocol (TCP/IP) or some other such protocol). A cyclic redundancy check (CRC) is performed on the packet contents to ensure that when the data gets to the destination node, all the data captured is correct.

A CRC-32 is computed as follows:

1. The destination, source, length/type, and data section are used to generate a number for function operations as follows:

$$G(x) = x32 + x26 + x23 + x22 + x16 + x12 + x11 + x10 + x8 + x7 + x5 + x4 + x2 + x1$$

2. The first 32 bits of the frame are complemented.
3. The n bits of the frame are then considered to be coefficients of a polynomial $M(x)$ of degree $n - 1$. The first bit of the destination field corre-

sponds to the $x(n-1)$ term, and the last bit of the data field corresponds to the $x0$ term.

4. $M(x)$ is multiplied by $x32$ and divided by $G(x)$, producing a remainder $R(x)$ of degree less than 31.
5. The coefficients of $R(x)$ are considered to be a 32-bit sequence.
6. The bit sequence is complemented, and the result is the CRC.

By using a 32-bit CRC check, the chances of bad data being received and not detected are about 4.3 billion (2^{32-1}) to 1. This number is important, as the error factor allowed indicates network reliability. When a packet is delivered, Ethernet provides a very reliable platform for LAN access.

In the case of IEEE 802.3, the packet format is slightly different. It is quite obvious that the TYPE field seen in the V2.0 specification is missing in the IEEE 802.3 specification. Without the type field, compatibility cannot be maintained among the two standards; there is no workaround. In fact, the same bit locations used for the type field in the V2.0 specification are used in 802.3 for a field that contains the length of the data.

Another anomaly is the option of using 48-bit or 16-bit node addresses in the IEEE specification. Because of this particular difference, when the 16-bit addressing scheme is employed, only 802.3-compliant nodes may communicate with one another. Another problem is the inclusion of IEEE 802.2 Logical Link Control (LLC) information in the beginning of the data section on 802.3 frames. LLC information allows the remote (destination) node to know what entity on the source node sent the packet. It also allows identification of the type of 802.3 frame, as there are different types (in accordance with IEEE 802.2).

Still a third format for the packet is a specialized one used for control messages, as provided for in the 802.2 network management specification and supported by vendors who offer the capability of producing Class I (control) packet types. The previously described 802.3 packet type is also known as a Class II packet, or user-defined packet.

Ethernet V2.0 and IEEE 802.3 are different enough as to be incompatible. Describing how such an incompatibility arose from political and technical disagreements is best left to historians and industry analysts. Let it suffice to say that you *must* be cautious when considering Ethernet V2.0 or IEEE 802.3. If your company is considering Ethernet, make sure that all cooperating nodes "speak" either V2.0 format or 802.3 format. Most vendors have developed controllers that understand both formats, but you must select them carefully.

Most vendors tend to support IEEE 802.3 rather than Ethernet V2.0, and for a fairly straightforward reason. With the impending implementation of a complete OSI-compliant network (with OSI-prescribed protocols at each layer of the architecture), it is important for vendors developing OSI-compliant networks to adhere to ISO standards. Since IEEE 802.3 is an ISO standard—as well as being prescribed for access at layers 1 and 2 of the OSI model—if a vendor wants to get the most mileage from its development effort, it should develop software and hardware around 802.3. There is nothing intrinsically wrong with the V2.0 standard, other than its being only a vendor standard and not complying with the prescribed ISO standard for the Ethernet-like network. For the future, all paths will inevitably converge on the 802.3 implementation.

The easiest way to express the functionality of Ethernet/802.3 is as a data "truck." Nodes wishing to communicate on the network allocate the truck, put their data in its trailer section and send it out. The truck delivers the data to the remote station but does not interpret, in any way, the contents of the trailer. The end effect is that data is moved around very quickly with minimal overhead, fast access, and a fairly efficient protocol.

A Technical Description of Ethernet Components

Ethernet, as previously described, is a local area network technology that is used to connect various computers or "smart" devices, typically (but not exclusively) in an office environment. Ethernets come in various "flavors," such as baseband or broadband, and may run on a variety of media, such as coax, twisted pair, and fiber.

An Ethernet is configured in a "bus" topology, consisting of a backbone (main) cable to which communicating systems and peripherals are attached (or "tapped"). Taps may be intrusive, in which the cable is cut to add the tap; or taps may be nonintrusive, in which the cable is drilled and a tap is added without disturbing the integrity or operation of the network. By definition, a baseband Ethernet (the most common) is tapped nonintrusively, and broadband Ethernets usually require intrusive taps for connecting nodes. Ethernets allow only 100 taps per master segment of 500-meter thickwire coaxial cable. This limitation also implies that if the cable is shorter, proportionately fewer taps are allowed.

Baseband Ethernet uses the entire cable for Ethernet communications. For simpler installation, management, and configuration, most customers should use *only* baseband. Also, baseband is more cost-effective per node than broadband.

In baseband, if a coaxial cable had a bandwidth of, say, 500 megahertz (MHz), the entire 500 MHz would be reserved for Ethernet traffic, even though Ethernet/802.3 requires considerably less than 500 MHz. A baseband Ethernet is terminated at both ends with 50-ohm terminators and is grounded *on one end only* to earth or building ground, depending on the ground potential hazard. (To prevent shock hazard, always have a licensed master electrician ground the cable: although the voltage level is not high, the number of amps can be high.)

Some locations have a serious problem with cable grounding between various facilities. Tests by qualified electricians and ground study specialists have found ground potential between buildings that has exceeded 20 amps! In such cases, workers connecting coaxial cable—especially cable that must be grounded, such as Ethernet cable—must take additional precautions so that the cable is not grounded improperly or between buildings. As such, any Ethernet connection between buildings must be done via fiber optic relay to preclude electrical hazard.

Moreover, the National Electrical Code (NEC) now requires special handling of cables that are used to provide network connectivity. For details, check with a local electrician and check the appropriate sections of the NEC.

Another feature of baseband, as mentioned, is that it allows nonintrusive tapping. Thickwire coaxial cable is typically premarked with a black ring every 2.5 meters for placement of taps. (Thinwire cable (RG-58), which is tapped at minimum intervals of 0.5 meters, is usually not marked.)

Baseband Ethernet can run on various types of media, each of which limits node proximity and total cable distances for a segment. Thickwire coax must be shorter than 500 meters, whereas thinwire coax (RG-58A/U, or R/U) can range from 185 to 1000 meters, depending on the vendor of the transceivers and the network controllers. Twisted-pair Ethernets (the 10-Mbps types) run from 20 to 100 meters, and fiber optic Ethernets run from 30 to 5000 meters. The various length restrictions have to do with specific media propagation delays and noise factors on each type of cable, plus logic restrictions in the controllers and transceivers.

While all types of media use the baseband method of transmitting data on the cable, not all cables can be directly connected to one another. A barrel connector cannot be used to connect a fiber to a thinwire; rather, a special type of repeater must be used. In some situations, however, thinwire can be connected via barrel connector to a thickwire baseband Ethernet, but the length restrictions on the overall segment vary depending on how much of the cable is thickwire and how much is thinwire. If you are considering such a hybrid of cables, use the following formula to calculate the total cable length:

$$(3.28 \times \text{Thinwire Length}) + \text{Thickwire Length} < 500 \text{ meters}$$

For example, if the thinwire section is 100 meters and the thickwire 50 meters, the total length of the cable, physically, would be 150 meters. However, electrically the cable would appear as a 378-meter Ethernet. So, thinwire can be connected to thickwire, but you must compensate for the differences in signal strength (thinwire has a higher signal-loss problem) and noise factors.

If baseband segments of different media are connected, a repeater or bridge is usually recommended.

Tapping a cable is obviously not sufficient to allow communications: an electrical interface of some kind is required. In the case of Ethernet, such an interface is called a transceiver. Transceivers come in many shapes and sizes (as well as price ranges), but they all perform one basic function: they allow a system to communicate with the cable.

A transceiver is so named because it transmits and receives simultaneously. When a system is sending information to the Ethernet cable, the transceiver's transmitting circuitry sends the bits of data while the transceiver's receiving circuitry listens to the transmitted data. If the transceiver detects that the data being sent by the transmitting side of the transceiver is the same as that being received by the receiver side, all is well. If, however, the two sides do not match, the transceiver presumes that a collision has happened and notifies the controller card on the host system. A transceiver is fairly dumb: it simply sends data, receives data, and notifies the host controller when a collision occurs.

Some vendors, such as Digital Equipment Corporation, have developed specialized boxes that allow more than one system to connect to a single transceiver tap. The Digital Ethernet Local Network Interconnect (DELNI) box allows up to eight systems to connect to the box, and a single Ethernet transceiver taps the eight systems onto the main Ethernet cable. (Other vendors make DELNI-like boxes, so the DEC box is by no means unique.) A by-product of the DELNI is its ability to stand alone and emulate an eight-tap Ethernet cable. Where systems are no more than 50 meters away from the DELNI or when there are no more than eight collocated systems that need to be on an Ethernet, the DELNI is more cost-effective—not to mention more convenient—than a chunk of Ethernet cable and eight transceivers. On the downside, the DELNI has its own power supply, so if it fails, up to eight nodes may be unable to access the network (if a single-level DELNI is cascaded, the loss may be much greater).

If a transceiver compensator box, such as the DELNI, is connected to the Ethernet segment, the overall cable length may need to be examined. An eight-connection transceiver compensator is equivalent to 20 meters of cable with eight taps. Thus the backbone cable's total length may need to be reduced to compensate for the attached transceiver compensators. Check with the Ethernet component vendor to ensure that the network will still be compliant after connecting such compensators, especially on very long segments (those that approach the 500-meter length restriction).

From the thickwire transceiver, a 15-pin cable (also called an Attachment Unit Interface, or AUI, cable) is run to a cable mounting bracket (called the bulkhead assembly) in the back of a system or peripheral (see Figure 1.8). The AUI cable is aptly enough called the transceiver cable. Transceiver cables come

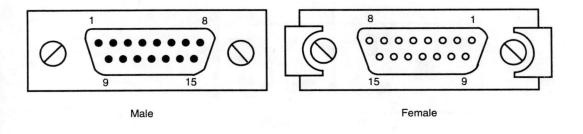

Male   Female

Figure 1.8
Attachment Unit Interface 15-Pin Connectors

in a variety of lengths, but more vendors limit transceiver cables to 50 meters; some require the transceiver cable to be somewhat shorter. The transceiver cable does more than provide the wiring for the data transfer and handshakes between the controller and the transceiver. Because the transceiver usually does not have a power supply of its own, the transceiver cable also has a wire (pin 13 of the connector) that supplies power from the host system controller to the transceiver.

A transceiver cable has to be carefully selected, as makers of different transceivers and controllers have different ways to connect the cable to the transceiver or to the system bulkhead assembly. Some vendors use a sliding-lock system as specified in the IEEE 802.3 specification; others opt for the traditional brass screws. While the sliding-lock connector is convenient, it is also easily disconnected from the cable. Installers should always use plastic tie-wraps or shrink tubing to ensure that the sliding connector will not become disconnected from either the transceiver or the system.

To connect the host system properly to the transceiver assembly, the host system needs a controller board or equivalent circuitry. Such controllers are usually add-on cards that system vendors provide for an additional cost (see Figure 1.9). Different systems have different connectivity requirements, so it is very important to get a controller that will match the system hardware and communicate properly with the host's networking software.

Controllers consist of at least three separate sets of functional components: the Ethernet interface circuitry; the on-board processor, microcode, and ROM/RAM; and a host system bus interface. The Ethernet interface circuitry is typically provided as one of the standard chip sets from Intel, AMD, or other manufacturers of chip subsystems. The processor, microcode, and ROM/RAM

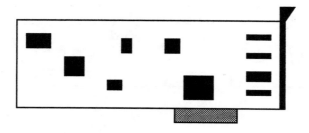

Figure 1.9
PC Network Controller Card

vary from vendor to vendor due to customers' different requirements and controllers' various functions.

Different Controllers, Different Capabilities

Different controllers from the same hardware vendor designed for the exact same host system may have different capabilities. Chip and controller speeds vary from less than 1.8-Mbps throughput to more than 9.1 Mbps. When selecting Ethernet controllers, consider the following:

- Will the controller support the selected software environment?
- Is the controller access speed well matched to the system capabilities?
- Is there a compatible transceiver for the controller?
- Does the controller have special host system requirements?
- Is the controller supported by the host system as a "native" controller?
- Are the levels of buffering in the controller adequate for the expected load factors?
- What are the controller's mean-time-between-failures (MTBF) and mean-time-to-repair (MTTR) factors?
- Does the controller support V2.0 or IEEE 802.3 or both?
- Is there host interface (drivers) software for the controller?
- Is the controller configurable by the customer?
- Is the controller programmable by the customer?
- Will the controller support a multiple-protocol environment?
- Will the controller experience problems if other Ethernet controllers are on the same system?

■ What software packages are available for the controller? Will they work concurrently on the controller and host system?

    Although technically not a part of an Ethernet, the host software is extremely important to Ethernet; in fact, any Ethernet is fairly worthless without it. As previously discussed, Ethernet is a "data mover." Just as the phone system carries voice but does not retransmit spoken words lost to static or failed connections, so Ethernet simply sends data on the network. If the packet arrives at the proper destination in one piece, great. If not, that's OK—there's plenty more where the last packet came from. The data that gets moved is whatever the host system decides to send or allows receipt of. In the case of Ethernet, the Ethernet packet protocol is fairly simple and well defined.

    On microcomputer systems, especially those that work with MS-DOS, one can usually select between a device driver for a particular protocol suite and a more generic driver that will work with multiple protocol suites. The protocol-specific driver, typically called a Data Link Library (DLL) driver, functions better with specific protocol suites that the driver was designed to work with. Generic drivers that adhere to the Microsoft specification, called the Network Driver Interface Specification (NDIS), or the Novell standard, called the Open Datalink Interface (ODI), tend to be somewhat larger and, in many cases, slightly faster, than the DLL drivers. On the negative side, all of a package's features may not work with the NDIS driver, while the DLL driver may provide full package functionality.

    In a recent test of controllers and associated drivers on a live Ethernet network, the device driver was shown to have a profound impact on network performance as well as controller reliability. In tests conducted on eight different controllers using different device drivers, not only did the same card exhibit different performance metrics with different drivers, but also, when the network load increased to 20 to 30%, many DLL drivers caused the microcomputer systems to hang or crash. Moral: The combination of device driver and device cannot be too carefully examined or too carefully tested and configured.

    How the host gets to the network is defined by the controller and associated interface software. Typically, a company would select a particular network architecture or technology approach that satisfies a specific requirement or group of requirements. This network technology would usually provide the connectivity required by utilizing a protocol or series of protocols over the Ethernet (the protocols used would be encapsulated in the data segment of the Ethernet packet). It is up to the host software to sort out the destination for various protocols used over an Ethernet: the Ethernet definition does not provide for any such screening or assistance. Since not all host software packages are capable of accepting multiple protocols or multiple types of Ethernet controllers, select and use protocols on the Ethernet carefully.

Host software packages range from terminal services packages to full-function network packages (program-to-program, file transfer, remote file access, virtual terminal support, and so on). In all cases, many packages expect to use either a particular Ethernet controller type or a class of Ethernet controllers on particular machine architectures. Some stand-alone, dedicated systems (such as terminal server systems) use a particular protocol that may not be modified and will work with only a fairly rigidly defined set of devices or services.

Ethernet/802.3 and Host System Software

Another issue in the selection of host software on Ethernets is the problem of base software architecture. Ethernet, when properly configured, is a fairly stable and reliable network. As a result, communications architectures designed for unstable network technologies (such as dial-up lines) will typically incur overhead that is counterproductive in a LAN environment. As such, most host communications software architectures usually fall into one of two categories:

1. **Connection-oriented protocol.** In this type of communications architecture, cooperating nodes on a network constantly send initialization (init) and "HELLO" messages to insure that the remote system is available and reachable. The init and HELLO messages are essential on unstable links and help guarantee that the links are available when required. This type of communications method is also called "circuit oriented."

2. **Connectionless protocol.** This type of protocol handling, while not unique to LANs, is ideally suited for them, as it makes best use of available resources. Typically, a connectionless-oriented protocol will send messages only when there is data or messages to send. If initialization or HELLO messages are required, they are sent only if the remote node does not properly acknowledge message or control sequences, or when a node is initially activating. Network technologies that take advantage of this type of mechanism incur less host overhead and reduce control traffic on the network. This type of communications method is sometimes called "socket oriented."

It is difficult to say which architecture is better: each provides a unique method of connection. In the LAN environment, however, traditional communications protocols from some network architectures may not be well suited for usage of Ethernet as a communications medium, so careful selection is a must.

By and large, however, connectionless protocols are better suited for LAN technologies such as Ethernet. Since connection-oriented network technologies usually require a good deal of synchronization, the overhead on the network can be extreme, especially if there is signal loss or errors on the line. Connectionless protocols help reduce overall traffic load and rely on a semi-reliable communications medium, such as Ethernet.

Summary

Ethernet/802.3 provides general, nonguaranteed network connnectivity facilities. Because of the bursty nature of traffic and the flexibility in network protocol support, a wide range of network performance metrics may occur. Configuring an Ethernet/802.3 network requires care and planning; it is not necessarily as trivial as some would have companies and network managers believe. Properly configured, however, Ethernet/802.3 networks provide high reliability and excellent performance.

Managing Ethernet/802.3 Local Area Networks **2**

In this chapter, I discuss the basic functions of network management for multiple-protocol networks. This information is essential for understanding the problems of providing a productive network, as well as the problems inherent in overall management. Before any user can take the network resource seriously, the managers must have the network working and must be managing it correctly.

Network Management: The Generalities

To many people, network management seems to be a mystical, incomprehensible entity. It seems that whenever the words are mentioned, people recoil in horror, mutter expletives to themselves, or spout arcana understandable only to those versed in witchcraft.

Actually, network management may be separated into levels of management that are well defined and easily understood. Not all levels have tools that may be implemented with the current state of technology, but we can define the functions and, as tools are developed, we can manage them better.

Level 1

The first level of network management is the basic cable plant of the network. This level would include all cables, connectors, interconnects, satellite equipment rooms (SERs), and so on. Level 1 support means that the network management team would provide error-free connectivity to the basic network backbone system from the source wall to the destination wall.

Tools to help manage level 1 include those for cable installation and repair, time-domain reflectometers (TDRs), bit-error-rate testers (BERTs), pair testers (for twisted-pair cables), fiber polishing and fusion equipment (if fiber is involved), digital multimeters, and other tools for managing, controlling, and maintaining the cable plant.

A set of tools is desperately needed to help network concentration devices monitor node addresses and, potentially, node names, as well as other bits of information about *what* is connected to the network and *where*. Some twisted-pair concentrators are starting to provide the basic facilities for such monitoring, but most do not even tell the network manager the node's physical address (in token ring and 802.3 networks), much less the node name (which would normally need to be provided to a database facility of some sort). Many products and tools can identify certain nodes on certain network segments, but none can record and store node addresses in files and then use the files with other management tools or provide listings to network managers for control of the network.

I recently reviewed for a customer of mine two different vendors' sets of offerings for twisted-pair concentrators. Figure 2.1 shows a typical concentrator. The customer was told explicitly by both vendors that the tools could identify specific Ethernet/802.3 addresses at each twisted-pair port. On examination, the first vendor's unit could enable or disable ports on the concentrator, among other things, but it could not provide, in any manner, the actual Ethernet/802.3 network addresses on each port. To collect this information using the first vendor's unit, the network manager would still have to go to each node on the concentrator and collect the information directly from the system connected to each port.

The second vendor's unit, while visually pleasing, could provide only limited information on the Ethernet port addresses and could not save the in-

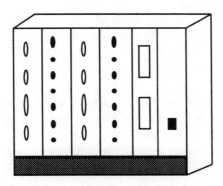

Figure 2.1
A Wiring Hub Concentrator

formation to a file or other system for later collating or reporting. Using this unit, the network manager would be required to go from concentrator to concentrator to find a particular node and write each address into a separate program (such as a word processor) to get a list. Although it is easier to identify an address with a particular port, this method still falls short of what the network manager actually needs to manage the network at level 1: a complete listing of each system type, node name, and node address, and configuration information for each node and port. This information is critical for system failure identification, network repairs, and other very important network management functions. Indeed, in order to upgrade to IPv6, the network manager must have such listings so that nodes and routers may be properly configured and tuned. Network map information is not optional; it is required.

One problem with address location information results from some protocols that do not provide the actual hardware card's address. Products such as DECnet Phase IV use a permutated software address generated by DECnet at network activation time (it begins with the prefix AA-00-04). As a result, the network node address at a particular port on a concentrator could change from time to time as the network manager changes the node address or system at a port. To really complicate things, it is not at all uncommon for DECnet nodes to be improperly configured during installation, causing two nodes to appear on the network with the same address. (Having two separate nodes with two identical Ethernet/802.3 addresses is grossly illegal from a standards point of view.) A tool that monitoring such situations and set off an alarm when necessary would be extremely valuable to the network manager—but such a tool would need all the concentrators to be connected and talking to one another.

Therefore, at level 1 we are still missing critical components to locate nodes on the network and to provide consistent network management information. We need automatic node recognition at a particular port on a particular concentrator. Notice the word *automatic*—we don't want to be crawling around behind systems and opening cabinets to find addresses at each port.

Level 2

Level 2 of network management involves the analysis of traffic and traffic patterns between nodes on the network—in other words, knowing which nodes are sending what traffic to which other nodes, how often, and how much. With the information collected, the network manager may then monitor traffic flow patterns and properly set up routers, bridges, and gateway buffers and resolve other configuration issues to ensure proper network performance. Also, through such analysis the network manager may monitor congestion pattern and potential security problems. For example, if one node is talking to many other nodes when normally that node talks to only two or three others per day, that could indicate a break-in attempt or a spreading virus. The manager can also keep track of unauthorized protocols on certain nodes, nodes connecting to sensitive (secure) nodes on the network, errors in packets, network-specific issues (such as collisions, short packets, long packets, babbling nodes), and other traffic-related issues that reveal problems with traffic on the network, not necessarily with any particular implementation of a protocol.

Figure 2.2 shows some tools for level 2 network management, which might include multisegment network management tools, such as Network Professor, Watchdog, and LANProbe; protocol analyzers, such as Sniffer, LANalyzer, HP 4972A, and EtherPeek (see Figure 2.3); specific-protocol management tools, such as the Simple Network Management Protocol (SNMP) management tool and Management Information Blocks (MIBs) for TCP/IP, DECmcc, Apple Interpoll, and SNA Netview; security monitors, such as the Network Security Monitor (NSM); and network mapping tools (such as the Network Mapping Utility (NMU)).

Level 3

Level 3 network management involves specific-component analysis for certain packages, products, protocol suites, and other network items that require detailed, specialized knowledge to troubleshoot, configure, analyze for performance, and adjust for proper operating modes. Management at this level relies on a series of "expert" individuals who can help solve network problems and help configure and expand the network when necessary. Under most operating circumstances, level 3 network management is seldom called upon, but

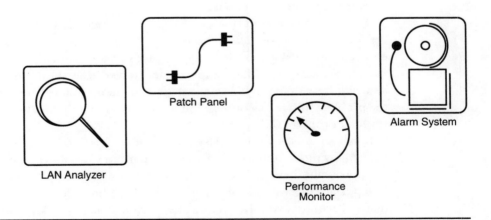

LAN Analyzer

Patch Panel

Performance Monitor

Alarm System

Figure 2.2
Network Level 2 Management Tools

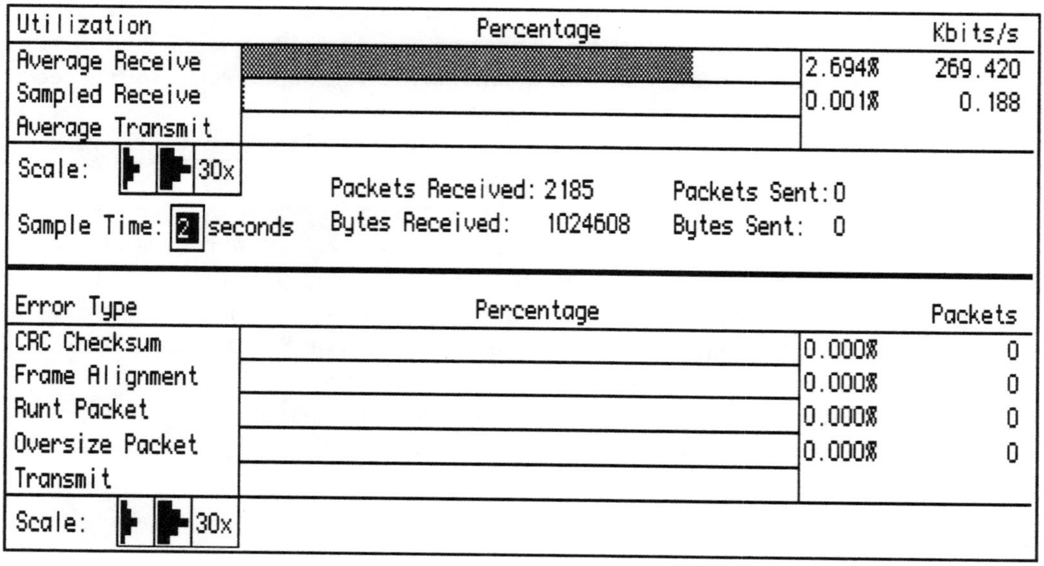

```
┌─────────────────────────────────────────────────────────────────────────┐
│ Utilization              Percentage                         Kbits/s        │
├─────────────────────────────────────────────────────────────────────────┤
│ Average Receive  ░░░░░░░░░░░░░░░░░░░░░░░░░░░      2.694%      269.420      │
│ Sampled Receive                                  0.001%        0.188      │
│ Average Transmit                                                           │
├─────────────────────────────────────────────────────────────────────────┤
│ Scale: ◄ ►30x        Packets Received: 2185   Packets Sent: 0             │
│ Sample Time: 2 seconds  Bytes Received:  1024608   Bytes Sent:  0         │
├─────────────────────────────────────────────────────────────────────────┤
│ Error Type              Percentage                         Packets         │
├─────────────────────────────────────────────────────────────────────────┤
│ CRC Checksum                                     0.000%          0        │
│ Frame Alignment                                  0.000%          0        │
│ Runt Packet                                      0.000%          0        │
│ Oversize Packet                                  0.000%          0        │
│ Transmit                                                                   │
│ Scale: ◄ ►30x                                                             │
└─────────────────────────────────────────────────────────────────────────┘
```

Figure 2.3

The Main Screen of the EtherPeek Protocol Analyzer

when the need arises (usually in times of crisis-mode management), level 3 network management is essential.

There are very few tools for level 3 network management. The best resources are usually people—such as in-house experts, consultants, or service-provider companies—who have extensive experience with a particular package or product set. (For certain products, expert system tools can also be useful.) The problem with developing in-house expertise is retaining trained individuals, and the problem with hiring outside "guns" is ascertaining that they can get things running properly.

Some vendors provide level 3 expertise in the form of dial-up or on-site support. Many times there are well-qualified personnel available to provide level 3 support, but these people may not be the front-line support technicians. It is important to have a list of experts available 24 hours a day for any problem that will require extensive technical expertise or in-depth knowledge of certain products or combinations of products.

Network management, broken down into its composite parts, allows the network manager to properly configure, control, and secure the network. At this time, not all the tools are available to control all three levels of network management properly, but products are still being developed by creative companies with expertise in network management. Until a full tool set is available, network managers will need to survive as we have for many years: on our own.

Managing Networks: The Tools

It's amazing to learn how many sites are searching for the ultimate network management tool. What's really interesting is how many people believe that one tool will solve all the ills of the network.

Sure. And there is one ultimate systems management tool, too.

It's reality time. No, there is not one package to manage the network, and no, neither SNMP, CMIP, nor any other four-letter word will save your network. It's easy to prove: Just try to find one tool that does everything. It doesn't exist, not for any price.

Why is it that everyone knows that it takes multiple tools to manage a system and yet people fervently believe that they need only one tool to manage a network? Probably because the cost of network management tools is fairly stiff. So managers may be inclined to believe that because something is expensive, it must do more. No, not true again. Network management requires lots of activities that call for diverse tools.

No One Tool Does It All

For systems management, the basic tool set includes functions such as backup and restore, user accounting, disk management (compression, statistics, and so on), tape library management, security (restricted access, statistics, alarms, and so on), image control and management, systems performance, problem tracking, and user support, among others. There is no one tool that provides for all these functions at the same time, although some utilities might combine two or three functions in one neat package. Some operating systems, such as OpenVMS, provide an extensive set of absolutely must-have tools, but the systems manager will still need to purchase additional tools—or write them with command procedures or program code—to get all the management features required for proper systems management.

Network management is no different. In most cases, network management involves many of the same tasks as systems management, as well as a few that are unique to networks. The big problem in network management is that every protocol suite has its own management utilities and style. So the network manager has to learn many different types of control and management utilities.

Actually, this situation is much like each operating system environment having its own set of operating system management utilities which, in turn, are different in command syntax and structure from other operating system environments.

Network managers use hardware and software tools to manage the network properly. Hardware tools include breakout boxes, BERTs, time-domain reflectometers, load generators, and other devices. Software tools perform functions including security, accounting, traffic analysis, performance analysis, reporting, and error detection and troubleshooting. No one vendor can provide all the parts and pieces required for full network management. Some vendors will tell you they have it all, but if you look closely, you will find that, practically universally, they all have some third-party tools and gadgets to help manage the network or some homegrown stuff to make management easier.

Networks are becoming much too complex for a single tool, anyway. If one tool did it all, there would be little of a system left over for any other function. Some vendors have tried to cover all the bases and have met with abysmal results, in both performance and features. Even with the push to use SNMP and OSI protocols such as CMIP (the Common Management Information Protocol), neither provide for a full-featured network management scheme that covers all aspects of network management.

Vaporware

One of my customers could not figure out which network management solution to buy to solve her network management problem. She had a legitimate problem: more than 1200 nodes of various operating systems and hardware technologies hooked up to LocalTalk, Ethernet, and token rings.

The most confusing aspect of the problem was "vaporware." Lately the industry has been deluged with torrents of vaporware announcements for network management tools that in fact do not exist. Some companies even claim to offer OSI compatibility simply because their marketing artists can draw network architectural diagrams in seven-layer boxes.

SNMP for Network Management

There is a great rush by TCP/IP customers to acquire management tools that implement SNMP. Although such a concept seems great on paper, there simply are *no* implementations that solve *all* of the problems of true network management. Worse, the industry media has been very quick to announce to the networking world that SNMP is the way to go and a real boon to the industry.

Don't misunderstand me. I am not bashing SNMP. In fact, SNMP is a clever protocol idea and has real potential. The problem is not SNMP, it's the vendors of supposedly compliant products.

In fact, for SNMP to work for TCP/IP customers, a few important steps need to be taken. First, all nodes that will allow network management via SNMP must support various network protocol inquiries, as well as support an MIB that must be implemented by the TCP/IP package being queried by a management server somewhere on the network. (To compound this problem, there are several MIB formats that may be used.) Second, there must be a node or nodes that implement SNMP and the appropriate MIB requirements to properly query TCP/IP nodes and control their activities. Therefore, having an implementation of SNMP is fairly worthless unless other nodes on the network cooperate with it. Implementing such cooperation is not as trivial as many vendors and others would have customers believe. If it were, we would have the implementations now.

Another problem with MIBs is that they do not contain information about specific applications that TCP/IP uses to implement its user functionality (such as TELNET, FTP, and others). Therefore, information kept in the MIB and used by the SNMP suite may be of limited value to network managers interested in specific management features of particular application protocols.

CMIP vs. SNMP

To compound the problem of implementing SNMP, there is the question of whether SNMP is the "right" solution for long-term network management needs. In fact, there is a push right now to implement the Common Management Information Service (CMIS) protocol, CMIP, over TCP/IP networks. Because CMIS will be part of the OSI management architecture and standards, and SNMP is only an Internet working group recommendation—not an international standard—this implementation recommendation would supersede SNMP.

Proprietary Enterprise Network Architectures

Some vendors have decided to pursue the proprietary route, as Digital has with its Enterprise Management Architecture (EMA). It's a great idea. Digital has some very nice brochures and data sheets and even claims to have products. According to the EMA architectural specification, Digital even has the right idea: it hasn't limited EMA to DEC products or architectures, and supposedly encompasses the needs of other third-party protocols (such as SNMP) and OSI protocols. The problem is that after detailed specifications are requested as to how a third-party vendor or original equipment manufacturer (OEM) might interface to the EMA architecture, such specifications never arrive—and further investigation proves that they are "still being refined."

Anyone can define an architecture. But the "architect" should provide interface standards for all to see. Theoretically, EMA has a unified user interface. This would mean that all networking packages that wish to use EMA would have some DEC-supplied standard by which user interfaces should be coded or to which they should be interfaced. However, even existent DEC network management interfaces for various products (such as TSM, DECnet, Polycenter, and RBMS) are inconsistent and do not follow their own recommendations. Someday they probably will, but in the meantime network managers have to learn all the different products in their workplace. Even then, other vendors are reluctant to "buy in" to the DEC method of network management and user interface style.

Some companies even have the gall to announce products and product lines before beta versions are even available. A couple of third-party vendors recently announced so-called network management tool sets, which, after much investigation, simply do not exist. One marketing rep told me that his company's announcements were meant to identify its intent to the market and secure market share for when the products do become available—later this year or next year.

Such activities border on the unethical. There are legitimate network management vendors in the industry with real products that solve real problems. Companies announcing vaporware network management products confuse the customer base and force legitimate vendors to spend an inordinate amount of time educating customers on the facts and fantasies of the industry. Worse, customers have to spend time investigating products that supposedly will solve their networking problems—only to find vaporware. This practice causes customers to bear ill will toward misleading vendors, wastes the customers' valuable time, and results in general confusion in the network management end of the industry.

Network management involves a whole slew of activities: accounting, maintaining historical information, performance analysis, troubleshooting, operational support, security, long-term trending, station-to-station traffic analysis, congestion analysis, among many others. More than a unified front end or a generic interface between tools, managers need real network management products that address their real problems. A couple of companies do have real products that meet many of the requirements just listed. Unfortunately, these legitimate multivendor, multiprotocol network management tools get lost in the vaporware shuffle generated by companies that have no real products and probably won't for a long time.

If it is true that the network is becoming the most critical aspect of the computational environment, then companies need to strive to implement network management schemes and tools. And customers need to look to legitimate products from legitimate companies and to realize that vaporware hurts everyone—especially them.

Network Mapping: What's Really Out There?

First we should answer the question "Why is a network map necessary?" The best way to start is to explain what a network map is. It is a topological representation of the nodes on a network and information about them. More than just a piece of paper with a bunch of boxes connected by a variety of lines, a network map should contain a range of information to assist the network manager in monitoring the network, finding nodes that will not cooperate, and tracking down network intrusions. A map should show the following information, besides other useful tidbits:

- Source locations for traffic analysis
- Proper spacing of systems on cables that are picky
- Node locations and maximum node quantities (for example, Ethernet/802.3 networks)
- Interconnect locations (repeaters, bridges, routers, brouters, knots of string, Dixie cups, and other connection devices)
- Addresses of all protocols on each node (most nodes run an average of two four protocols)
- Names of all nodes for each protocol (many nodes have two to four different node names, depending on the protocol and the particular time)

Another major reason for keeping a good map is to manage the transition to IPv6 and OSI, and to isolate nodes that may violate corporate security restrictions. OSI naming services and X.500 directory services require a fairly detailed listing of what is on the network, and where, so that connectivity services may be provided. As such, there is little choice but to collect the information for inclusion in OSI naming domains and other database products for the network.

Now that we know what a network map contains, *why* would one be useful? Some reasons are quite obvious: A map helps keep the network up when situations surface that are contrary to proper operations. When users call the network support hotline, they need to provide some bits of coherent information regarding the node they are on, so that network operations personnel can begin to identify the problem. Most users are hard-pressed to report information about even the physical location of the system, much less any addressing or naming information. Once the mapping exercise is complete, the user should be able to give such physical location information, as well as the map itself. Using that map, network operations personnel should, at a bare minimum, be able to identify the node; verify the location; and determine what is installed on the system, which protocols are used, what services are present, which systems function as clients or servers to the user's system, and other information to help isolate the problem.

Although it may seem silly to go to such extremes, believe me, it's necessary. Ask any user in your organization to describe what is on his or her system; even the most technical users rarely know for sure. Then start asking about node names, addresses, and connection paths. Without such information, no network operator or manager has a hope of finding the conflict or problem quickly. Oh, sure, the problem will eventually be isolated, but not without some serious digging around. Some problems, as usual, will be obvious, but don't kid yourself: a good map simplifies network management and troubleshooting, big time.

Now that we know what a map is and why one is needed, the next problem is generating one. Some companies have taken it upon themselves to provide tools and programs to help network managers identify node names, addresses, and other basic information on a package-by-package basis. A good example is the venerable NETMAP program written by Stan Rabinowitz at Digital some years ago. NETMAP used the Network Information and Control Exchange (NICE) protocol to poke DECnet Phase III and IV nodes on the network and have them send information about their DECnet environment back to the requesting node. From there, the program would then create a map of the network with some basic information about each node (such as machine type, name, and versions). Although NETMAP could not gather physical location information, the network manager could take the program's output and begin to track down such information. NETMAP found its way onto the DECUS VAX SIG tapes some years ago and has been around in various permutations since.

Even a couple of years ago, Jim Miller from Digital contributed a large amount of code that was used to demonstrate a network control center at the worldwide Digital trade show, DECWorld. It was nice that Digital did such a thing, but the features demonstrated should be a permanent part of DECnet—not an unsupported, ad hoc set of capabilities that most people would have trouble getting running without compilers or expertise in network operations.

In the last year, some tools have appeared on the market that make it easier to create network maps and inventory listings. Products such as the Network Mapping Utility (NMU) from Network-1 greatly facilitate the automatic generation of network maps. What makes NMU unique is that it can "learn" about Ethernet/802.3 addresses, protocols per address, names per address, and other information that is essential to network management. Best of all, NMU is automatic, requiring minimal management intervention. Also, as new nodes appear on the network, NMU automatically updates the maps for the Ethernet/802.3 network.

Since most protocols (including DECnet) lack any facility like NETMAP, it is up to the network manager to create a map the hard way. In the scheme of network management, as we saw previously, this task is often called a level 1 operation. Collecting such information involves a complete inventory of all systems on the network—a challenging, grubby, and thankless job. Challenging? Yes, because all network nodes change configurations, many times without the knowledge of the network operations staff, so the need to reinventory configurations is a never-ending quest for some tool to do it with. Unfortunately, people still have to do so the old-fashioned way, by hand.

When you are collecting information for the map, it helps to make a checklist of required information before going to each system and collecting the information. I have condensed my checklists to two pages that represent sufficient information about a node to build a good network map.

Recently, at a large network facility, I developed a program for a PC so that technicians using handheld PCs could collect and enter information as they went merrily from system to system. The handheld devices could accept data via a keypad and then generate a bar-coded sticker, which the technician would place on the system. I admit, I stole the idea: at an automated rental car agency, I had noticed that the personnel did the whole operation in the lot with handheld terminals and printers. Why not do the same with nodes on the network? The bar-coded ID marker tells anyone that the system is in the inventory, thus the system's network information can be retrieved easily—the user simply tells the support center the number on the sticker. In the future, as maps are being revised, the system's information can be retrieved via a simple scan and then updated easily. And when the system moves, network managers can track it as it wanders through the corporate maze.

You do not need a PC to collect the information for a map, but I can guarantee that spending half a day with dBASE, 4th Dimension, Paradox, Oracle, Ingres, or even a spiffy command procedure can make a major-league difference in collecting, sorting, collating, and tracking node information as the network grows and changes.

To make network mapping work for the network management team, they have to realize that the information is essential. You can prove this gathering useful information and putting it to work. To start with, list the following information:

- Node names for each protocol
- Addresses for each protocol
- Hardware addresses for controllers on LANs
- Version numbers of system and network software (especially for packages that use the networking protocols installed in the system)
- Objects that the protocols have installed
- Clients that the node connects to
- Servers that the node connects to (such as disks or printer servers)
- Load hosts (if any)
- Nodes that are loaded by the node (if the node is a load host)
- Types of hardware connections (some nodes have many, especially routers)

- Physical location
- Environmental problems (say, the node is outside in a dusty area)
- System manager's name for the node
- Phone numbers of the system's repair center and of its technical assistance center
- Other information that may be useful in identifying the node's location, who "owns" it, and its configuration

Oddly enough, none of this collection operation is terribly difficult. It is, however, time-consuming. Either a visit to each node or a rigid installation procedure is required to enter information about a node when the node is activated. If non-systems personnel are to do the inventory, a "crib sheet" of software commands will be needed to get some of the information on protocols, names, addresses, and so on.

One site I helped set up some time ago needed a lot of help in this department. Since they had more than 1000 PCs, I decided to have the PCs report the information about themselves. By putting collection programs and batch files on file servers and modifying AUTOEXEC.BAT files to run the collection routines at boot on the 1st and 15th of the month and then to copy the files to a specific directory on a specific server, the information about each PC was eventually collected. Now such collection is automatic. Though this method does not record physical location information—so it is still necessary to gather that by hand—it does provide a pretty full-featured start in the collection process. In practice, this setup is no more burdensome than installing a new package or distributing an update.

Another site purchased a bulk floppy copier and periodically sends out updates to all users on the network, like a vendor sending a software update. However, the support team acts like a vendor of services and will not work with a user until the package is installed on his or her node. When a user calls in with a problem, a team member checks to ensure that the caller has the programs on the node. If not, the support person talks the user through the installation procedure and activates that user for support. Though tedious, this procedure does get the job done, so the network can be controlled.

With the impending migration to OSI, the need for such information will be essential to properly configure OSI products such as the X.500 directory service, distributed data dictionaries, distributed naming services, and other network products and databases essential for operations in the OSI environment. Sites that lack a node inventory will find it practically impossible to properly configure an OSI network and set up all the node recognition software and databases. A network map will not be optional with OSI—it will be required.

Network mapping is a tedious, dirty job, but someone has to do it—usually the network management team. At first, team members generally resist the assignment, since it is a pain to do. But in the long run, a well-maintained map makes their job easier, and can provide a highly maintainable network environment, resulting in reduced network downtime as well as powerful expansion and day-to-day management capabilities.

Managing Multiprotocol Networks

Networks used to be easy: buy the wire, a single network software package, and the controller for the software and the wire; load the software through an exhaustive generation procedure; start the product; crash the system. Then repeat—this time with the proper network parameters—and enjoy some basic networking using one single protocol.

Not anymore. Now we have protocols for each and every application need. Maintenance Operations Protocol (MOP) downline loads operating systems to remote machines. Local area transport (LAT) allows terminals on certain types of terminal servers to connect to host systems and allow virtual terminal communications (CTERM does the same thing for other network packages such as DECnet). We have data-link level protocols such as Digital Data Communications Message Protocol (DDCMP), High-Level Data Link Control protocol (HDLC), Synchronous Data Link Control protocol (SDLC), and many more. We have protocols for internetwork routing (Internet Protocol, or IP), protocols for guaranteed message delivery (transport protocols), protocols for session management (session control, such as Network Services Protocol, or NSP), and protocols for network management (such as Management Information and Control Exchange, or MICE)—and there are more on the way every day.

There is no single protocol on a network anymore. There used to be, but that was back in the Dark Ages of networking (around 1970), when computing was done with automatic abacuses. Now the network of today will run an average of two to four data-link protocols on each system and as many as 12 or more combinations of protocols that are combined or excluded to form a monolithic tower of communication called a protocol "stack."

Why So Many Protocols?

Protocols have propagated for the same reason that there has been a surge in differing computing systems: the need to solve a multitude of difficult networking problems. With specialized protocols, the need to do very difficult workarounds is reduced and problems are solved. To perform disk input/output (I/O) across a network, many vendors have developed very specialized protocols to handle the various stages and problems of network-based disk access, as well as record- or file-locking issues among multiple systems. Certain protocols have indeed emerged as very good solutions to the problems for which they were designed. But some protocols are being used in areas for which they were never designed, resulting in performance and implementation problems.

To understand multiprotocol networks, it is necessary first to understand the theory behind protocol exchanges and the problems involved. The first issue to address is the type of hardware the network architecture will use and how reliable the network hardware technology will be.

When selecting network hardware technology, the protocol architect must use mechanisms to figure out how to handle the various types of problems and errors that will be encountered. To this end, two basic types of construction methods for network protocols have appeared: connection-oriented protocols and connection-less protocols.

Connection-Oriented Protocols

Connection-oriented protocols are network protocols that have been created with the understanding that the communications medium (hardware technology) will not be "trusted": that is, the communications medium will most likely have more than its share of problems. A typical analog telephone line is a good example of an "untrusted" medium. While a telephone line may easily be installed and used, it is frequently plagued with noise, static, and other problems that have to be heard to be believed. As a result, the network software cannot guarantee that everything placed on the cable will actually make it to the destination in a pristine condition. As a matter of fact, odds are that there is a much better than average chance that data will be lost during the transmission and that many of the network protocol packets that appear on the communications medium (the phone line, in this case) will be damaged by various points of interference.

The network protocol architect must therefore account for the fact that the network medium is inherently unreliable and design a protocol that not only handles the specific network problem but also provides a guaranteed delivery path between the connected machines. To do this, the connection-oriented concept of networking is applied. Under a connection-oriented network service (CONS), connection points between, say, two machines are carefully monitored by each end to make sure that the connection is still operating properly and that packets are arriving in sequence and without error.

Connection-Oriented Properties

Connections between systems have certain characteristics that you should keep in mind when examining or constructing a CONS protocol. First, a connection between two entities does not necessarily represent a physical connection. For example, a program, which is not a physical entity, may connect to a remote program, which itself is not a physical entity. The programs could be on separate machines, which would require a physical connection of some sort, or they could be on the same machine and use a network architecture connection—*not* a physical medium.

Second, for a CONS protocol "suite" (group of protocols) to work, several properties must be established. One of these, time, requires periods of inactivity to ensure that the link still exists and still works, be it seconds or hours between actual data transfer. Another property, sequenced delivery, requires that the CONS suite allow the accurate delivery of the protocol(s) in an uncorrupted way. So each packet must arrive in order and without error. If a packet is missing, retransmission must occur. If a packet arrives as a duplicate, it must be discarded. Another important property is flow control. CONS suites must make efficient use of buffers on the connected systems and compensate for message arrival speed versus CPU capability, intermediate baud rates, and other issues that could cause underflow or overflow of information. To do this, many CONS protocols contain transmission "windows" that allow a node to send a "chunk" of packets and receive verification of transmission before sending the next chunk. In this way, message flow may be controlled, and losses on the network are minimal, somewhat predictable, and correctable.

For a CONS protocol to work, several phases of connection must take place. First, a relationship must be established between the communicating entities. This is done via a connection request of some sort and usually involves the exchange of basic information required to set up or reject the link. Such basic information might include the following:

- Error-recovery mechanisms
- Class of service (such as throughput metrics, message size(s), and so forth)
- Name of the remote party (system, program, gateway, and so on)
- Accounting information
- Network management information
- Signaling and message synchronization techniques (if negotiable)

Once the link is established and the two entities are connected, the data transfer phase begins. In this phase, data packets are sent between the entities in sequence. This transfer may be half duplex (one side at a time) or full duplex (both sides simultaneously) and may involve differing volumes of data, depending on the work being done.

The final phase of a CONS connection is the disconnect or release phase. How the disconnect is done depends greatly on protocol restrictions, as some CONS protocol suites may cause data to be destroyed on disconnect. Other CONS protocols allow for total closure and cleanup of all structures before the disconnect—so the realm of possibilities is wide indeed.

During the transfer of data or during idle periods, CONS protocol suites may periodically send messages to remote systems to make sure that they are still connected. Typically called "HELLO" messages, they are sent so the remotes will know that a particular sender is still alive and available for service. In some situations, if a host system does not hear from a remote within a certain period of time, the host may send an INIT or HELLO message to see if the remote is alive. In this manner, the remote may respond if it is alive, or not respond if it is overloaded, busy, or not available. If it gets no response, the host system declares the node unavailable and may kill any links it thinks are in progress or notify other nodes of the connection failure.

A good example of CONS protocol suites is the use of DMR-11s between two VAX systems. The DMR-11 is a serial, synchronous communications device that allows speeds up to 1 Mbps between two systems. The DMR, however, has on-board DDCMP protocol that allows packet sequencing and ACK/NAK services in the cards. As a result, CONS capability exists between the two systems, and sequencing errors, synchronization errors, and a multitude of other issues are handled by the boards without interference or assistance from the host systems. Since the boards handle the CONS facility, the connection data delivery is guaranteed at layer 2 (data link) of the OSI reference model. In this case, DDCMP may be viewed, by definition, as a data-link CONS protocol.

However, DDCMP is much too versatile to be used strictly as a CONS protocol or only at layer 2. Some implementations of DDCMP are at layer 2, but others are at layers 3 and 4 of the OSI model.

Another very popular CONS suite is Transmission Control Protocol (TCP), which is often used with the routing protocol Internet Protocol. Figure 2.4 shows the TCP frame format. TCP is a highly reliable, connection-oriented protocol that is ideal for use in communications-hostile environments, such as leased lines and X.25 long-haul connections.

CONS suites are very useful for networks whose hardware medium is inherently unreliable. They are also useful where network nodes themselves have timing sequences that are obscure or difficult to configure—which would normally cause "unconfirmed" messages to be discarded or ignored, since the system was busy or not available to the network at the time of data transfer.

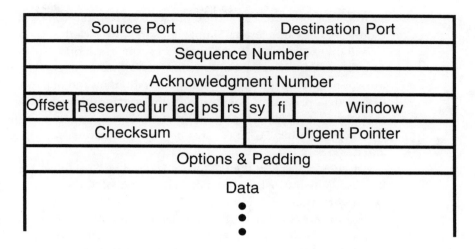

Source Port		Destination Port					
Sequence Number							
Acknowledgment Number							
Offset	Reserved	ur	ac	ps	rs	sy	fi	Window
Checksum				Urgent Pointer			
Options & Padding							
Data ⋮							

Figure 2.4
TCP Frame Format

Connectionless Protocols

There are times, however, when network hardware mediums are fairly reliable, usually in higher-speed networks such as LANs. LAN architectures usually span the range of speeds from 1 Mbps to as high as 10 Gbps. With high data rates, the network medium must be inherently reliable to achieve the rated speed; therefore, such a medium is not as susceptible to noise and other interference as more traditional networks would be. In these cases, a CONS mechanism would incur a great deal of network overhead that may not be needed and could significantly degrade the network.

To solve this problem, another class of service, called a connectionless network service or protocol (CLNS or CLNP), was created. CLNS suites evolved, basically, from networks that have multiple distribution paths. The CLNS relationship from one entity to another is a transient one at best, with each network operation being independent of the others. Because of this independence, CLNS protocol suites *do not* guarantee delivery or sequencing of data and are usually at the lower layers of the network architecture.

Like CONS, CLNS has connection phases, but only two. The first phase involves the access to the medium being used, usually via a controller and the appropriate software. The second phase is the transmission of the data, which is done as a one-time event. Simple and straightforward.

A good example of a CLNS protocol is the usage of the Internet Protocol (see Figure 2.5). IP is used when a TCP packet wishes to connect to other networks. Since IP does not guarantee delivery of data and makes a best effort to deliver data packets, it demonstrates the usage of the CLNS service. At the same time, it also shows the problems of CLNS: no guaranteed delivery of data. To accomplish this, TCP must provide the mechanisms for proper sequencing and delivery of data.

Another example is the IPX protocol used by Novell NetWare (see Figure 2.6). NetWare is capable of using various protocols for transport of packets between systems on the network, but IPX is preferred for connections on LANs such as Ethernet because of its speed and reasonable network overhead.

Some applications, such as bar-code reading, credit card verification, broadcast-oriented data transmissions (such as news wire services), and others, may benefit from CLNS protocol suites. By and large, however, most functioning network architectures utilize CONS, with some hardware mechanisms supporting CLNS for access to a specific medium (such as Ethernet).

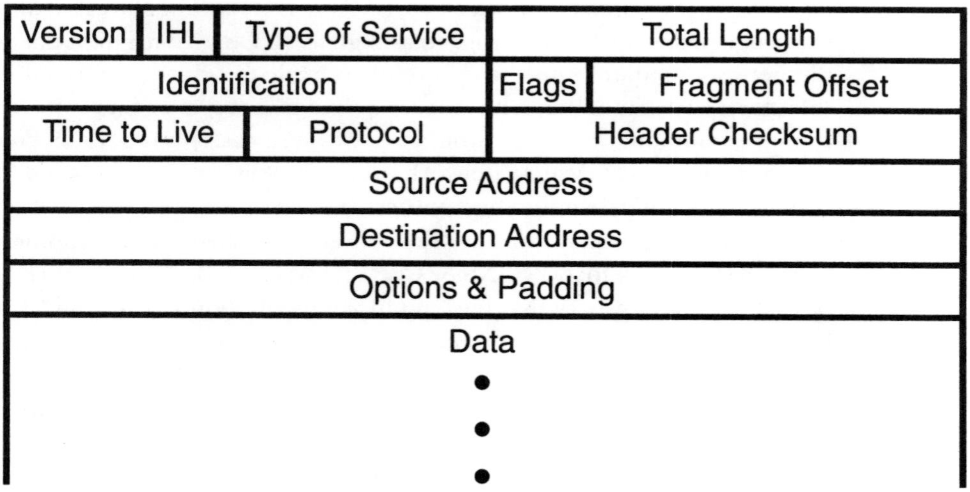

Version	IHL	Type of Service	Total Length		
Identification			Flags	Fragment Offset	
Time to Live		Protocol	Header Checksum		
Source Address					
Destination Address					
Options & Padding					
Data ● ● ●					

Figure 2.5
IP Packet Format

Checksum (Always FFFF)	16 Bits
Packet Length	16 Bits
Transport Control/Packet Type	8 Bits/8 Bits
Destination Network	32 Bits
Destination Host	48 Bits
Destination Socket	16 Bits
Source Network	48 Bits
Source Host	32 Bits
Source Socket	16 Bits
0–546 Octets of Data	Lots of Bits

Figure 2.6
IPX Packet Format

Which Protocol to Use?

In these days of LAN dominance, it seems that networks suffer from protocol schizophrenia: the same functional capability exists in various protocol suites. For instance, there are at least six different virtual terminal protocols available for Ethernet access. Only one, OSI's Virtual Terminal Protocol (VTP), is an international standard, but it has a very low usage metric at this writing and will probably be low for some time to come. Other protocols, such as LAT, are very popular these days due to vendor support and vendor products (such as DEC's popular DECServer line of terminal servers). The problem with LAT is that it runs, at present, only on Ethernet—other networks need not apply! VTP, however, is at a higher level of network protocol than LAT and, therefore, may traverse very different networks and provide terminal support in places LAT currently does not roam.

So which one is best? That depends. Understanding multiprotocol networks begins with a grasp of the following issues:

1. There are very few accepted international standards that truly work well and efficiently above OSI layer 2 (data link).
2. Vendors have all developed their own protocol suites based on whatever network architecture they sell.
3. Some vendors' approaches work well on CLNS hardware and CONS hardware. Others often work well on one or the other but not both.
4. Some vendors lobotomize their protocols or create new ones to solve connectivity problems that arise when they support new hardware technologies that their network architecture was never designed to handle.
5. When a hardware technology becomes popular, vendors adapt (or "port") their protocol suites to that hardware to take advantage of market demand, no matter what the consequences are.

What does all this mean? Simple: multiprotocol networks are not going away, at least not for a long time. Because of the politics and functional issues involved, very few network architectures are at great risk of disappearing due to lack of international standardization. While we all might lust for OSI network protocols on our VAXes, there will still be many a Local Area VAXCluster (LAVC) customer utilizing Systems Communications Services (SCS) protocol over Ethernet. SCS is not a standard (yet) and not a part of OSI. It will still serve LAVC nodes happily at the same time DECnet is generating HDLC packets with OSI upper-layer protocols on the same cable—and possibly from the same system.

So, multiprotocol networks are not going away. What about the future?

At present, network technologies continue to use new protocols for a variety of needs. Recently a company I work with a lot needed to tie together dissimilar systems on a network to collect and analyze network traffic. Although they might have used an existing network protocol, it was deemed necessary to create a new, application-specific protocol to get the speed required to provide useful statistics in real time, as well as provide a multisegment, multitechnology collection capability. To do this, a new protocol was created that would allow the described connectivity. Voila! A new network protocol.

Network architectures are changing to take advantage of internationally standardized network protocols, as well. Frankly, this development tends to disturb me, as I have been involved with various standards committees for some time. Some of the protocols being standardized have dubious capabilities (that is, they may not work in certain environments). Yet it seems that everyone is on the OSI bandwagon, hell-bent on standards whether they work or not. Eventually they will work, but standards force many network vendors to change their outlook on protocols on a network.

New Protocols Mean New Philosophies

For instance, DECnet-VAX (and other DECnet operating environments) under Phase IV guarantees delivery of data at the data-link layer of Digital Network Architecture (DNA). This means that, where possible, the hardware may be tasked with sequencing and retransmission of data. When DECnet takes the leap to Phase V, the OSI architecture will require that sequencing and retransmissions happen at layer 4, the transport layer. Also, the pre-scribed layer 2 protocol, HDLC, would replace DDCMP on ISO-standardized hardware implementations (such as 802.3 CSMA/CD networks and 802.5 token ring networks). Just those two simple actions—sequencing and re-transmission—require that DECnet under Phase V (that is, OSI-compliant DECnet) undergo big-time modifications, not only to the protocols involved but also to the philosophy of DECnet operations. Will this increase the pro-tocols on networks? Yes. HDLC will make its appearance, as will higher-layer protocols. Will DDCMP go away? No. Phase IV nodes will be supported by Phase V nodes and will continue to use DDCMP (as will non-OSI hardware controllers).

There are some very nice features about OSI that any company would be happy to get hold of. But still there is the problem of multiple protocols on the network and how to manage them all. Moreover, with each OSI layer being rigidly defined, there will be more "imbedded" protocols in an HDLC packet than there are now in a DDCMP packet.

The Problems of Multiple Protocols on a Network

Under OSI, each layer of the network architecture "wraps" a protocol around the previous layer. While other network vendors would like most buyers to be-lieve that their network architecture does the same, most of the time that claim is a lot of hype. Many architectures today generate a generic protocol packet in their defined protocol that contains option bits that redefine the intent of the packet based upon the bit settings in the optional area. This means that the same basic format is used for all protocol formats, but the data contents of the packet may actually be user data or predefined network architecture data (such as a routing or HELLO message) based on bit patterns in the optional field(s). As a result, breaking down some protocol suites with network analyzers and filtering tools on network bridges may be very difficult and time-consuming.

Some Bridges Are Your Friends

Very often a network is interconnected by devices called bridges (see Figure 2.7). A bridge is not a router; it simply sends protocol messages over a connection medium to a remote network of the same or different type, but it does not change the basic content of the message being passed along. In the case of networks such as Ethernet, bridges are used to connect various Ethernet segments into a cohesive uninterrupted network, from a software point of view. Since bridges function at layer 2 of the network architecture, the connection of the segments is transparent to most network architectures and the systems think that the network is one large continuous segment.

Bridges, however, may be very intelligent. In this situation, a bridge may be programmed to send *only* the packets that are truly destined for a node on an

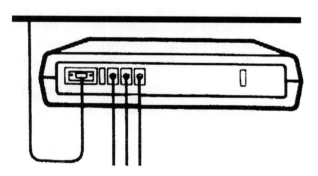

Interchange 4-Port Brouter

Interchangeable Port Configuration
    4 Thickwires
    4 Thinwires
    4 Twisted Pair
    4 Local Fiber Interconnect (with Transceiver)
    Any combination of the above with up to 4 separate segments

Figure 2.7
Multiport Bridge

adjoining segment. If the packet seen on a network is destined for a node on the same side of the network (on the same segment), the packet is *not* sent over to the adjoining segment, and as a result, traffic is reduced on the second segment. Bridges may be smart enough to filter traffic based not only on destination address but also on protocol type, source address, and, in some situations, content of data fields.

In a multiprotocol network, bridge filtering may be very useful to reduce traffic load and to keep the wrong messages from propagating all over the network. To get optimum filtration effect, however, the network manager must program the bridge with the knowledge necessary to filter traffic properly. This programming may be on a protocol-by-protocol basis, so protocol format knowledge is imperative if the filtration effort is to be successful. The downside is that the more options the bridge is looking for, the more time it takes to filter all packets, which can severely decrease overall network throughput as well as cause bridge congestion and packet loss.

Gateways and the Translation Problem

Another problem of multiprotocol networks is protocol translation. Protocol translation is usually accomplished with the use of gateways, which usually provide two-architecture conversion. This means that a specific gateway would translate between two architectural entities only. An example is a DEC SNA gateway. The SNA gateway uses DECnet for connectivity to other DECnet nodes on the network on one side of the gateway, and SNA for connectivity to IBM or SNA-compliant nodes (such as Wang or UNISYS systems). The translation is not DECnet as much as connection to both sides via their respective native-mode architectures and emulation of a connection type that is suitable to both sides. For example, starting a connection as logical unit 6.2 (LU6.2) from the IBM side to the DEC side is fairly easy, since the connection "looks" and "feels" like a real LU6.2 connection. From the DEC side, however, the connection does not look exactly like a standard transparent DECnet-VAX connection. It's close, but not the same (a normal DECnet connection does not use program routines such as SNA$ACCESS and SNA$BIND). Therefore, a gateway is more like a facilitator than a full translator in this case.

Full-translation gateways are beginning to appear, however. One from a company in the Midwest will allow DECnet-VAX connections to appear as a TCP/IP connection to a UNIX or other TCP/IP node in a completely transparent way. While expensive and powerful, it does provide true transparent gateway access to multiprotocol applications. Such connectivity is not without a pricetag, however, so it is not available to those without deep pockets— yet.

Network Management Problems

One last problem of multiprotocol networks is network management. Many companies are facing questions of how to control and manage the network resource as well as provide meaningful usage statistics, network accounting, and other related functions. Providing such capabilities in a multivendor network is difficult at best and usually requires some very heavy duty network applications and CPU horsepower. Since all protocol suites are different enough to be incompatible, and since the base philosophies of network architectures are different enough as to cause serious problems for network management tools, it is virtually impossible to monitor and maintain multiprotocol networks without a lot of different types of tools and without a lot of training.

One or two products may be able to monitor multiple protocols and network packages, but the product has not yet been built that can provide a full multiprotocol management facility. There have been some valiant attempts at such a feat, but most have concentrated on a couple of the more popular protocols and architectures associated with them. With network architectures changing as much as they do, even vendors of these tool sets have a hard time keeping up with the changes, so many may provide the features, but the features for full multiprotocol networks are still far off.

Multiprotocol networks are here today—and here to stay for a long, long time. Even the OSI model allows for multiple protocols at each layer of the OSI architecture, so even OSI nodes will be running multiple protocols. But whether the protocols are connection oriented, connectionless, or both, having multiple protocols means dealing with multiple products offering multiple solutions via multiple nodes on multiple networks, supplied by multiple vendors.

Trying to Minimize Protocols Doesn't Work

Many companies want a network these days. In times of economic hardship, organizations will attempt to make do with what they have, computationally—and make better use of it. Installing and using a network can help a company be more productive at a reasonable incremental cost, allowing access to resources that would otherwise be unreachable or unusable.

When any company embarks on the network trail, the first issue that most people focus on is which protocol suite to use. There seems to be this fixation that for the network to be manageable, only one protocol will do, and that a company should try to standardize on one protocol suite. Not only is this archaic thinking, but it is absolutely impossible on most commercial networks, since many times the suite chosen has more than one internal protocol.

To compound network agony, new customers often push to hire personnel who specialize in only one or two protocol suites. Many people assume that each networking protocol suite is so difficult to learn that there must be a pool of experts for each one.

What most network novices do not realize is that about 60 to 75% of a network specialist's experience is common to practically all protocol suites; only the remainder is protocol specific. All network managers and technicians have to possess a certain base of knowledge and training that transcends particular networking protocols and products. This foundation of knowledge covers the proper control, maintenance, and management of a network, including topics such as communications theory, LAN and WAN architectures, routers, bridges, interconnects, modems, and many others. None of these topics is necessarily protocol specific; many of the protocols used on most networks will support one or more of these technologies, and many will in fact have more than one hardware and long-haul technology for multiple protocols.

In short, protocol suites have a lot more in common than most people realize.

The reason we have to place so many differing protocols on the network boils down to the human condition: everyone thinks he or she has a better mousetrap. In fairness, the evolution of networking technology alone is going to produce bigger and better protocols to solve the connectivity needs of a growing industry. Some vendors have chosen to hang their technological hats on protocol suites that are well established and highly functional, such as TCP/IP. Others have opted for a proprietary solution, such as DECnet, SNA, AppleTalk, and others. For most users, a protocol suite will meet their network needs if it offers these four basic network services:

- File transfer
- Electronic mail
- Virtual terminal
- Program-to-program

Practically all network protocol suites provide the same four basic features, either in the suite itself or with low-cost add-ons from other companies. Some enhancements, such as file sharing, printer sharing, distributed database support, and other applications-related facilities, are also useful, but if the basic four facilities are there, users tend to be satisfied, at least (not ecstatic, just content with basic network features).

If you compare your current suites of protocols running on your systems right now, you will find that, for the most part, they all provide the same four basic facilities. So why are there four different suites on your system? Politics.

Yes, politics. There are very few technical reasons why a specific suite or multiple suites must be implemented. DECnet may be the main suite because the

VAX systems were installed first and staffers have expertise in that. TCP/IP arrived because the UNIX folks insisted that it was a better solution for UNIX and was interfaced better to the user shell than DECnet. AppleTalk arrived because it was in the Mac systems and no one wanted to buy DECnet or TCP for the Mac at the time. And so on, and so on.

Yes, these are political decisions. The network protocols did not decide all on their own to invade the sanctity of your systems. Some *one* made a choice. Software and hardware cannot do that. The decision to run a suite or suites of protocols was probably up to some power-that-be who had not the foggiest idea what he or she was deciding upon and probably never really knew what the protocol suites did. To that person, one additional feature in one suite made all the difference. This one is easier to use on this machine. Whatever the reason, if a human made the decision, it was politics.

The problem with all of this is that there is only one safe bet when considering networking solutions: design a network in such a manner that it can handle any protocol. That does not mean that all protocols should be used, only that the network, on demand, should be able to support any protocol in use on the networking hardware platform selected.

For instance, if 802.3 (a.k.a. Ethernet in IEEE clothing) were the prescribed network hardware solution, systems should be configured in such a manner that they could support any protocol levied upon them to solve network connectivity problems. A PC may require NetWare (IPX protocol) today, but next month because of an office move and department management switch, it may need to support PathWorks for DOS, which uses a variety of protocols (LAT, DECnet, TCP/IP, OSI, and others) in the same package. If the PC were configured with an 802.3 controller that supported one and only one protocol suite, this would be an unsupportable situation and would require a hardware reconfiguration. If the microcomputer configuration specialist had been thinking ahead, this would not have been a problem, since there are a couple of 802.3-class controllers for PCs that support all the protocols used by PathWorks as well as NetWare. If such a choice had been made, the worst that would happen is a software reconfiguration.

The general trend in the industry, especially where Digital is concerned, is to provide all protocols on the desktop for all possible application needs. With the arrival of products such as PathWorks, customers now purchase a package with a large number of network software and hardware solutions bundled in, so they can install an easy-to-use, inexpensive networking package for a reasonable price.

Once a company installs a multiprotocol solution such as Pathworks, it must ask, as previously mentioned, which protocols to use and which to focus on for network management needs. The answer is all of them. Whether corporate and network management like it or not, the users will activate all the protocols, eventually, no matter how strict a management structure is placed on what can and cannot be done on a network. Why? Because users have the power of the MEMORANDUM: such features will be implemented because Bob in Building B is using the feature and "I need it to do my job." Some may think that users are not smart enough to figure out that the unimplemented features do not exist. This is a great untruth, especially with the current crop of college grads invading the workplace, who had to have four years of microcomputer experience simply to make it through college. The days of hiding features and capabilities by un-information are over.

So what does the prudent and proactive network manager do? Learn it all. There is simply no other solution. And for those waiting for OSI to solve all the world's networking problems, I have a news flash for you: it won't—and you will still have to use the existing protocols for some specific networking product areas (such as file servers) or learn another 40 protocols for the OSI suite alone. OSI is multiprotocol as well.

The moral is this: To be competent in network management, network personnel will need to learn many protocols. This lesson applies even to single-vendor solutions (Digital alone has quite a few completely distinct protocol suites on the network already) and even to networks with a small number of nodes. In most networking environments, there is a minimum of four protocols seen on the network; many have an average of eight to ten distinct protocols in use. Some of these solutions have one package per protocol, and some have multiple protocols per package. In all cases, one-protocol experience is not enough, right now—and it will only get worse with multiple-protocol packages such as PathWorks.

Get ready for multiple protocols now. You probably already have them, you just don't realize it. And remember, with multiple protocols come multiple headaches, such as performance, security, accounting, addressing, and other issues. Prepare to deal with all of these issues, because multiple protocols on the network are not disappearing—they're growing.

Security Issues for Multiprotocol Networks

In most traditional networking environments, there is an extreme amount of gnashing of teeth when people decide which protocols to place on which machines to satisfy user access requirements. By implementing specific protocols and packages on certain systems, the systems may communicate with each other using the selected protocol suites. Some systems need to communicate with more than one system type, and this usually requires more than one protocol suite—not because all systems have specific suites, but because many vendors implement a certain suite of protocols on a certain systems architecture in a more "seamless" manner than they do other protocols.

Some of the matches of operating systems and protocols are obvious: UNIX and TCP/IP VMS go with DECnet or SCS. Macintosh goes with AppleTalk. MS-DOS goes with NetWare or LAN Manager. Datapoint goes with ARCNET. MVS goes with SNA. There are others, of course, but you get the point: some vendors have, for some time, hitched their products to a particular suite of protocols.

Although all vendors are migrating inexorably to OSI, companies will not give up their investments in existing protocols and packages simply because OSI is available. Also, since OSI does not solve all the evils of networking, many packages and protocols will be around for some time after OSI becomes a staple simply because they provide features and services that OSI cannot.

The real problem with packages like PathWorks, which offer an extensive suite of protocols, is that systems using such packages now have newfound access to certain systems. With the new accessibility comes not only the opportunity to connect with new systems and services but also the opportunity to exploit the security of systems on the network.

Disreputable nodes possessing new protocol suites can now exploit systems that may not have proper security access controls and methods. Also, each systems manager now has to worry about a much larger contingent of systems that have potential access to his or her system. Previously, if a node on a network had to worry about only 50 nodes that possessed TCP/IP, what about now that there are over 500 nodes that could attempt access? What about the statistical chances of a larger number of disreputable nodes attempting break-ins? Systems managers now have to secure their system from 500 possible points of intrusion instead of 50.

For example, if all PCs possess multiple-protocol suites, a user wishing to access files on another PC may be foiled by security features in one protocol suite but could easily copy the same file to his PC using another protocol suite with more liberal (or nonexistent) security features.

Sound implausible? How hard is it to break a protocol, considering that the makeup of almost every protocol is published in either specifications or books available to anyone? How much security exists in protocol suites? Sure, some have authentication security, in which a receiving node requires an originating node to provide either a password or an encrypted key to verify who is who. Following authentication, however, traffic is sent in the clear and may be viewed by someone using an analyzer or, if on a LAN, placing the system in collect-all-packets mode and viewing same. Even if a protocol were completely encrypted, by using a multiple-protocol suite package, a user could easily use another suite if the first one selected had superior security.

Multiple protocols is not analogous to multiple languages on a system. Languages are still subject to the operating system capabilities and security features. Sure, some languages may have a slight edge in security-bypass capabilities, but not on well-designed systems. Protocols, however, are unique: each package has its own security nuances—or no security at all. Worse, the implementation of protocols on various operating systems provides the opportunity to exploit security features on systems that have implemented a protocol suite but do not make adequate use of security restraints.

This may sound like an overreaction, but it's not. More than 86% of all *documented* system break-ins happen because internal personnel use the network resources available to exploit systems on the network. This statistic, about two years old, was calculated before users got the opportunity to install and use multiprotocol networking solutions on PCs and other systems. This statistic also came before the massive explosion in network connections that has happened in the last two years. So the chances of systems being exploited by break-ins via the network have increased dramatically, not to mention the fact that the sheer number of systems and the number of systems now connected to networks has increased dramatically as well.

Summary

Network management in the Ethernet/802.3 environment is not simple—and not as easy as many vendors tell you it has to be. For a network to perform properly and reliably and for users to be satisfied, there is a lot to do.

Ethernet/802.3 Performance and Management

3

To properly understand Ethernet/802.3 performance and management, you should acquaint yourself with some of the issues involving Ethernet/802.3 performance. Though a variety of products generate a wealth of performance information for the network manager, he or she must be able to understand those metrics to be able to adjust the network and provide meaningful information to others.

Performance with Ethernet/802.3

One problem common to all networks is performance. Network performance is multidimensional, comprising hardware design and architecture, protocol design and architecture, types of protocol activity (connectionless and connection oriented), queuing delay within software (both in the controller hardware and on the host operating system and host network software), and many other components.

Most users of networks lump their reviews of performance into one statement: "It's slow, so there is a performance problem." Though there is some truth in this type of logic, the slowness of response, which is the typical user complaint of slowness, has nothing to do with overall performance. The system and network could be running at peak efficiency and processing data packets at blazing numbers per second. But if the response is slow on an individual basis, people generically categorize the network performance as slow.

Assessing performance on Ethernet/802.3 networks is a tricky proposition at best. Ethernet, which is predominantly hardware, gets blamed for many performance problems on the network. Sometimes such blame is justified, but most often the performance of Ethernet/802.3 is directly dependent on many other collateral components that have little to do with how Ethernet/802.3 moves data around.

Studies of Performance

For many years, one of the biggest myths surrounding Ethernet/802.3 has been the existence of "studies" of its performance. For one reason or another, many of these so-called studies have been only theoretical; and believe it or not, most do not take into account the actual way Ethernet/802.3 works. For example, a few years back, one supposed study claimed that an Ethernet/802.3 network degrades at 37% of line utilization at 3 Mbps (*not* 10 Mbps—this one gets misinterpreted a lot) utilizing minimum packet length. There are a few interesting items to note about the study:

- When packets were 256–512 bytes in size, the utilization of the cable was near 100%. Only when the packet size dropped to minimum packet size did the performance drop to 37%.
- The analysis was not complex and was judged to be "preliminary."
- Performance was for a 3-Mbps network within a fixed environment.
- The analysis was theoretical in nature and did not necessarily encompass actual live network performance.

There have been other theoretical studies as well. Practically all early studies were made against the known configuration issues of the initial Ethernet/802.3 specification (3 Mbps). Some transmission rules, electrical time frames, and other figures in the Ethernet/802.3 specification are "hard" and specific to Ethernet/802.3 configurations. Since some of these rules are difficult to model, due to lack of technique or other type of modeling method, substitutes were introduced that were "similar" in nature, but they still did not work exactly like an Ethernet/802.3 in a live environment. This substitution meant that many theoretical studies—some of which have been at the root of the performance myths—were based on performance "assumptions" that are inaccurate in a live 10-Mbps environment. Here are some of the studies' assumptions, each of which is followed by more realistic observations:

1. Ethernet's 1-persistent CSMA/CD (in which there is a probability of 1 that a station which is ready to transmit when the channel [cable] is busy will send its data when the channel is free) is similar to models of nonpersistent CSMA/CD (in which a station waits a random amount of time if the channel is busy).

Some studies modeled p-persistent CSMA/CD (in which there is a probability of p that a station will transmit immediately; otherwise, it will wait to transmit). Modeled data for nonpersistent protocols will show that low-load networks deteriorate and high-load networks perform better. However, this is not how Ethernet/802.3 works—it is 1-persistent, which changes the entire modeling metric.

2. Networks have a simple distribution of data that is typically Poisson.

Simple distribution of data is a relatively reasonable network behavior. Real networks do not behave reasonably.

3. Stations on networks are spaced equally or at least predictably.

How often is spacing predictable on a real Ethernet? Ethernet/802.3 configuration rules are very frequently violated by vendors and customers alike.

4. To help simplify the model, the host system and host controller buffering are given "rules."

This simplification is not realistic. Different types of operating systems, different implementations of the same networking software, different controller software drivers, and different controller input/output queuing buffers will vary dramatically from system to system and vendor to vendor. The effect is that no two systems, even with the same hardware and host networking software, may be buffered alike. This discrepancy affects whether data is properly buffered, is lost due to lack of buffers, and is subject to other calamities.

5. Most network models assume fairness in acquiring the network channel.

This is simply not true in real life. I know of one workstation vendor that has changed the backoff timer on collision detection to make its system attempt to reacquire the network faster than other systems. This adjustment is great if you are on that system, but it is grossly unfair to people on rule-abiding systems on the same cable. If stations are not following the definition—which happens much more often than you may believe—the network is unfair and will react much differently than predicted.

6. Many theoretical models use one or more fixed packet sizes to show two or three possible ranges of performance.

However, because Ethernet/802.3 is used by many protocols, both documented and undocumented, packet sizes differ greatly, depending on the protocol—as does the frequency with which the packets are generated by the host (called the interarrival packet gap). The network is a microcosm of humanity: at one instant there may be a myriad of network packet sizes, arrival gaps, and other performance-affecting conditions.

7. The size and population of the network are static.

Live networks do not fit nice, defined quantities with known available MIPS on CPUs, well-behaved software, and other commodities.

The bottom line is this: there is very little "real" data on Ethernet/802.3 performance that is reliable for a live network. Worse, some of the theoretical performance data that we have all come to quote and rely on may be "tainted" in favor of certain metrics that have nothing to do with how Ethernet/802.3 actually works. This means that configuration rules in some situations may be too conservative or too optimistic. Worse, it may mean that actual Ethernet/802.3 performance is much different than what many studies have shown.

Which Study to Believe?

So, what should the network manager believe when it comes to Ethernet/802.3 performance? Here are a few interesting things to consider:

1. It is difficult to test Ethernet/802.3 performance in all situations. Setting up an office environment showed that using short packets with lots of close-together stations (more than 90 on one segment) was more efficient than having the same number of stations far apart in "clumps." Other studies have shown that this is a function of collision resolution issues: the closer the stations, the more quickly collisions are resolved and data begins to resume on the network. Therefore, even issues such as node separation affect real network metrics.

2. Generating packets from one host to another for testing in a real environment requires premeasurement for each situation. Collection systems on an Ethernet/802.3 generate predominantly short packets (on average, 64 bytes) and therefore are easy to predict and measure. Bigger, interactive networks generate many small packets (64–128 bytes) and occasionally larger ones (1 kilobyte or larger), but the interval for generation of short versus long packets varies greatly from network to network and application to application. Longer packets increase the efficiency of the network, keep down the total packet count, and reduce the possibility of collisions.

   To really understand a network, data has to be collected for a while to model the network properly and observe the mix of traffic sizes.

3. Improperly built controllers that do not follow the rules cause inaccurate estimation of network performance. In today's market, there are several situations in which this is a fact. This makes the network unfair and causes performance degradation for some networks.

4. The performance of Ethernet/802.3 is one issue, the performance of network software protocols is another. The Ethernet/802.3 channel is quite capable of handling up to 10 Mbps (the low number of systems with large packet sizes will demonstrate this). Few software packages were originally

designed with Ethernet/802.3 access issues in mind. As a result, Ethernet/802.3 performance usually is quite good. The problem has to do with software overhead, interrupt latency, queuing problems, and other issues on the host system. Some packages, such as DECnet, implement flow control; other protocols do not and demonstrate completely different metrics. All have varying performance in Ethernet/802.3 configurations, depending on a mass of variables that has to be seen to be believed.

A Case Study of Performance Testing

To find out some of the limits of performance on Ethernet/802.3 controllers for the microcomputer bus architecture called EISA (found on popular PCs), we tested an Ethernet/802.3 LAN utilizing a specific test suite and protocol components that were judged to be stable and practical.

Figure 3.1 depicts the results of a series of tests run on several popular microcomputer controllers with various drivers. The controllers were tested with the PathWorks software package for MS-DOS, and either the DLL or NDIS drivers were used with each card. In some cases, both drivers were tested for performance with the same card to provide statistical evidence that controller *and* driver combinations affect node throughput and performance (which they do).

In the first test, a 1-MB file was transferred from a VAX system to the microcomputer system being tested. The protocol used was DECnet Phase IV; the microcomputers were Intel 80386 systems running at 33 MHz.

The controllers being tested were the following:

- Intel EtherExpress 16 with a DLL driver
- Digital DEPCA-TP with DLL and NDIS drivers
- Hewlett-Packard EtherTwist with a DLL driver
- 3Com 3C509 with DLL and NDIS drivers
- 3Com 3C507 with a DLL driver

As the network load increased, more of the systems "hung" or crashed. When DLL drivers were used with specific controllers, the controllers failed earlier in the test than they did with NDIS drivers.

Also, the actual throughput of the controllers was, uniformly, lower than the vendor rated performance figures for each of the controllers. This is due to the test including throughput of protocol and not just raw measurement of traffic collection capabilities.

In the test, the packet size average was 572 octets and was measured with two different external protocol-analysis units to verify packet performance. In

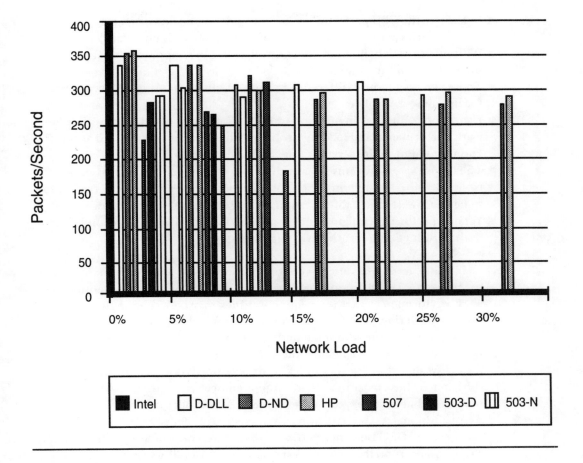

Figure 3.1
The Results of Performance Tests

no case did any controller reach the potential performance of approximately 6750 packets per second (the theoretical limit of performance at 572 octets for the Ethernet/802.3 network type). The best performance metric seen was slightly over 400 packets per second under optimal conditions.

With the increase in network load during the test, eventually all but two configurations locked up the microcomputers, causing test failure for the affected configurations.

Here are some of the conclusions we reached regarding the test:

■ Cable speed is not the problem in most 10-Mbps Ethernet/802.3 environments.

- In all tests, the CPU performance on both sides of the link never reached 50%, so CPU performance on properly configured systems is not a factor.
- Without exception, none of the controllers began to approach total potential throughput on the network.
- There can be a radical difference in throughput when using different drivers for the same controller.
- Use of the controllers in question under network load could cause serious network performance and loading problems when they are configured as servers and user count to the server is not carefully considered.
- The failure rate of systems (PCs in this case) will rise for certain classes of controller-driver combinations as the network load increases. Failure rate needs to be the lowest in just this situation, because users rely on the network.
- Vendor performance figures never matched live-environment testing figures in the production network environment tested.

In short, testing of various vendor components in an environment similar to the eventual production environment is essential for properly planning network performance. Further, vendor statistics may be exceedingly optimistic when considering performance criteria for controllers on the network.

Of interest are the additional statistics seen when very powerful systems were used to communicate the same file over the networks. "Powerful" in this case means systems that are very quick in terms of MIPS rating, fast internal I/O subsystems (bus structures), and large memory setup (over 32 MB of memory); and that have very fast Ethernet/802.3 controller capabilities.

An addtional test was run using a VAX system model 4000-100 with the DEC-engineered SGEC Ethernet/802.3 motherboard controller-on-a-chip. We put a range of users on the network, varying from 25 to 100 active users. The 4000-100 is an inexpensive and yet very powerful desktop or tower machine with the best, state-of-the-art Ethernet/802.3 chip set on the motherboard. This chip set, when tested with packet counting in promiscuous mode, was capable of achieving a sustained network packet rate of more than 9.1 Mbps. Considering the desired network maximum rate of 10 Mbps, this measurement indicates that the controller chip is capable of achieving almost cable speed in actual data-transfer activities.

In the tests, it was shown that under the highest user access level (100 users on PCs attached to the VAX system), the system would not generate more than about 1100 packets per second at 572 octets per packet. When the load was artificially increased on the network to more than 75% of network capacity, the system's packets-per-second rating remained the same. In all tests, the system overhead loading never exceeded 72% of potential load on the VAX, the bus structure was never even taxed at all, the I/Os per second on the disks never exceeded 21 per second (the disks used were capable of more than 40

I/Os per second), and the user activities were normal for the load and the system.

In theory, if the controller were the bottleneck, as network load increased, the packets-per-second rating for actual user data would decrease and the throughput would decrease, as the controller would be more heavily burdened with monitoring network activities and searching for packets rather than actually transmitting data to the network. This situation never occurred. Therefore, the controller, even under very adverse conditions, never reached saturation, nor did the system and its peripherals.

This conclusion leaves one culprit: the protocol suite itself.

By changing protocol suites for the same file transfer and file access mechanism, the packets-per-second rate increased slightly and still leveled off at about 2200. When faced with this problem, we decided that it was time to prove the theory. The only way to do so was to write a file transfer protocol that would provide nonblocking and non-timing delay services. In short, the protocol would transfer all data as fast as possible and would attempt to use as much of the network bandwidth as possible.

When we wrote the protocol to transfer data and then connect to the remote systems, a peak transfer rate of more than 6000 packets per second was achieved, even at network load of more than 50%. Without much of the protocol suite that manages sessions, error control, and all the facilities and timers that most protocols require to survive in a multiusage environment, the network was properly and adequately used.

What does this mean? Network systems are attaining enough speed and capability that they are no longer the bottlenecks that plagued network transfers in the past. To use faster network hardware technologies in the future, we must reengineer our thinking in network protocol design and architecture, so that the protocol suite itself does not hinder LAN performance, as is the case today with many popular protocol suites.

Practical Suggestions for Performance

There are many other less tangible Ethernet/802.3 performance issues. In the examination of recent "live" studies and my own experiments with a multi-segment analyzer, here are some suggestions for a high-performance Ethernet:

1. Keep packets as long as possible. Doing so reduces collision contention and protocol overhead (allowing more user bytes per protocol overhead per packet).
2. Keep cables short and connect distributed systems with bridges or buffered repeaters (not bit repeaters). Divide your systems into func-

tional groups and try to keep the traffic localized to that segment for that group.

3. Keep systems close together. Closer systems take less time to resolve collisions and will result in decreased overhead on the network (a 500-meter thickwire segment requires about 10 microseconds for a round-trip delay; a 23.4-meter segment requires virtually no delay).

4. Make sure that vendors have "followed the rules" on backoff timers, channel acquisition timing, and other Ethernet/802.3 rules. An unfair network configuration does not perform consistently well for all systems connected.

5. Keep the theme of the Ethernet/802.3 to a particular class of application. Real-time doesn't mix with commercial applications: the performance of both will suffer, especially under load.

6. Controllers should be able to buffer several packets at a time. The more buffering that is available, the better the performance will be.

7. Packet gapping may be an issue for some protocol types. If a high-speed system produces back-to-back packets between two systems on the Ethernet, the slower receiver may not have enough transition time between interrupts to capture the next packet on the network. By increasing the gap interval between packets, the link will be slightly slower but there may be fewer retransmissions, which may in turn increase network performance. Some software packages can adjust the packet gap between transmitted packets.

Is a 10-Mbps Ethernet/802.3 Network Fast Enough?

The answer, for today and for the near term (about three years), is a resounding yes! But the real question should be this: If 10 Mbps is fast enough, why is my performance so poor?

Most Ethernets experience a loading factor of between 1% and 7%, on average. Of course, there are times when the load reaches 100%, but this happens typically for very temporary burst-mode traffic and does not reflect the normal operation of most Ethernets. There is a rumor going around that an Ethernet/802.3 loaded at 20% average load is overloaded and cannot handle the data throughput needs of Ethernet-connected systems. Not true! If only 20% of a resource is being used, there is still another 80% to go.

Fairly intense studies of Ethernet/802.3 performance have observed 20% loading of the cable—indicative of a reasonable amount of data, yes, but very often the data present on the cable is retransmissions, which artificially inflates the actual amount of original traffic on the network. This happens because some component in the transmission hierarchy is either not accepting Ethernet/802.3 packets or destroying them.

For practically any application, 10 Mbps is a perfectly acceptable speed. Some companies use Ethernets for full-motion video (with compression) on the cable with no difficulties, even between multiple workstations running the video software. The problems, more often than not, are those related to controller congestion, bridge congestion, poorly designed and installed Ethernets, or abused Ethernets that perform poorly because systems are configured poorly.

The single most common problem with Ethernet/802.3 performance is controller congestion on connected systems. The controllers on systems connected to an Ethernet/802.3 may not be powerful enough to read the packets on the cable fast enough, so they cannot capture all the packets offered to a system the first time.

For example, a MicroVAX and a network analyzer were placed on a thinwire (RG-58) network with no other nodes of any type. At that point, a small MACRO-32 program was written that placed the VAX Ethernet/802.3 controller on the MicroVAX in promiscuous mode (forcing the controller to collect *all* packets seen on the network) and then did nothing else but count the packets seen on the network. The analyzer was programmed to generate previously recorded LAT packets at the rate of 20% of the capability of the cable speed (14,700 packets per second at 64 bytes is possible, and the analyzer was generating 3000 packets per second at 256 bytes).

The results were less than favorable. Of the 3000 packets per second offered on the network, the MicroVAX was able to count only an average of 1156 packets per second, with a peak of 1520.

Although the study was not scientific, some variances were done to further test Ethernet/802.3 throughput versus cable speed. The testing did prove out a few conclusions:

1. Cable speed does not hinder packet transmission or protocol type. That is, the cable is not the speed problem.
2. The ability to collect data from the cable at 10 Mbps on the controller is not questioned. The ability to get the packets, once collected, to the host on a consistent basis is seriously questioned.
3. When tested with different controllers on the same network and same analyzer generating the same traffic, substantially different speeds were seen. This is attributed to faster CPUs on the host system and faster Ethernet/802.3 controllers with better buffering. In two cases with a faster controller on a large VAX, well over 2500 packets per second were collected.
4. Higher speeds of traffic produced the same collection results on the MicroVAX. This means that a faster rate of transmission by another node would cause generation of more packets per second on the cable, but the MicroVAX always collected the same average amounts per second.

5. The direction of traffic flow has a dramatic effect on overall throughput. When our test sent data from a faster system to a slower system with no delay between packets, the slower system missed a substantial amount of packets the first time (retransmissions were required to get the message over the network). When packets were sent from a slower system to a faster system, virtually no packets were missed and there were very few retransmissions.

6. Faster controllers may not mean better throughput. In one test, when a faster controller was connected to the MicroVAX, the MicroVAX became saturated before the controller did, and performance stagnated.

7. Packet transfer through intelligent bridge units caused very different performance metrics, depending largely on bridge model, number of protocol or data filters involved, bridge CPU power, and other factors.

8. Shorter packets with a smaller time gap between packets were seen less often than larger packets with a delay between packets. Further investigation showed that packet delay in most networking software is not used by default, so packets are transmitted without delay until the sender receives a flow control message from the receiver. With increased delay between packets, packets were sent more slowly, but there were substantially fewer retransmissions (A DECnet session was used to try this; the gap was adjusted with the CIRCUIT parameter TRANSMIT TIMER, which is in 1/16th-second values.) This adjustment effectively almost doubled the test case's throughput.

One caution: Many vendors claim bandwidth capabilities that appear to be the same as Ethernet/802.3 speeds. Bandwidth is the possible; throughput is the actual. Throughput is a function of hardware speed, software speed, CPU power, overhead, and many other considerations. In other words, bandwidth is nice, but throughput is what is important. What good is a bandwidth capability that exceeds the capability of the CPU and related hardware?

Many vendors will produce performance information that makes their products and technology appear to meet your needs. In practice, many times such capabilities are inaccurate in real honest-to-goodness user environments. Tests that involve sleight-of-hand programming do not reflect reality. We send files, mail, and, unfortunately for performance, SET HOST or TELNET sessions on the network. This is the reality of networks, not the theoretical, highly tuned network performance figures we are given. The cable speed of Ethernets, with the exception, possibly, of 1BASE2 802.3 networks (1 Mbps), is not a problem with most applications. The problems are numerous, but many of the performance problems start with systems that cannot make effective use of the available cable speed.

Summary

Ethernet/802.3 performance is much maligned and misunderstood. Don't confuse the problems of Ethernet/802.3 performance with network software performance, queuing delay in operating systems, bus latency, bus contention, or any of a group of possible problems that contribute to network performance and delays. Most of all, don't get caught up in hype: insist on performance fact.

Ethernet/802.3 Network Planning   4

Planning a network for proper functionality in the Ethernet/802.3 environment is just as critical as properly installing and using it. In this chapter, we explore the various problems of network planning and upgrade planning for Ethernet/802.3 networks.

What's a Network Plan?

One of my customers recently complained about their inability to predict their network configuration needs for the next year. They wanted to know how much it was going to cost to install new components, but they had no idea what it was going to take to satisfy upcoming network needs—and therefore had no idea how they were going to budget for the network. Worse yet, they did not know the proper components to buy for the overall network to solve their long-term needs.

I suggested that they needed a network plan. Their response, which was typical and expected, was "What's a network plan and why do I need one?"

Fair question. A network plan is a proactive tool that companies are starting to use to plan for network needs. It is a fairly detailed document that analyzes the current need and, through a technique called predictive analysis, allows a network designer to compose a step-by-step plan to help companies implement their network—now and in the future. Companies need a network plan to keep from buying the wrong components and installing ill-conceived and ill-planned network technologies that will not fit together in the "big picture" as the network matures over the years.

I've been doing network plans for years. Oddly enough, few other designers provide such services. Sure, there are plenty of folks who will design a network to solve current and short-term problems, sometimes correctly so. Unfortunately, problems surface not in the next year, but in a couple of years, when the network must be expanded and there is no clear vision as to what to do next. The kinds of cables, bridges, repeaters, interconnect technologies, protocols, servers, clients, and other technologies that are needed can be predicted and planned for with a little care and proper updating of a consolidated, complete plan.

You "Needs" a Needs Analysis

One mistake most companies make with any mix of technologies is not completing their needs analysis when they are solving a problem. Sure, they decide which database technology to use today to solve a problem, but what is the next technology after the current one? For instance, if a company were to install a relational database today, what is the next evolution in technology in databases? What should a company do now to get ready for that advance, so that current technology does not need a total rewrite and components do not need reinstallation to migrate to the new technology?

To answer the question properly, one must be cognizant of the technologies being developed and techniques used today in relational databases. Obviously, heuristical techniques will be coming into use. Large amounts of "unformatted" data, such as voice and video, will need to be stored. Total database distribution will be necessary to all networked nodes. Dissimilar operating environments will want to share common data. Graphical input and output of information will be necessary, as well as combinatorial searching of stored information in different databases on different networks. In short, a graphically oriented, network accessible, fully distributed, highly available, relational-compatible, high-density storable, user-friendly database technology is coming—in other words, a spatially related database.

Spatially related? Sure. Obviously the next step in database technology is the need for object-oriented storage. Some technology has to provide that capability, and the technology is the use of a spatially related database. Spatially related database technologies use a mathematical technique called triangular irregular networks (TINs) to store and retrieve very large volumes of three-dimensional and other types of data. Using this technique, the database designer may store vast amounts of dissimilar types of information and relate the information both locally and through a distributed method. While limited space here prevents a suitable treatment of the technologies surrounding spatially related databases—and after all, this is supposed to be a networking book—the existence of such technologies and even some products testifies to the probabilities of such a distributed database environment that solves a great many needs. Digital even has a couple of test technologies up (DICES and

Spatial II products) that are used in specific vertical market areas—proof that the technologies are being developed. Further research into spatial structures and technologies shows the opportunities and capabilities to solve a great many problems that will be faced by database designers and users of the future.

What does all this have to do with a network plan? Everything. Just as database technologies may be predicted by using research into new technologies as well as correlation to expected problems (and using static predictive research techniques), networks may be similarly predicted and planned for.

How to Start a Network Plan

A network plan begins with the overall conditions of the current network and the overall technical environmental concerns that affect the network's makeup and growth. This list would include the following:

- Reasons why the network has grown the way it has
- The technological decisions that were made, and why
- The types of applications and market area the network is used to support
- The overall operational control and network management technologies
- The overall network goals and satisfaction criteria (what it takes to keep the users happy)
- Known problems and technological issues that are currently unresolved

This list of requirements is not easy to satisfy, but by spelling out your needs and then analyzing the collected data, the network planner can get a good sense of the customer's present status and what led to that status.

The next step is an examination of the attitudes of the company as a whole. This step is necessary to provide a plan that fits the corporate network growth style of the company. This process includes interviewing decision makers and asking senior managers what they expect a network could provide to meet their goals, what are the overall management trends in the company, and what are the expected corporate growth and facility growth, as well as a myriad of subjects that tell the network planner "what" a company is and where it is headed.

After collecting data, the network planner must search for anomalies in that data. One of my customers always grows much faster than they expect, and they are growing at a rate they did not ever predict. It is easy, however, to understand why, as they have consistently set networking goals over the years and consistently exceeded them. So when I designed their network plan, I added a factor of 5 to 10 to everything they told me they wanted to do, and then I planned accordingly. That method proved highly accurate: they are in their second year of the plan and are already ahead of schedule. Anomaly analysis helps the network planner consider all aspects and needs of the network and produce a migration plan accordingly.

After examining the data and anomalies, the planner should have a good idea of what has happened and why. Then the network planner can use growth acceleration curves, which are very similar to market growth analysis techniques, to predict what size the network may achieve. Also, besides helping with proper sizing, the curves allow the planner to examine chokepoints in the growth.

A chokepoint is a point in the network life cycle that tells the network planner that a problem in configuration will arise when a certain number of nodes or when the load factor reaches a certain level. By identifying such points, the network planner may configure solutions to conquer the problem and provide measurement metrics to the customer, so that they will know when they are approaching a chokepoint. When a chokepoint is reached, the network plan should prescribe solutions that are in line with overall network plans and goals—and that will allow a smooth transition to other future technologies. In this manner, a total growth solution is achieved; no one needs to guess "what to do next" in the network life cycle. The plan also provides a high degree of cost control and budget prediction, which are essential today, when network costs are far exceeding system costs and rising rapidly.

Measurement Criteria

The network plan also includes measurement criteria for expanding, consolidating, integrating new systems and networks, merging networks (in the case of acquisition of another network), and other activities that will occur in the life of the network. The measurement criteria cover the inevitable eventualities as the network evolves. Usually, such eventualities are highly unplanned and require a reactive action. Such a predicament results in ill-planned solutions that eventually cause portions of the network to be rebuilt and can be very expensive over time to work around or replace. The network plan enables a company to respond to new networking situations proactively, not reactively. In this manner, even if there is no time to properly analyze what needs to be done in a crisis, the network plan allows for proper implementation of solutions, not installation of the wrong thing at the wrong time. This foresight can result in significant cost reduction over the life of the network.

A proper network plan does not have calendar dates. Instead, a plan helps identify certain event modules, which allow measurement of criteria that affect the next step in the network life cycle. Instead of stating that 50 terminals will be installed in January, the plan would call for a solution of adding 50 terminals. When the network reached a certain loading factor, the plan would call for certain actions to take place to allow proper implementation of a solution.

Not all future technologies are predictable, but they do not have to be. A network plan should provide a solid basis for a time frame of two to five years, with specific recommendations. Following that time frame, a general goal and trend method should be included. Every two or three years, the customer should revisit the plan and ensure that it is updated to reflect the current network technologies and corporate goals. In this manner, the network plan allows the customer to benefit from current, near-term, and long-term technologies in a planned, methodical way. A network plan that is a "living" document should never be out of date and should always reflect the corporate vision for the network, as well as how to implement it.

How Much Does a Network Plan Cost?

Some companies claim that network planning is expensive. Most do not realize the expense of a poorly planned network. In my experience, a good network plan runs from $10,000 to $50,000 for larger networks, with the average in the $10,000 to $20,000 range. That's cheap insurance considering that if two bridges are placed remotely in the wrong place, the cost of replacement will run about $10,000 to $20,000. For smaller networks (those with five to ten nodes), a complete plan may not be necessary. As the network grows, however, proper planning will save big bucks. Is the cost of one screw-up worth the cost of a plan? The answer is yes.

Want proof of what happens without a network plan? Look at your own network and computing environment and see how many hardware and software components are tossed aside before their time. Look at all the modems and controllers lying around that have lost their usefulness. How about the replacement components that *had* to be put in because the original stuff was obsolete when it was installed? How much recabling was necessary in the name of expansion? What happened the last time a crisis occurred? Did your company analyze the situation, plan the solution, map it into the overall network goals, and purchase equipment to solve the short- and long-term needs? Or did the company simply find a component that patched the situation and hope for the best? With a plan, you can avoid much of this waste and experience a proper migration.

Good network planning does not have to take months or years, and it does not have to cost much if properly and competently done. Look for network planners with vision and a good track record, and remember that a good network planner asks not only technological but also managerial questions. A good planner will drive you and your organization nuts for a few days and will dredge up all the weaknesses and foibles of your network. After the planner is done, however, you will have a goal, a plan, and direction. You will be ready for the next expansion crisis and you will be able to provide thoughtful, knowledgeable solutions that fit the overall goals.

Planning a Network Plan

Full-featured network implementations have a well-designed strategy for justification, planning, implementation, and post-installation expansion plans. For any company to realize its potential to properly utilize components efficiently and cost-effectively, it will need to take a cautious, thorough approach to implementation of any networking components. This includes any office or facility that will be connected to the network, as well as all components at all facilities.

The following items should be completed to ensure proper implementation of the network and all associated management resources. By using a stepwise, methodical network planning method, the network will provide highly reliable, cost-effective, and low-overhead services. Using sound management planning techniques, the network may be implemented properly and quickly and still provide proper migration paths to follow-on efforts, without duplicating work or making current products obsolete.

To implement a full-featured network properly, study the following list of activities and seriously consider executing them. Based on previous design experience, proper implementation of the following steps provides a low-risk, high-availability, cost-effective network solution that may be tailored at any time, as well as a proactive network posture for the organization.

Complete Steps for Creating a Network Plan

Note: Following the name of each step is my suggestion regarding who should carry out that step.

1. **Feasibility study** (customer, with assistance, if required, from consultant). This document states the need for a network, where networking is necessary, the set of services required to satisfy corporate goals, the life cycle of components using the network, the potential fiscal savings by using the

network, the overall scope of the project, and the steps to accomplish these things.

2. **Network functional specification** (customer, with assistance from consultant). This is a "what" document that describes, in management terms, what functions and features will be provided to satisfy corporate networking requirements. It also lays out the phases of the project, the goals for each phase, acceptance criteria, financial reporting and budgeting criteria, approval criteria, management reporting criteria and formats (if required), progress reporting, review requirements (not dates, since no technical information is available at this stage), interconnect possibilities, growth requirements (estimated), external assistance requirements and criteria, and so on.

3. **Functional review** (customer sites only). This step is a review of the functional specification by all affected entities to ensure that the document is complete, properly covers all phases, and addresses all concerns for *what* the network is supposed to do (not *how*).

4. **Criteria for network design services** (customer, with assistance from consultant). This is a short document listing required services from a potential agency or vendor of network design services, including required documents, assistance, financial and management reporting, selection criteria, customer contact points for questions, and other information required to properly select a network design company. This document also frequently serves as a request-for-proposal (RFP) document for the network design.

5. **Selection of the network design services vendor** (customer). This document provides the rationale for selecting the vendor and offers a written explanation of the vendor selection for future needs; it also documents various management reporting criteria.

6. **Network technical specification and design** (consultant, with customer input). This is the "how" document that explains, in great detail, how the network and all components for each phase will be implemented and what components are required. Topics usually included are network rationale, current components and their integration, network goals, network entities, overall design criteria, potential technical risks and problems, unique problems and solutions, cable plant makeup, interconnects, traffic modeling analysis, protocol recommendations and protocol performance analysis, expansion model, installation plan, expansion plan, training plan, network management plan, troubleshooting issues, migration and enhancement issues and planning, network technical cost analysis (if required), testing criteria, test methods, acceptance testing, product interfaces for multiple products on the network, application issues, maintenance issues, personnel needs and skills criteria, management (people)

review criteria, overall application and network software and hardware management needs and solutions, recommended products for various components, standards adherence, and other required technical issues that must be addressed to provide a well-behaved, solid, low-risk network implementation.

7. **Network plan** (consultant, with customer input). This document provides customer guidance regarding expansion of the network in a proactive, cost-efficient way rather than a reactive way, as tends to be the norm in many networks. By implementing a well-devised network plan, the installed network may be expanded predictably and efficiently and can be budgeted for before components are required. Basically, the network plan provides network measurements and chokepoints that allow the network management team to know when components will need to be added to expand the network. Further, the plan gives the customer total control over the expansion, so that goals are met and unnecessary components are not added in haste. Wasteful expenditures are also eliminated, as costs for components are controlled and all components installed properly match the expansion plan of the network (no extraneous hardware, software, or consulting is needed).

8. **Network operations plan** (customer, with consultant). This document explains, in detail, how the installed network works and includes a complete map and inventory of all components so that operational staff can properly control and manage the network. The operations plan also includes a troubleshooting guide, contact lists, vendor contacts, decision trees (if required), reconfiguration information, testing, problem/trouble logging, security monitoring, problem reporting, management reporting, performance monitoring and data collection, and other required operational control issues.

9. **Network training document** (customer, with consultant). This document provides detailed training plans for all classes of users of the network resources and products. Plans would include network management staff training, systems management staff training, and various levels of user training. Remedial training as well as new user/staff training would also need to be addressed. Plans should also include potential training for new offices added to the network and new products added in the future (this would include new functionality or rewrites of existing components).

10. **Network audit document** (consultant and customer). In all government facilities and most larger businesses, occasional scheduled network audits as well as surprise audits are commonplace. This document allows preparation for such an audit in a methodical, detailed way without resorting to half-implemented preparation when an audit is announced. The document does not cover the audit procedure but does cover how to prepare

network facilities for an audit and what reports and other items would be required for management and for archival purposes. Also, action plan sequences for post-audit work would be included to provide full benefit of the audit function.

11. **Add-on request mechanism document** (customer, with consultant). This document provides a mechanism by which the organizational entities that use the network may suggest improvements and enhancements that match the plan or allow the plan to be modified, properly, to achieve the long-term results desired and required to be successful. It should be brief and provide sample suggestion formats, line-of-authority requirements, approval chain, feedback mechanisms, disposition reporting, and appeal facilities in case of disputes. In this way, changes may be addressed in a formal, objective way, using a tool that will incorporate required facilities that users will need in the future that may not be envisioned today.

If a company uses this network implementation and planning model in a considered, thought-out way, it will be very successful in its networking plans and will implement a cost-effective, maintainable, reliable, and very usable network. Failure to properly plan and implement the network will result in wasteful network components, manual overhead, slowness in delivery of network resources, and other cost- and manpower-intensive activities.

Planning and Retooling

In our industry, we constantly get these little unwelcome reality checks that we wish we could explode into certain oblivion. One of the most pervasive is the problem of change. Often I am asked when the next whatever is going to come out, or when the next version of something will be released. In all situations, the fundamental issue is change. We have to do it and there is little choice in the matter. The problem is convincing management that we have to do it and there is little choice in the matter.

About every 18 to 24 months, by my clock, we get a revamping of basic get-the-work-out-the-door technologies: printers, disks, CPUs, and network connectivity. Look how old your current technologies are and then examine how often they have been upgraded in the last five years or so. Sneaks up on you, doesn't it? I had to upgrade one of my VAXes, so I started to look into what I needed to get the job done. I then started considering upgrading my venerable MicroVAX II to a 4000-200 system (the board/memory swap kit from Digital). I came to realize that my 3100 is only 15 months old and the II has been here only about 29 months and already it is obsolete (try to buy a new one). Considering the fact that since the 3100 was formally announced on January 11, 1989 (I was there), it already has undergone a couple of major reengineerings (from 2.5 VAX units of performance (VUPs) to 10-plus is a considerable jump) in less than 30 months, it leads one to think that we need to reengineer our ideas of upgrades and version numbers to reflect the reality of computing. We need major upgrades about every two years, to keep up with the new overheads of software and the demands of users.

No one thinks twice when each year the major automotive vendors introduce new car models. In fact, we would all be aghast if they did not revamp some product lines, big time, every year. Why is it that engineers, any engineer, cannot leave things alone. I *liked* my 1977 Volkswagen Rabbit L. I drove it until it died a miserable and undeserved death (it helps to add oil every once in a while, I discovered much too late). When it came time to find a new car, the new Rabbits were now called Golfs and drove like golf carts. The new model was supposed to be superior to my 1977 model, but while it shared some of the same lineage, it was far from the same. Further investigation showed that there had been four major changes to the line in six years. No one complained, no one wanted his money back, and we all upgraded our cars as we went.

We expect some technologies to be upgraded every year, but when it comes to computers, our management is frequently aghast at the facts of upgrades and replacements and cannot understand why we have to upgrade and replace so often.

Software Enhancements and Planning

One of the major reasons for upgrading is software enhancement. My VAX-11/780 in 1978 was quite capable of supporting 15 to 20 users in 4 MB of memory with an RP06 176-MB removable disk and two DZ11-Es. That same system could function today, but the maintenance costs alone would make it grossly uneconomical and the software overhead of the operating system environment and user graphical environments would leave me with a single-user system that would create a useful computing environment for very few. No, I am not waxing nostalgic or wishing to return to the "large-iron" environment. It is a simple fact that VMS, applications, network software, and practically any other type of code you care to think of have gotten *huge* in size and complexity. This girth translates into big efforts by all and much greater horsepower requirements for user satisfaction.

Want proof? Take a perfectly good VAXStation 4000 and fire up the "old" VWS interface. With this, and 16 MB of memory, you could probably support 10 or so All-in-One users with a reasonable response time. Replace VWS with

DECWindows and the latest version of VMS or its suitable substitute, and the 10-user workstation becomes a single-user workstation. Add high-resolution color and VAXCluster capability and performance starts to take a hit, even for a single user. Argue all you want, say what you will, but there is no denying the fact that more sophisticated software packages and more new features and services *must* require additional computational horsepower.

Microcomputer applications are much the same. Three years ago, word processing with mice and icons was pretty much seen in only the Mac environment. With MS Windows V3.0 and new word processing software, graphical access to word processing became available. Integration of graphics, spreadsheet information (such as Object Linking and Embedding, or OLE), database access from applications, integral network support, and a myriad of other computation- and memory-intensive applications leads to the inevitable conclusion that more CPU power, greater memory, and larger disk space are essential to support the same applications we had three years ago. Look at the size of a file that contains clip art versus a file with the same text and no art. Sure, the art gives the document life, but it kills the system and the disk storage availability.

Already there is a standards committee working on standards for 100-MB 3.5-inch floppies. We already can purchase and use magneto-optical, read-write-erase removable disks that store 128 or 256 MB on a 3.5-inch disk that you can slip into a pocket. RISC machine technologies will give way to MISC and VLIW technologies in the next few years. We will be upgrading as never before.

The one constant in the computer business is change. There are so many vendor consortiums and standards committees working on new goodies, it surely boggles the mind as to how we will consume it all. We are getting into the same situation that many industrial businesses have had to deal with for some years: we are going to have to either retool every two years or so or fall by the computing wayside and be unable to get our jobs done. Many of us will resist changes, myself included, but there is no denying change when you wish to retain telephone support, vendor support, new features, and other desirable items that we all want to keep our computing facilities state-of-the-art and our users happy.

Ethernet/802.3 Retooling

Ethernet/802.3 networks get retooled as well. The original Ethernet developed at Xerox in 1976 ran at 3 Mbps. Later, version 2.0 specified a network that communicated at 10 Mbps. IEEE's 802.3 committee established the subsection 1BASE2 as a 1-Mbps CSMA/CD network, as well as 10-Mbps variants for thickwire (10BASE5), thinwire (10BASE2), twisted pair (10BASET), and later for fiber (10BASEF).

In the current IEEE 802.3 standard, cable speed is never explicitly specified. In fact, the standard provides for minimum and maximum round-trip times for signal propagation and for various configurations of cable and interconnection facilities. Therefore, there is no reason why Ethernet/802.3 networks cannot be configured to run faster than the popular 10-Mbps variant. In fact, the intent to make the same connection technology (CSMA/CD) much faster than most basic variants on the market is in the master game plan of the IEEE and 802.3 vendors.

The Future of Ethernet/802.3

In the future, the use of the 802.3 Manchester encoding technique for networks may be made obsolete by more "advanced" techniques, such as the 4b/5b encoding technique used by the Fiber Distributed Data Interface (FDDI). Using 4b/5b encoding, a full signal transition is not required for "bit" identification, and therefore a much higher bits-per-second rate is possible as a lower signaling rate. For instance, a 10-Mbps Manchester-encoded signaling system, such as that used by 10-Mbps baseband standards, requires about 20 MHz of signaling for the 10-Mbps speed. If 100 Mbps were provided using this technique, over 200 MHz of bandwidth would be required of the medium used. This would exceed the capabilities of many twisted-pair copper cables and would violate FCC Class B signaling requirements in the United States as well as other countries such as Germany. By using a different encoding technique (as well as token passing), the 100-Mbps speed is achieved at 125 MHz instead of 200 MHz.

What this means is that to achieve greater speeds efficiently with low-cost components, signaling techniques will have to change, which means the future demise and replacement of the Manchester signaling technique. Since much of the Ethernet/802.3 standard is wrapped around the concept of Manchester encoding, this may mean that when speeds of up to 100 Mbps are required, FDDI, or another type of medium besides fiber, may be required for greater speeds. FDDI has been demonstrated and used on fiber optic media, but vendors have also taken the signaling and encoding techniques of FDDI and placed them on unshielded twisted-pair (UTP), shielded twisted-pair (STP), and thinwire RG-58A/U cable.

From a longevity point of view, the ability to support differing signaling systems on UTP, STP, and thinwire cables is important for long-term network solutions. This may indicate that Ethernet/802.3 networks that use these types of media as the preferred solution today are well poised for conversion to the 100-Mbps FDDI/CDDI technology network of the future.

At the writing of this book, the IEEE is in the process of evaluating not only the usage of other types of medium for 802.3 but also the increase of cable speed to 100 Mbps. Whether this speed catches on before the whole world gets 100-Mbps-happy remains to be seen. It is, however, a midlife upgrade that may be useful for some sites that will require additional speed but not a full hardware platform changeout.

In the foreseeable future, Ethernet/802.3 networks will tend to migrate to twisted-pair connectivity as the medium, as well as fiber and, later, wireless connectivity. With each type of Ethernet/802.3 medium there are advantages and disadvantages. Since this chapter is devoted to planning and retooling, it is appropriate to discuss these available and upcoming technologies and find out where they do and do not fit in network configurations.

Further work on 100-Mbps Ethernet/802.3 via UTP is being considered at this writing, either by speeding up the medium access control interface (MAC submission) or by using the four wires of the two pair of UTP in a new way (100BASEVG submission). Which, if any, will make the 802.3 standard series is anyone's guess at this point, as both are still experimental and neither are standardized. Experience with standards committees also promises that whatever comes out in the standard will not be the same as the submission from either faction, so anyone who purchases either solution at this writing may be looking at replacing or upgrading equipment to be compliant with the standard when approved and completed.

With time, 100 Mbps of anything will be too slow, so the smart retooling network person knows that media is more important than speed. Will your media selection support gigabit and terabit speeds? Will your media upgrade to support types of network technologies other than 802.3 and other current off-the-shelf solutions? These are more pressing problems for a long-term solution than if 100-Mbps will solve the short-term problem.

Twisted-Pair Ethernet/802.3 (10BASET)

A question that is constantly posed to most network designers is "What kind of cable should I install for future network technologies?"

It's a fair question. Of course, every vendor has their answer, and they all want every customer to believe that theirs is the only answer for future network cable needs. In fact, the ultimate future network cabling system may be no cable at all. We already have hints of this system with infrared networks such as PHOTONET and radio-oriented networks. Also, with the development of technology such as Code Access Multiple Access and Code Demand Multiple Access, the evolution to the use of non-cable-oriented transmission technologies is real. In the meantime, we still have a need for cable to slake network thirsts. The problem is which cable to use.

Ask any vendor, and the two most common answers for future network technologies are twisted pair and fiber. In fact, it is widely acknowledged that fiber to the desktop is the "wave of the future." Both fiber and copper twisted pair have been around for a while, but the main difference today is that developments in transmission technologies allow usage of the media in new ways and at much higher speeds. Of course, fiber may give way to radio-based networks, and then later to light-wave networks (that is, cableless media). But we'll save that scenario for later in this chapter.

Twisted Pair and the Future of Ethernet/802.3

Putting fiber aside for now, the real controversy these days involves twisted pair and its vendors. Some vendors tout unshielded twisted pair; others focus on shielded twisted pair. Both cable types have merit, but only one, STP, can really provide a very long term solution without recabling for some time—until the need for fiber arises.

In my experience with twisted pair, which extends over 20 years, the main problem is that sales and support teams, as well as customers, do not know what twisted pair is and when it should and should not be used. There are situations in which twisted-pair cabling is a superior solution that will last for many years. There are also cases in which twisted-pair cabling is the proverbial Pandora's box. In all cases, twisted pair is frequently misunderstood and misused in network applications.

Twisted-pair cables came into use as a result of early multiple-pair, multiwire cables (untwisted) and a problem called crosstalk. Crosstalk, which is basically interference, occurred between voice pairs in the multiwire when energy radiated from one pair and "spilled over" into another. It was discovered that if the pairs were twisted together, with each pair twisted at a different twist rate, the radiated energy from current flowing in any one wire would be almost completely canceled out by radiation from the same current on the return wire of the pair. In this manner, the energy radiated into the other pairs in the cable is minimal and nondisruptive. No crosstalk! (Or very little.)

A side effect of twisting the wire is that the pairs become less susceptible to external noise, provided that they are properly twisted, terminated, and used.

This technique is all well and good for voice transmission. At voice frequencies, the physical dimensions of the pair of wires and the average twist length (the distance between successive twists) are much shorter than the wavelength of the signals placed on the wire. Theoretically, the twist "balances" the cable: at any point in space along each wire within the pair, the energy is equal. The compressed voice signal on a telephone pair may have a frequency as low as 1 kHz, with a wavelength that is almost 115 miles. The typical twist length of telephone cable is 6 inches, so it is theoretically and realistically possible to balance the energy.

However, as the frequency of signals increases, the probability of problems increases as well. The problem for twisted pair occurs with shorter wavelengths, that is, at higher frequencies. The theoretical balancing of the energy cannot be accomplished, as the probability of crosstalk and external noise interference increases exponentially with frequency. In other words, with telephone twisted pair wire, the shorter the wavelength, the greater the chance that distortion and interference will be generated. This phenomenon is especially pronounced with the introduction of megabit-level data communications.

Extensive research has been done by very large computing companies and other entities, who compared different twisted-pair environments and the effects of shielding the twisted pair in various noise-generating environments. NCR, for instance, showed in 1984 that on unshielded twisted-pair cable, if the data rate was increased from 1 Mbps to 4 Mbps, the peak noise amplitude increased by almost an order of magnitude. Moral: the faster the data rate on unshielded cable, the more susceptible it is to noise and interference. Other studies showed that when unshielded twisted-pair cable was used in an office environment, devices that use highly inductive switching technologies (such as electric motors, fluorescent lights, typewriters, copiers, and postal machines) cause serious interference if the unshielded twisted-pair cable is close to the device (within 6 feet) generating the signal. If the signal exceeded 1 volt, the 6-foot distance from the noise sources was not always sufficient to preclude the interference from affecting the unshielded twisted pair.

To further complicate the issue, at high frequencies, unshielded twisted-pair cable still generates energy. The FCC in the United States and equivalent authorities in other countries have announced some serious restrictions on radiation emissions above 30 MHz. This means that most unshielded twisted-pair installations can be used up to about 10 Mbps before the FCC regulation kicks in (10 Mbps signaling requires frequencies higher than 20 MHz to function). Rates higher than 10 Mbps will require add-on filters or another cable technology.

An obvious but resisted (no pun intended) answer is shielded twisted pair. By placing a shield on each wire of a pair and then twisting the pair, interference becomes almost a thing of the past. Tests of shielded twisted pair have demonstrated very little, if any, interference from the same sources of interference for unshielded twisted pair and do not exceed the radiation emission requirements of the FCC (estimates show that shielded twisted pair can achieve rates more than 50 times 10 Mbps and still not exceed FCC radiation restrictions). Shielded twisted pair, however, does impose a penalty: shielding causes a capacitance problem that translates to shorter allowable cable runs than unshielded twisted pair.

What does all this mean for the average network installation? Plenty. Long-term networks will require speeds that far exceed 10Mbps, and unless FCC regulations are modified, unshielded twisted pair restricts growth over currently proposed cable speeds. A longer term solution is to run shielded cable, but the proposed 10BASET does not provide for that type of cable in the current standard draft. Further, distance limitations imposed by shielded cable may cause problems at some sites. There are many sites that are planning to use currently installed unshielded twisted pair as 802.3 10BASET media in the future. Here are some items that bear thinking about:

1. 10 milliseconds of noise at 9.6 Kbps is a lot different from 10 milliseconds of noise at 10 Mbps. The faster the transmission, the more important it is to carefully install cable away from electrical interference and other potential noise hazards.

2. Punch-down blocks, connectors, and other required connection points may introduce noise into the network. Recently a twisted-pair repeater "hub" that had two open sockets for connection to segments of twisted pair caused all segments off of the hub to have noise and distortion problems. By putting in dummy terminators in the open RJ-11 sockets of the hub, the problems disappeared. The vendor told the customer that this was not necessary, but analysis of the cable showed that it was, and it did correct the problem.

3. Shielded cable is not standard, but it is beneficial and good for the long term. Many sites are choosing such cable (frequently referred to as IBM Type 1 cable), but the need for shorter lengths of twisted pair requires more careful layout of runs and more hub locations. In turn, the expense increases, not only in cable cost but also in the number of interconnects.

4. Shielded twisted-pair cable may be used with many different types of networks, such as CSMA/CD (Ethernet as well), token ring, ARCNET, and others. Not all networks support unshielded twisted pair as a valid cable media type.

5. Because of the small amount of connectable metal in twisted-pair connectors, they are highly susceptible to corrosion in hostile environments. One of my customer sites had installed a twisted-pair network and was using RJ-11 (4-wire phone plug) connectors. Because the customer utilizes chlorine and other volatile gases at its facility (and it is in a marshy area), the connectors regularly fail, causing noise to be introduced on the network,

and require frequent replacement. The section of network next to one of the twisted-pair configurations is composed of thinwire and has not had one cable fault in four years. The twisted pair is two years old and has required more than 30 repairs in the last 18 months. Twisted pair is definitely not for all environments.

Oddly enough, one of the bigger proponents of unshielded twisted pair, Digital Equipment Corporation, carefully states in some documents concerning 802.3 twisted-pair networking that "thinwire is the optimal media to deliver 802.3/Ethernet to the desktop." Then again, maybe that position is not so odd, considering that thinwire (RG-58A/U coax) is practically immune from noise (when properly installed) and does not exceed FCC requirements coming down the road.

Many solutions on the market for unshielded twisted-pair 802.3/Ethernet do not meet the standard in many ways, depending on the vendor. About the only thing in common with 10BASET is the cable type. Variances in connectors, signaling rates, peak-to-peak voltages, and other critical components can cause supposedly standardized components not to communicate when connected. It is very important that sites that are not 10BASET-compliant become so after the standard, to ensure that expansion of the twisted-pair network does not become a nightmare with no end due to the variety of connection methods and the restrictions imposed on the network by each vendor.

When considering the use of twisted pair as a cabling standard or for a "one-cable-fits-all" situation, unshielded twisted pair is fine if you do not expect to exceed about 10 Mbps. If, however, a truly long-term solution is required and minimal noise aggravation sought, shielded twisted pair is the way to go. In both situations, proper analysis of network longevity and needs is required before any decision can be made. This means that a proper network design, with all the bells and whistles, needs to be done to ensure that the correct solution is selected and achieved.

Problems with Twisted Pair in Real Installations

Let me start by saying that I like unshielded twisted pair. I use it, when appropriate, for many types of networks and terminal connections. While it is new to LAN technologies, I have been using it for many years and have installed it for many, many LANs. But, like any technology, it has its drawbacks and cannot be used everywhere, contrary to anything any vendor might tell you.

I recently had to work with a cable vendor to install an unshielded twisted-pair network. Against my professional judgment, at this particular site, the customer insisted that such cable type be used. A fairly typical office facility, it should have been well suited for the unshielded twisted-pair experience. After all was said and done, we ended up with some areas cabled with unshielded twisted-pair 802.3 10BASET-compliant cable and the rest cabled with non-standardized shielded twisted pair and thinwire (RG-58A/U) 802.3 cable.

The problems started innocently enough. One of the sections of UTP ran too close to the copier. You know the type of copier: you insert trees and steel in one end and collated, stapled copies come out the other end. Copiers can generate some serious EMI, and UTP makes a wonderful receptor of such noise and static. Since the UTP concentrator/repeater was in the closet next to the copier, it was similarly affected, as the UTP cables from the nearby offices were terminating in the closet and also contributed to the overall noise problem coming in to the concentrator. How did we find out? The concentrator, smart little guy that it is, decided that the error counts on 7 of the 12 ports were too high and shut them down for us. How wonderful technology is!

Well, thinwire solved that issue, since moving the copier was out of the question and we still needed to connect the offices. We could have used shielded twisted pair, but the customer had a thinwire repeater they wanted to use. No biggie—so far.

The next problem was on one floor up. Same symptoms: the concentrator decided that there was much too much garbage on a couple of the UTP lines and automatically shut them down. No equipment nearby, no visible source of interference, no obvious source of the problem. Replace connectors, check out concentrator, no problems. Replace concentrator. New concentrator shuts down same two ports, same error messages.

Was Rod Serling nearby?

Just for giggles, I ran a piece of thinwire to the office via the hallway and cabled up the system. No problem. I put an analyzer on the thinwire segment; no problem. I put an analyzer on the UTP segment and got all kinds of framing errors. A-ha! Noise had returned. The big question was from where?

I popped the ceiling tiles and began my search. Nothing obvious. I checked the physical perimeter of the offices and found that in the next room, separated by a heavily insulated wall, there were various printers and output devices. Surely they could not be causing the problem, could they? Too unbelievable to consider. I continued to look for a source of my problems, but I kept coming back to the printer room. Finally, I called a cable guru friend of mine and gave him my analysis of what I found.

His response: "What kind of studs are they using in the walls?"

What the hell does that have to do with the noise problem?

"Well, those newfangled aluminum studs do a great job of transmitting static from other locations if they are connected together somehow. It's kind of like wiring cable together—the studs make contact with each other when assembled for the office walls, and any nearby noise gets transmitted to the other studs and pretty soon there is a static problem traveling all over the office area. We see it all the time. The only solution is to run shielded twisted pairs or coax. You'd be surprised how often it happens."

He's right. I would. So I proposed a semi-scientific test. If all the printers were turned off and disconnected from the walls, the problem should disappear, yes?

Guess what? Problem went away. You learn something new every day. So we changed the cable to individually shielded pairs and the problem evaporated.

Another telephone closet, another problem. This time, the concentrator was complaining that seven ports had errors. The problem was, the ports didn't have anything connected to them: they were empty! Well, since this was the concentrator near the despised copier, EMI was a possibility. I called the vendor of the concentrator and asked if EMI would be a problem in an empty port on the concentrator.

"Surely you can't be serious! No, not a problem."

More investigation. Called a customer who had the same concentrator from the same vendor and asked him if they had the problem.

"Oh, yeah! We solved it by putting these little RJ-11 terminator connectors into the unused ports. Turned out to be a noise problem."

Where'd you get the terminators?

"From the vendor. They knew all about it."

Hmmmm. Another call to the vendor, and this time I got someone at the corporate facility, who seemed to have her head screwed on straight. I asked her about the mysterious empty socket problem and she confirmed what the customer had told me. She also sent me a box of the little terminators.

I installed the terminators and, again, the problem vanished.

At this point, I had about 75% of the systems up and running and what should have been a one-day job had turned into six days. Then the customer asked me a very good question: "Are all installations as much of a pain as this one? I know we are getting things fixed, but if you weren't here, we wouldn't know what to do or who to call, much less fix the problems."

A fair assessment. After thinking about it for a while and comparing other UTP installations I have been involved in, I concluded that I have had similar experiences. Usually one or two problems per site, but usually not as diverse a range in one site. I have had problems with corrosion at industrial sites, where the RJ-11 and RJ-45 connectors quickly get corroded because of the environment at the facility, but thinwire and thickwire components do not seem to suffer as much as the components that have contacts; they are either protected or have a much larger metal surface area and are not as dramatically affected as the smaller surface areas on the metal contacts of the RJ-11 and RJ-45 connectors.

Noise is always a problem with any unshielded cable. Normally noise is not much of an issue in an office, but with more and more office equipment actually being used in the area near the connectors and the workplace, there are more sources of noise. In the olden days of computing, we ran terminal cables to the office and all the systems were in a large room. Now, there is a general tendency to provide office-environment systems and workstations at the desktop. This alone promotes more hardware closer to the workspace, which can help contribute to the problem, especially with FCC Class A equipment.

For instance, my old GRiD Compass II, a Class A device, when placed next to my little portable color TV, completely blows away any reception. The same TV, however, when placed next to my Mac Plus, is happy. It is happy next to my Mac IIci and even my 386-based PC, but not happy when next to the external 100-MB hard disk. While the hard disk is a Class B device and therefore better shielded, it has a fan, which seems to like to interfere with the TV. The TV is not too thrilled being next to a MicroVAX setup, either. Obviously, if I can interfere with a television, UTP is only a step away.

Moral of the story? UTP is great as a convenience. If it is already installed, it may be usable for some classes of network. Care in installation, placement of cables, connectors, and concentrators is all-important. There are still a great many locations where UTP should not be considered, especially if there are noise sources and higher LAN transfer rates are required. A 10-millisecond burst of static at 9.6 Kbps causes much less damage than the same static at 10 Mbps, so LANs running UTP cannot be considered the same way that terminal or low-speed networks are set up, especially when considering interference metrics.

How Many Pairs of Twisted Pair?

Which do I prefer, shielded or unshielded? It depends on what I am doing. But I am awfully fond of shielded twisted pair. Especially since I plan on upgrading my twisted-pair network to 100 Mbps or better over twisted pair, shielded is the only way to go. And 16 pairs (yes, 16 pairs) to each location, too. Why? Because it's simple, as this list shows:

- Four pairs for a LAN
- Four pairs for voice
- Four pairs for alternate LAN
- Four pairs for alternate LAN

Although using fewer pairs may be functional, it is much more difficult to manage in a live network environment. Most networks will be upgraded in the future, even twisted-pair networks, and this will mean parallel network connectivity for a period of time while the new network is being tested and the old network is running.

A more powerful reason for the numbers of pairs of cable is the problem of pair identification. Trying to figure out what pair is connected to what in a telephone closet is incredibly difficult on a good day, and trying to reconfigure each location can be very tedious. By running a separate pair or combinations of pairs for each network type or communications function, the pairs may be color coded for ease of identification and configuration. While this may seem trivial, it's not when most network sites now have well over 100 nodes. As multiple network technologies are integrated into the site—and this is the trend—the need to run multiple network technologies simultaneously will be required. Trying to keep sorted out as to which pair at which work area is which type of network will be difficult and very time-consuming. Color coding the pairs is a great help in managing the multiple Ethernet/802.3 configuration as well as multiple network technologies. It not only saves time, it will reduce downtime, increase flexibility of the network cable configuration, and allow more rapid troubleshooting and reconfiguration.

Wireless Ethernet/802.3 Networks

As I write this book, I've been designing and implementing my latest wireless network. This one was a bit unusual because it is wireless not only for data but also for voice. The other unusual thing about this network is that it is the first one that I have done completely in the United States. All other wireless networks that I have put in, especially for voice, have been in Europe in the last two years; now the trend is reaching this country. Some of my university customers have been approached by regional Bell operating companies to participate in wireless PBX and localized voice access experiments. They have also been approached by wireless data network vendors regarding putting in wireless data networks for micro- and minicomputer access.

Wireless networks are by no means new. In the late 1960s, the University of Hawaii activated ALOHANET, a packet radio network (see Chapter 1). The military uses packet radio for a variety of applications (for example, the Naval Tactical Data System, or NTDS II), both classified and unclassified. Commercial packet radio networks are at work in police cars, emergency response systems, and even shipping and delivery companies (take a glance inside a Federal Express truck sometime).

I've been harping about wireless networks for some time. Years ago, I was involved in the innovation and implementation of a wireless network for a shipping company, and I have seen the network grow steadily to thousands of nodes in 21 countries. Cellular phones, now the norm, have always been wireless, so wireless voice has not been a mystery to anyone in a long time. Wireless PBXs, however, are new in the United States, even though our colleagues in Europe have been using them for a couple of years now. But lately there has been an enormous push to adopt wireless networks in this country for both voice and data. There are *a lot* of companies jumping on the bandwagon now, much earlier than many observers (including myself) expected.

Why the big rush? Well, many companies and organizations need the flexibility of being able to move workstations and microcomputer systems around. Wiring expenses have gotten outrageous, due to the labor costs involved. The need for faster networks has caused some cabling technologies to become obsolete in a very short time, due to their vendor-defined speed and transport limitations. As a result, buildings have had to be recabled long before anyone expected them to be. The cable of the future is no cable at all—and that cable is here now.

Some networks, like Motorola's Altair 10-Mbps 802.3/V2.0 frame-compliant wireless network, are making high-speed wireless LANs possible with little installation effort and with maximum availability. Areas difficult to cable are now trivial to access, and when a department moves, the network moves as well. Installing the entire network now takes hours instead of days, and installing a new node on the network takes minutes instead of the hours it takes to install cable, connectors, and other required components to bring the node up. While networks like Altair are severely more expensive than equivalent cable-oriented networks, eventually the costs for a wireless hookup will be equal or below that of a wire-oriented network connection today. This cost reduction may happen much sooner than expected if the concepts of wireless networks catch on in the mainstream corporate installation.

Some smaller and slower wireless networks, such as Local Area Wireless Network (LAWN) and PHOTONET (a LocalTalk-compatible wireless solution), have been around for some time. More expensive than wire-oriented networks, they are very useful for quick network installation requirements and for those locations where the workgroup will be moved around or mobilized.

Wireless networks, however, have to be even more carefully designed than cable-oriented networks, due to the potential of greater sources of interference and distortion. Further, the basic network design precepts of workgroup placement, traffic matrix isolation, and many other issues still apply; they do not evaporate when the cable does. Imagine trying to figure out traffic patterns and connectivity matrices between nodes when there is no defined cable path! There are also some pretty serious FCC restrictions in the United States that must be adhered to, as well as the standard National Electrical Code, EIA/TIA, and other standards that are designed for networks, electrical equipment, and their respective needs. Some states even require that the cableless plan be approved by a licensed professional engineer. So installation of a wireless network, while technically straightforward, comes with a baggage load of paper that must be addressed if the network is to function properly and within legal tolerances required by governmental agencies and the vendor of the hardware for transmission and reception of data.

While wireless data networking concepts and technologies have been around in the United States for some time, in Europe a new telephony standard called CT3 has been slowly but steadily increasing its foothold. With CT3, users carry their telephones with them, and base station repeaters strategically placed in the work vicinity allow users to communicate with the PBX system. CT3 phones may be used outside of the office in a manner similar to a cellular phone, because base stations may be installed on the tops of buildings or at special pay phonebooths (in the United Kingdom, these booths are marked—all you have to do is be nearby). With CT2, the predecessor standard, a phone user could originate calls but could not receive them. CT3 removes this limitation and provides an inexpensive, wireless network connection that "follows" the user of the phone system as he or she moves within a facility. The phone becomes a personal communications tool and enhances the ability of coworkers and supervisors to access each other without being tied down to a particular physical location.

One nice thing about CT3 is that it can be integrated with the Integrated Services Digital Network (ISDN) technology that is starting to get a foothold in some countries. In this manner, CT3 evolution will surely allow low-speed (up to 64-Kbps) data access via the phone, as well as voice access.

As previously mentioned, the implementation of cableless networks is fast and efficient. At one site I recently worked on, it took over two weeks to wire up four stories of a building for unshielded twisted-pair network access and phone access for 500 workstations and phones. Another week of testing ensued, and then the add-ons started to trickle in. At another physical facility for the same customer, we installed a wireless data network and a CT3 test plant. The entire base station network was installed in three hours, and the required repeaters for the wireless data access took about six hours. The system was tested the next day, and on the third day 622 workstations were active and running with the same speeds and voice/data access facilities as the UTP installation that took over two weeks. Talk about instant gratification! This, however, is not unusual with wireless networks and can provide a company a very fast activation curve with quick results and productivity.

Summary

Planning for the network of the future is always a guessing game at best. The odds-on favorites for the long term are fiber and wireless, but in the meantime, the Ethernet/802.3 network of choice will tend to be twisted pair. Not because it is superior to thinwire, thickwire, or any other alternative medium, but because about 80% of all businesses already have twisted pair installed and *it is available*. It is not necessarily cheaper or easier to maintain.

Proper planning precludes major mistakes. Remember that Ethernet/802.3 networks require planning to survive the long haul, and proper planning is just another part of efficient network management.

Workgroup Placement, Bridges, and Brouters: Improving Ethernet/802.3 Performance

Many times Ethernet/802.3 performance can be dramatically improved by isolating workgroups via bridges and bridge/router combinations, called brouters. This chapter focuses on what workgroup placement is, the differences in bridges and brouters, and how to utilize the technologies effectively to improve Ethernet/802.3 performance.

Workgroup Placement

Recently a site wanted to upgrade their Ethernet/802.3 DEMPR (thinwire multiport repeater with eight thinwires connected to one thickwire—see Figure 5.1) to multiple bridge units to reduce traffic on the network.

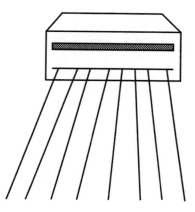

Figure 5.1
Thinwire Multiport Repeater (Stand-alone)

They had put a protocol analyzer on the network and found that everyone was transmitting traffic all over the network. The theory was simple: if they could cut down the amount of traffic on the network, the network performance should improve. It's a sound theory—if every node on the entire network is connected on the same logical segment of cable (or wireless medium), each node must look at every packet to see if the packet bears its address.

Obviously, there is a finite amount of computing power in the node's Ethernet/802.3 controller, and a finite amount of RAM as well. So there is a finite amount of packets that any Ethernet/802.3 controller may process in a given time period. If you can reduce the number of packets that the controller sees but that are not destined for the node viewing them, then you can reduce network overhead and improve throughput on that node. Also, if the buffers in a controller are full of other nodes' traffic, then packets destined for a particular node will be "ignored" by the controller, since there is no RAM available for storing them. If you reduce the amount of traffic that a node must examine, you will reduce retransmissions and improve throughput.

This site had looked at some of the new multiport bridge units on the market and decided that they would implement one. Installation was easy: disconnect the DEMPR from the thickwire and the eight thinwires and connect two new four-port bridges (see Figure 5.2). The installation took about 10 minutes and the bridges came up fine.

The network, however, proceeded to go into the sewer. Response time became very bad and there were all kinds of network disconnects and timeouts. And those were the good features!

The problem was not devils in the bridge units. Far from it. The problem turned out to be which systems were connected to which segments and which

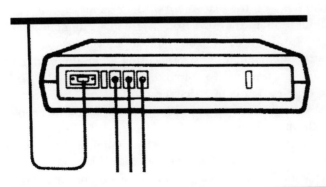

Figure 5.2
Four-Port Multiport Bridge (High Speed)

nodes were talking to which. With all nodes in the workgroup configured on the various segments, the repeater never degraded in throughput with this configuration. When the repeater was replaced by the bridges, however, problems surfaced.

The Purposes of a Bridge

One purpose of a bridge is not only to segment the network electrically but also to segment traffic that appears on the network. To do so, the bridge unit "learns" which side of the bridge a node is located on by listening to all packets on all connected segments and creating a table of source addresses. In this manner, the bridge discovers which systems are on which segment. When a packet arrives at the bridge, the bridge looks at the destination and source addresses and decides if the packet should be forwarded to a segment other than the one the packet originated on. Thus, packets that originate at a node on segment A with a destination of another node on the same segment are not forwarded to another segment. This method allows traffic to remain on the necessary segments but it does not affect segments on the network that do not need the packet.

When replacing the multiport repeater with bridge units, it is important that the traffic patterns be studied carefully, first to determine which nodes are communicating with other nodes and then to attempt to place them on the same physical segment whenever possible. This placement allows the bridge to do its job properly and not get overloaded attempting to filter packets that it cannot possibly filter due to traffic path.

In our example, when network performance suffered heavily rather than improved after installing bridges, the problem was not with the bridge units. The problem was with the placement of the systems on the segments. In the actual configuration, the network nodes were PCs, minicomputer systems, and various servers and disk servers on the cables. Because the disk servers were on different segments than the systems using them, the bridge was not filtering but forwarding packets. To compound the problem, the bridge units had to examine each packet before deciding to forward them. Since this activity takes longer than forwarding bits without examination in a repeater, the network throughput suffered.

Placing workstations that need to work together or share data on the same segment is not a new concept. What is new is the idea of placing nodes on the network in such a way that nodes that need to communicate with each other are on the same physical segment on the network. This placement allows nodes to continue to communicate with each other and also allows the bridge to properly filter traffic that appears on each segment.

Replacing Repeaters with Bridges

The moral? Chances are very good that as networks mature, multisegment repeater units, such as multiport repeaters and some twisted-pair repeater types, will be replaced by multiport bridges. Though configuration and installation of such a device is easy, one still needs to be extremely careful to ensure that the bridge can do its work. When the multiport units are configured into the network, the network designer and installation team need to make sure that nodes that will be communicating frequently are on the same physical segment. Although it may not seem important, traffic-wise, at the time, misinstallation will eventually cause problems and require reconfiguration of the network.

Electrical Isolation

Another benefit of proper network segment configuration comes if a repeater or bridge fails. If the units that need to communicate with each other are on the same physical segment(s), then in the case of repeater or bridge failure, those units may still continue to exchange data—but not with any other systems on any other segment. When cooperating systems are on the same segment, they may continue to work even if there is a problem interconnecting to other systems. If, say, the shared disk units were placed on another wire, then the nodes lose the ability to recover and continue to work; thus the network configuration is substandard.

Placing nodes on any ol' cable is not good enough. You will hear this advice often enough from the network vendors of the world. Proper placement of nodes on the network ensures proper fail-over now and proper conversion in the future. Remember that after the vendor has sold you his wares and left, you are on your own—you still have to manage and control the network. You also have to provide adequate performance.

Bridges and Brouters

There are substantial differences between bridges, router units, and the new hybrid systems called brouters. To properly understand which unit is best for what, you need to know what each component is.

First there is the venerable bridge unit. Most bridge units provide a certain forwarding/filtering rate: one rate tells the customer how many packets per second (pps) can be processed by the bridge's myriad of "if-then-elses"; the other rate tells the customer how many packets per second may be sent between segments, flat out. Since there is no defined industry standard, filtering rates and forwarding rates are often interchanged in vendors' promotional literature.

Basically, since an Ethernet/802.3 segment under "full-tilt" load can generate more than 14,800 pps, the need to pick the packets off of one segment and get them to the other in one quick hurry is a biggie. It is even better yet if the bridge unit can process each packet to see if it is appropriate to send the packet from one segment to the other (that is, if the source machine and destination machine are on the same side of the bridge, it is not appropriate to move the packet over to the other side of the bridge). What governs how many packets may be processed includes bridge CPU power, memory, proprietary algorithms, queuing delay, network activity levels, and many other issues.

By default, practically all bridge units will "learn" which source nodes are on what side of the bridge and then filter traffic to determine if the packets generated by either side of a two-port bridge should be sent to the other side. This takes a goodly amount of horsepower to do correctly and quickly. Some bridges can be configured in such a way that they may also restrict certain sources or destinations from being accessed across the bridge; still others allow further restrictions on protocol types, even down to patterns of data being sent around. The more filtering and options implemented, the more horsepower—and money—is required.

Bridges are handy also because some networking protocols, such as MOP and LAT, are not classically routed. In other words, there is not a routing function designed into the protocol architecture; the protocol suite expects the network to provide a certain uniformity of speed and access. This type of protocol can also translate into problems in network configurations if a node running a nonroutable protocol needs to connect to another node on the network that is not on the same physical segment. If the interconnection between the segments does not support the protocol in question, connectivity is not allowed. If the protocol is not routable, then a bridge—which is protocol independent—can solve the problem.

Since pure bridges do not have routing algorithms in them, as a rule they cannot answer requests for information or for assistance from specific protocols. They may forward them to other LAN segments, but it would be handy if they could respond to specific network requests such as address resolution, node availability status, and other items that would keep packets from wandering all over the network.

What Is a Brouter?

A few years ago, some bridge vendors started to support multiple LAN connections to the same bridge. This innovation introduced a new concept called a brouter. The first brouters could be connected to two or more segments and would determine, based on source node and destination node addressing information, which of its segments should receive a packet. This proved to be a valuable facility, because intermediate segments (a segment between two other segments over which traffic must flow) could now be "routed" around, and performance between connected nodes could be increased. These initial bridge/router (brouter) combinations did not support any specific protocols, but the support and forwarding of multiple-segment packets was beneficial and useful. Though there has never been an industrywide naming convention for these units, they are generically called Class A brouter units (units that route based on source and destination information in a packet).

Since the initial brouter introduction, some companies, such as Vitalink, Cisco systems, and Wellfleet, have introduced bridge/router units that not only fulfill the Class A requirements but also allow inclusion of official honest-to-goodness protocol routing functions.

Routing Algorithms

In these newer types of brouters, a routing algorithm—such as Bellman-Ford-Moore, Open Shortest Path First (OSPF), ISO 8473A, or some other algorithm—is actually coded and included in the bridge unit. This allows the bridge to function as a traditional router for specific protocols and as a regular source-destination bridge filtering unit for nonroutable protocols. On a well-designed network, this reduces traffic from segment to segment, where the routing algorithms are capable of supplying routing service functions to the specific protocols (such as address translation, node availability, and other features). This type of device, which combines bridging, source-destination routing for multiple LAN segments, and traditional protocol routing for specific protocols, is commonly called a Class B brouter.

Configuration of Class B brouters is much different from that of a bridge, because Class B units must account for protocol overhead, network protocol loading, configuration of the routing database, protocol nuances, filtering, and many other issues. It can also get a little confusing for the network designer, who has to think of such devices as bridges for some protocols and routers for others (this difference increases the complexity of network traffic modeling tenfold). The benefits of a Class B brouter, especially in environments where the predominant network load is caused by a routable protocol, far exceed the aggravation of configuring it; they should be carefully considered for network expansions.

As our networks expand and we incur the overhead of new protocols and facilities, we will need to deploy ever more brouter units. Class A units are very useful where there are a number of in-building LANs that require high-speed forwarding and filtering. Class B units are especially useful where there are phone-line interconnects between LANs or where workgroups have been carefully segmented and designed and can make optimum use of the separate protocol traffic a Class B unit brings to the table. For best results, look for bridges and brouters that can be upgraded from to Class A and eventually to Class B. On Class B brouters, configure tables and buffers carefully for optimum performance. And finally, don't scrimp on a brouter's horsepower—you will suffer in the end if you do.

Improving Performance with Bridges and Brouters

Follow these steps to get better performance on your Ethernet/802.3 network via workgroups, bridges, and brouters:

1. Carefully collect traffic on the Ethernet/802.3 and analyze which node is communicating with which other nodes. This information will provide the volume of traffic between nodes and allow analysis of what system is communicating with what. Knowing this is important if you want to configure a bridge or brouter unit properly on the network

To collect the data for who-is-talking-to-whom, a protocol analyzer is not enough. In the networking world, this activity is called traffic analysis and it is not trivial. What has to be collected is not difficult to isolate. Trying to do it for every combination of nodes and protocols at the same time is what is difficult.

Enterprise-wide network management tools can help, but there are still very few that provide a full report on who is talking to whom. Network security tools, such as the Network Security Monitor (NSM), must perform traffic analysis as part of their normal function to detect network security breaches and, therefore, provide a secondary benefit besides network security monitoring.

2. Once node combinations have been identified, nodes that can be physically connected to the same Ethernet/802.3 cable should be. This means that nodes accessing a file server most of the time should be connected

on the same cable. Nodes in a local area VAXCluster should be on the same cable segment.

3. Cooperative nodes on cable segments should be isolated via a bridge or brouter unit. Which unit is best depends on whether the protocols being used between systems are routable or not. For instance, if the protocols are TCP/IP, DECnet, NetWare (IPX), AppleTalk, or another popular protocol, a Class B brouter unit would be a good candidate. For other types of protocols, a Class A brouter or a filtering bridge would be appropriate.

4. Based on the traffic rates seen during the initial data collection effort, select the bridge or brouter capabilities. Some sharing protocols, such as LAVC and NFS activities, should never be allowed to traverse bridges, due to performance problems. If the protocols can be isolated by the bridge or brouter, the appropriate protocol filters should be installed in the bridge or brouter unit(s) to keep the traffic isolated between segments.

All of this seems pretty straightforward; from a logical point of view, it is. Unfortunately, the politics of which workstation is located where and the problems of data collection and analysis do not make this effort any easier. Remember that what is convenient and easy for humans to understand and deal with is not trivial for technology. Technology does not understand that half a workgroup is in building A and the rest in building B and that both buildings are separated by a bridge or brouter unit. All the software and hardware knows is that to get from A to B, they must traverse the bridge, and over they go—much to the degradation of all nodes on the network and the bridge or brouter unit.

The 80/20 Rule and Traffic Isolation

As a general guideline, it is a good idea to try to isolate traffic and nodes based on the general networking rule of 80/20. The rule is pretty simple: try to keep 80% of the traffic between nodes on the same physical cable segment and isolate that segment from other segments. This usually means that the remaining 20% of traffic will need to traverse the bridge or brouter units. If, however, 80% of the traffic is between segments and only 20% on a segment itself, then a repeater is better suited to the task (purely from a traffic point of view). Putting in bridges and brouters, unless they are very swift, between segments where 80% or more of the traffic traverses the bridge or brouter may only cause more degradation.

One exception that comes to mind is when one segment has nothing but systems that will be talking to the rest of the network. For instance, if a segment of Ethernet/802.3 cable had nothing but terminal servers or X Window terminals on it, 100% of its traffic would need to go to other segments.

On the surface, it would appear that the proper interconnect device in such a case would be a repeater. The real question is whether 100% of the traffic on the *other* segment should be repeated back to the segment with all the terminal servers. In this situation, the answer is probably no. Since terminals are not as overhead-intensive as file transfers or other streaming types of activities, the chances are very good that a bridge or brouter would be more appropriate. Yes, 100% is headed "down" to the other segment. Is 100% also headed back up, or does only 5% of the total traffic need to go back? Also, if all the traffic is sent to the original terminal server segment from the other segment, the terminal servers now must deal with a much higher traffic load than before, and with a multitude of packets not destined for them. With a heavy traffic load, the nodes on the network will miss the traffic actually destined for them, as they will be examining traffic for other nodes. This causes the problems described at the beginning of this chapter, which is the reason for installing a bridge or brouter.

Multisegment (Multiport) Bridges

Every once in a a while, a new technology rears its ugly head and sends an orderly technical world into a chaotic "OK-what-do-we-do-now" mode.

Such products do not arrive every day. The smart technical type recognizes them and knows what to do: Learn. Quick.

Multiport bridges are one such product. Though previously unknown, the units were recently announced. Some have better features and different configurations from others, but they all are quietly throwing things for a loop in the subtle world of Ethernet/802.3 configurations. The problem is not whether they work or not. No, the problem is that they create so many new configuration opportunities for LANs that design criteria for 802.3-class LANs will have to be revisited and revised.

Currently there are rules for cable lengths, distances between nodes, propagation times for signals on the network cable types, and so on. These rules, properly applied to network topological design, allow the network designer to create and implement a functioning network that meets performance and expansion criteria as prescribed in various networking standards, most notably the IEEE 802.3 CSMA/CD standard.

Though 802.3 does not prescribe any rules for the incorporation of LAN bridge units in an 802.3 network design, there are some de facto rules of configuration that have evolved over the years when configuring bridges into a network. There are some explicit rules for repeater configurations, but there are also some pretty hazy areas, such as how many repeaters are allowed in a connection path. Without explicit speed information on bit propagation times from the vendor, it is difficult to know how many repeaters are actually allowed in a path.

One very popular type of repeater used in the 802.3 world is a device known as a multiport repeater. A multiport repeater typically allows 2 or more segments of 802.3 cable to be connected to the same box; all data seen on all connected segments is repeated to all connected segments. Most repeaters of this type have a minimum of 2 segments, but the more popular ones have 8 or more segments on the same physical box (one I know of has 12 connected segments on the same repeater). They can cost anywhere from $1000 to as much as $6000, but most are in the $3000 to $4000 range. Multiport repeaters typically connect thinwire (RG-58A/U) cables to the box and then connect the box via an AUI to a thickwire (if required). If there were, say, eight 189-meter thinwires connected to a multiport repeater, the repeater could connect 29 taps on each of the 8 thinwires, with a ninth 15-pin port connecting to a backbone thickwire. In this configuration, 232 connections are possible (the 30th tap on each thinwire is to the repeater itself) on each repeater off of the 8 thinwire segments. Since a 500-meter thickwire could accommodate 100 of these multiport repeaters, the number of machines connected to one thickwire via multiport repeaters could get silly really fast! Add one level of DELNIs in front of the repeaters and the total count is multiplied by a factor of 8—still off the same thickwire backbone.

Most vendors of thinwire multiport repeaters do not allow other repeaters or bridge units to be connected on the subordinate segments of the unit. This is usually due to potential propagation problems, but some vendors have other reasons as well. In short, multiport repeaters allow massive expansion capabilities at reasonable cost.

Some vendors allow different types of media on the repeaters. One vendor allows six thinwires, two thickwires, and two fiber connections on the same repeater. Others offer six thinwires and six twisted pair. There is a myriad of combinations allowed with various multiport repeaters, and since there is no standard as to how they should be configured, it is up to each vendor to stipulate any connectivity criteria.

The problem with repeaters is that they repeat—everything. In a lightly loaded network, this is not a big deal. But as the network grows and users become proficient in using the network, the need to isolate traffic to specific segments and reduce overall network load increases. Further, since most multiport repeaters will be connected to a backbone of some sort, there will eventually be a need to isolate traffic on the repeater from the backbone such that only traffic destined for the backbone should really be on the backbone, thus lim-

iting the amount of traffic on the network to what really needs to be there—
not every bit that appears on any cable.

It would seem logical to place a bridge unit between the repeaters and the
backbone to reduce the traffic load, but this means reconfiguration of the network and usually some additional "intermediate" segments to keep everything
legal and tidy. It also means that more hardware is added to the path, which
will cause the network troubleshooting matrix to increase, as well as introduce
additional points of failure into the network path.

Redundant Bridge Configurations

Another issue is the increased need to configure redundant network connections between systems. If, say, four network segments needed to be redundant
between each other, a minimum of eight bridges would be required to connect the four segments redundantly. This would mean stacking four segments
and connecting two bridges to each segment, with the bridges connected to
the next segment. The next segment would have four bridges connected to
it—two to the previous segment and two to the next segment in the stack, and
so on. The final segment would be connected via two bridges back to the original segment. While this setup provides some levels of redundancy, it is not
completely redundant to all segments, only to the next segment in a stack; thus
it is not a full network-redundant configuration.

Spanning Tree

For redundant bridge configurations, the 802.1d algorithm known as spanning tree is required. Spanning tree, developed at Digital Equipment
Corporation by the inspired Dr. Radia Perlman, who is now at Novell, allows a
"root" bridge to learn about the network topology of other spanning tree
bridges and to stop loop connections as well as allow bridge fail-over for segments that are connected by more than one bridge between the same two segments on the network.

Unfortunately, Dr. Perlman's original version of spanning tree, called DEC
Spanning Tree, is incompatible with the IEEE 802.1d flavor, which causes massive problems in mixed bridge algorithm environments. If the two types of
spanning tree algorithms are seen on the same network at the same time, in-
variably some of the bridges will, at a minimum, flush path tables and, at a maximum, crash and force a bridge reboot (this is the more common reaction). It
is exceedingly important to keep the algorithm selection for *all* bridge units
that "see" each other on the network to the same spanning tree protocol type

(DEC or 802.1d) to keep the units functioning, even if they are not placed between the same two segments.

For a more thorough treatment of spanning tree and other routing protocols, refer to Dr. Perlman's 1992 book *Interconnections*. It offers detailed explanations of routers and bridge units, while showing the amount of wit and humor required for a good technical book. I highly recommend it.

Multiport Bridges

In some cases spanning tree is overkill, and alternative hardware solutions may be preferred. Enter multiport bridges, especially in local network configurations. Local configurations are those where the bridges are within 50 meters of a segment of cable or adjacent to all other cable types. In other words, the segments are configured in such a fashion as to be connected over 2 kilometers without the use of telephone connections or fiber connections.

If we were to use a four-port multiport bridge to connect four segments, the configuration might look like the following.

When the same four segments of 802.3 cable are connected with multiport bridges in a redundant manner, only two of the four-port bridge units are required to connect to the four segments. Since the bridges are spanning tree-compliant and can "learn" about each other, they can be connected to the same segments with one bridge functioning as the live root bridge and the other in a hot standby mode in case the primary path should fail.

The cost benefits are serious. If a normal, local, two-segment bridge were used, the cost would be about $5000 to $8000 per bridge, with eight bridges required (about $40,000 to $64,000). Add in transceiver cables ($1600), power connections, and all the other sundry equipment, and the configuration can get right expensive. Add in the fact that there are many more bridges to configure into the spanning tree (this causes computability problems for the root bridge node), delays through all the bridge paths, and other tangible performance-related events, and the overhead gets fairly serious. Oh, it works—but not without serious management and loss of data in high-volume environments.

In the case of multiport bridges, only two devices are required and the number of transceiver cables is cut in half. Since multiport bridges cost about $15,000 (maximum list), total cost is about $30,000 in bridges and another $800 in cables. The result: fewer components to fail, better management, faster recovery in case of bridge disruption (spanning tree in the root bridge has to manage only two bridges as opposed to eight), simpler installation, and better expansion facilities with less hardware.

If multiport repeaters had been used in the network configuration, they could theoretically be replaced by a multiport bridge, with each segment's traffic isolated to the segment it is on—assuming that the segments were configured properly to start with.

Another benefit of a multiport bridge is that it does not have to follow the general rules of repeaters and therefore may allow repeaters to be located off the segments of the bridge. This allows a company to retain its investment in repeater technology by moving the replaced repeaters to the bridged segments. Because normal rules do not apply, additional multiport bridges may be located off of segments of a multiport bridge, allowing for some very creative network configurations.

Multiport bridges are useful in many configurations. Some of them are capable of supporting thickwire, thinwire, fiber, and twisted pair at the same time on the same bridge, enabling media translation. Others allow bridge management via SNMP and other management protocols. In short, they are powerful, true bridge units that can provide highly connected, redundant paths that are cost-effective, as well as powerful configurations for networks with a lot of systems. Care, however, must be exercised in their configuration if the bridge units are to reach their fullest potential of performance and capability.

A Case Study: Workgroup Placement

A large telecommunications vendor called me once and asked me to come analyze their Ethernet/802.3 network for a potential performance problem. Having heard all the problems before, just like any consultant, I started to ask the obvious questions, beginning with the very first one: How much load is on the network?

"Average load is about 45 to 57% and peaks at 100% every once in a while," they said.

Bleah! Most Ethernet/802.3 networks average between 3% and 15% and peak occasionally at 20–40%. This was obviously a busy network. The problem was that, although there were only about 200 nodes on the network, there was an inordinate amount of checksum failures and framing errors.

The First Step: Topological Mapping

The first thing to do was to get a topological map together to find out what node was on which segment and communicated with which other node. This is not always easy to do, but it is required if the network is to be properly analyzed for performance. (For a discussion of the basic formats and rationale for network maps, see "Network Mapping: What's Really Out There?" in Chapter 2.)

For the purposes of this book, the main reason to have a network topological map, replete with the exhaustive concordance of information about each node, is to know what resources are on which node and to know where each node is located on the network. "Where" means (a) which logical segment of the network the node is located on and (b) the node's physical location. The problem with network mapping and physical locations is there is no tool anywhere that can automatically tell any network manager where a node is located in the physical plant.

Another major reason to have a map is to help ease the transition to OSI. OSI naming services and X.500 directory services require a fairly detailed listing of what is on the network and where, so that connectivity services may be provided. As such, there is little choice but to collect the information for the inclusion into OSI naming domains and other database products for the network.

Automatic Network Mapping Products—An Example

A toolkit called Network Mapping Utility (NMU), from Network-1, aids in the discovery of nodes and protocols on the network. NMU was designed to simplify, as much as possible, the problems of creating topological maps of computer data networks.

NMU automatically "learns" about systems on the network, their protocols, addresses, names, aliases, and many other informational items, and allows the system or network manager to print out a variety of network maps based on the information collected by NMU. Very little input is required to generate high-quality, accurate network maps, and unlike other network mapping tools on the market, it calls for practically no system setup or predefinition of system information.

NMU is different in various ways from other manual network mapping solutions on the market:

- It learns about nodes.
- It has no protocol bias.
- It is vendor independent.
- It monitors for new nodes.
- It supports more than 488 protocols.
- It supports OSI naming standards.
- It supports CCITT naming standards.

- It provides mapping filters.
- It is a software-only product.
- It requires little expertise to use.
- It is cost-effective and fast.

The NMU Automatic Collection Facility

When NMU is activated on a VAX/VMS system, two special system processes are created that collect and analyze incoming packets from the network. Special memory tables and disk files are created with an extensive set of facts that are used by NMU to generate network topological diagrams of systems on the network.

NMU is preprogrammed to acquire as much information as possible about each major protocol, network address prefixes, node activities, and many other items. When the network or systems manager asks it to generate a specific map of the network, NMU analyzes all collected information against a set of defined rules within its inference facilities. These facilities are used to define information about nodes, learn about node names, where possible, and provide useful information on what is on the network.

All nodes on a network generate traffic. By monitoring each packet and then identifying its protocol, the vendor of the network hardware (this may be obtained by viewing the address prefix range that is allocated by the IEEE or ISO to each vendor's address range), and the source and destination addresses, NMU can combine these facts with higher-layer information to create a full map. And because NMU automates much of this effort, network security is enhanced: normally new nodes and protocols are added all the time with little regard as to who is doing what to whom and where the nodes are even located.

If a node's name is not available or has not been defined by the systems or network manager, NMU attempts to identify the LAN hardware vendor and other potential items that may indicate, at a minimum, the system vendor or system type. As more information about protocols and activity is collected, it is automatically added to the node's information base and presented on subsequent maps, when requested by the systems or network manager. For instance, a map may be run on Monday. On Tuesday, Novell NetWare 386 is installed. If a new map is generated on Tuesday after the installation and after the node is up, the new map will reflect that the node is now running Novell NetWare in addition to TCP/IP. If TCP/IP is removed from the system, the systems or network manager may remove that protocol from the node's profile. Should the protocol be reactivated, NMU will automatically record the protocol activity and produce an accurate map of the node with the protocol reenabled.

NMU Maps and Reports

When the network or systems manager requests a map or report, NMU creates one of various network maps or text files with listing information suitable for inclusion in word processing documents or as stand-alone reports.

NMU may create one or more of the following network maps:

- All nodes—simple master map for the entire LAN
- All nodes—simple master map for a particular segment
- All nodes—consolidated map for the entire LAN (all protocols, all information)
- All nodes—consolidated map of a particular segment
- All nodes running a particular protocol on a particular segment
- All nodes running a particular protocol on all segments

The availability of a report depends on the protocols that NMU discovers during its collection of information from the network. Obviously, it makes no sense to produce a report on a protocol that does not exist on your network. Therefore, NMU only allows reports on protocols that have been seen on the network.

NMU maps can be printed on any type of printer and displayed on any terminal that supports the ASCII character set. Further, NMU maps may be included in any word processing document supporting text input.

NMU also supports combining collected information from more than one NMU installation. In this manner, maps of the entire LAN may be made.

Who's Talking to Whom?

After you identify what is on the network, the next step in isolating the performance problem is to identify who is talking to whom and when.

One set of questions that most professed experts on Ethernet/802.3 network performance and management overlook is very simple:

- Which node is talking to which other node?
- How often?
- How much?
- Which protocols?
- How much per protocol?
- What time of the day?

Sounds easy? It's not. Try figuring out all of these items, at the same time, for every possible node-to-node communications linkage possible on the network, and you will see how serious and difficult this task becomes. The purpose of such an analysis is simple: learning what is normal for communications between two particular nodes at a particular moment and what is the current situation seen on the network outside the normal operating parameters that are usually observed for that type of data exchange.

Such data is collected with network management tools, of course, preferably those that are focused on network performance and management. Although quite a few network enterprise monitoring systems are quite capable of collecting the required information for network analysis, most do not provide any type of real-time alarming system for performance problems that require action by the network manager. By collecting as many packets as possible and then using sorting and collation software to figure out which node is connected to which node at which time of the day, these tools provide an analysis of the connectivity matrix that allows the network manager to determine a normal operating pattern for the protocols and nodes on the network. Deviation from this normal pattern may indicate a network problem, security breach, or other issue that requires network management intervention and potential corporate intervention.

For example, a microcomputer running MS-DOS and using the TCP/IP protocol connects and communicates with a node called PUFF every day between 8:00 a.m. and 3:30 p.m. During that time, only the TCP/IP protocol is used, there is an average byte-per-packet load of 200 bytes between the nodes, usually no more than 500,000 packets are transmitted between the nodes, and those 500,000 packets usually do not exceed a total byte count of about 20 MB of data for the time frame. This pattern is repetitive and is fairly indicative of the network node-to-node relationship between the two systems on the network on a day-by-day basis. Further analysis shows that there is very little, if any, activity on Saturdays and Sundays and that between 3:00 and 4:00 a.m. every working day there is a flurry of activity between the nodes, while a node-to-node disk backup is done. These routine figures reveal an operational pattern between the two nodes.

Automating Traffic Analysis

Doing such an analysis "manually" is not trivial. It could take hours and hours after the data is collected just to figure out which node is connected to which other node. It is important to analyze the traffic patterns between the nodes, because any deviation from the established normal operating pattern might indicate a security problem in addition to a performance problem. Also, identifying the performance matrix of traffic between systems helps clarify node-to-node relationships, which is essential for proper workgroup isolation.

In one case, data was collected to identify the who-is-connecting-to-who relationship. The following issues were found to contribute to the overall problem of Ethernet/802.3 performance:

- Most of the network was connected via 802.3 multiport thinwire repeater units, which allow all bits to be seen by all nodes. There is no traffic isolation or filtering.

- Some of the protocol choices being used for node-to-node connectivity were of an ACK/NAK nature. This means that for each data packet transmitted from a node to another node, the destination node must issue an active acknowledgment. Thus there is one overhead packet for each data packet. This also means that timing between the cooperative systems using the same protocol is very important, and exceeding certain time-to-acknowledge requirements was causing massive amounts of retries between the systems. This problem artificially inflated the packet count (due to retransmissions) and the network suffered as a whole.

- Use of unshielded-twisted-pair components caused the network to reflect noise on the cables and interfered with the normal operation of the network. This increased the numbers of retransmissions.

- Quite a few of the cooperative nodes were engaged in the usage of computer-aided design (CAD) software. CAD software files and applications are the size of Godzilla on steroids and can severely affect network performance when shared over the network, which is exactly what was happening with 30 of the workstations. CAD files were not the only ones getting bigger: so were word processing files (because of clip art), spreadsheets (because of embedded voice notations), electronic mail, and other types of files. This means that when the network is used by the components, performance suffers due to file size and other attributes.

- The customer told me during interviews that the company intended to begin using an image processing system to share visual images around the network. This meant that the worst case seen so far was nothing compared to what was going to happen. CAD files are large, but image files are huge.

At this point, a protocol analyzer was connected to the network in various spots to verify current network performance levels and to ensure that the collisions, CRC errors, and other errors were not isolated on a particular thinwire or twisted-pair segment on the network. It is also important to collect thorough and complete performance information before any network modifications are made, to ensure that modifications were beneficial and to measure improvement: If you do not know what is bad and where, it is hard to tell when it has gotten better. Reference points are essential to proper management.

What to look for in an Ethernet/802.3 protocol analyzer is covered in Chapter 8.

Those CADs

After analysis of the collected data, we decided to isolate the CAD users first to verify that the analysis was on track. It also happened to be one of the easier isolation facilities to do.

Isolation was done by separating the multiport thinwire repeater with the 30 workstations on it from the rest of the network with a local bridge unit. This unit, which cost about $2500 (at the time), was connected to the building thickwire backbone on one side of the bridge and to a small piece of thinwire cable on the other bridge connection port. On the thinwire, the multiport repeater was also connected, so that nodes wishing to connect to other systems on the network could continue to do so.

Following the connection of the bridge, the protocol analyzer was connected to both the backbone and to the new "separate" segment for data measurements. To ensure fairness of network performance measurement, the users were given a specific set of activities to perform before and after the network modification. By measuring the effects of the modification in a known environment, it was found that the overall load had been reduced from 42% to less than 10% on an average. Also, error rates that had reached as high as 14% of the total network bandwidth were now down to a tolerable 0.5% of the overall bandwidth, at worse case.

Overall, the network performance improved remarkably by placing a bridge unit at the right place on the network. Further analysis allowed placement of two more bridges in the same facility and eventually reduced the segment-by-segment loading to a very tolerable 5–7% (about the average for most well-behaved Ethernet/802.3 networks).

The key to good performance improvement was not just using a bridge but using it in the right way and placing it properly on the network. This resulted from mapping the network carefully and then analyzing who is talking to whom. Only after performing these steps will the network manager be able to isolate workgroups properly and improve network performance.

Summary

Isolating workgroups and installing bridges and brouters at the appropriate locations on the network can be very useful for isolating traffic and improving network performance. Care must be taken in proper network analysis before the bridges and brouters are installed to ensure that the network configuration adequately matches the network load metrics and access matrix.

Collision Management 6

Contrary to popular belief, there is nothing wrong with the occasional collision on an Ethernet/802.3 network. In fact, papers published by the original designers of Ethernet (Robert Metcalf and David Boggs) state that collisions are normal. There is a great deal of misunderstanding as to what a collision is and when one is bad. This chapter discusses collisions, when to get concerned about them, and what to do about it.

How Many Collisions Is Too Many?

One question constantly asked by many system and network managers is "How many collisions is too many collisions on Ethernet/802.3?"

It's a fair question. Of course, it's discussed in all the available Ethernet/802.3 documentation and is easily remedied by looking there.

Right.

In fact, there is no set rule. Ethernet/802.3 is basically a half-duplex network (one station sends at a time on the medium), and if a collision occurs, the current sending station is interrupted and no other station may send. (See Figure 6.1.) The two or more stations colliding with each other are not real thrilled, either.

How efficient the Ethernet/802.3 network is in resolving the collision depends on a variety of factors, including roundtrip bit propagation time (the quicker the collision is resolved, the more efficient the network becomes) and node "clustering" (how close groups of communicating nodes are placed, electrically). Therefore, depending on the network topology, location of nodes, and other things, there can be a wide disparity from Ethernet to Ethernet in the amount of time it takes to resolve a collision.

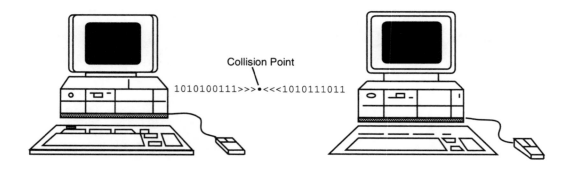

Figure 6.1
Sample Collision Action on the Network

Common Causes of Collisions

Before we can discuss how many is too many, we must first examine the conditions that may cause collisions. Here are the most common reasons for collisions (listed in no particular order):

1. **Propagation delay.** Different types of media have different propagation delays, as do traversing repeaters. For instance, a 23.4-meter thickwire Ethernet/802.3 has no discernible propagation delay. A 500-meter segment of thickwire has about a 10-microsecond propagation delay. Put a repeater between two local segments and you add another 10-microsecond delay, at least. If the nodes are far apart on long segments, there is a greater chance of collision due to propagation delay, especially in high traffic environments. Add repeaters to the configuration and the probability increases. Therefore, the length of certain types of Ethernet/802.3 media can have a dramatic effect on whether collisions occur.

2. **Nodes not following the rules.** Those rules are the collision-detection and retransmission rules established in Ethernet V2.0 and IEEE 802.3 specifications. Some vendors think that they can violate the rules and get away with it (you know who you are). In most cases they might, but when a vendor violates the rules on collision detection, it hurts everyone. The 802.3 specification states that after a collision, retransmission of a packet should occur after generation of a random amount of timer delay not to exceed 512 slot times (a slot time is defined as 51.2 microseconds for 10-Mbps

cable plants). This means that if a collision happens, a jam is sent, a random number is generated, and the controller waits that long before retransmission. The controller then acquires the cable (after listening) and sends the packet again. The wait interval is supposed to be between 1 and 512. In fact, some vendors violate the rule, setting a ceiling lower than 512, thereby not allowing random numbers higher than a predetermined value. One vendor I know of waits only between 1 and 16, thus allowing their systems to acquire the network quicker than those who generate a higher random number in accordance with the standard(s).

3. **Noise.** This cause is pretty obvious, but it still bears stating. Noise can come from a variety of locations, including external sources (such as a large motor) or harmonic distortion. With the increase in the use of unshielded twisted pair, the incidence of collisions caused by noise on UTP installations is increasing. In many sites I work with, we have more problems in the configuration of networks with UTP than we ever had to deal with when using straight coax or fiber network media. Various everyday office equipment also causes noise problems (copiers, laser printers, ballast transformers on fluorescent tube lighting, HVAC motors, and others). Even in the "benign" office environment, noise is a real problem.

4. **Node clustering.** Some studies suggest that clusters of nodes resolve collisions faster, since they are physically close together. These studies also go on to imply that physical clusters that attempt intracluster communications may experience a greater chance of collisions than close-together systems on shorter segments.

5. **Long segments of cable.** The longer the distance between nodes, the greater the chances of collisions. Some people configure networks incorrectly and unintentionally "logically" exceed the rules regarding cable length (such as when adding DELNIs and when directly connecting thickwire and thinwire cables to each other).

6. **Improper segmentation of cable.** Thickwire cable should be cut in accordance with the standard(s) and at specific lengths (for example, 23.4, 70.2, or 117 meters, and so on), which is something few companies do when installing their Ethernet/802.3 segments. Improper segmentation can cause noise problems and harmonic distortion problems, thus increasing the likelihood of collisions.

7. **Babbling transceivers.** When a transceiver loses its mind and begins to spew all kinds of trash on the cable, collisions inevitably happen. Locating a bad transceiver is an exciting experience, but that's a story for another time.

There are plenty of other situations that may cause collisions, but this list shows the most common ones.

Only a Transmitting Station May Collide and Detect

When a collision happens, *the only component that may detect it is the transmitting station.* Receiving stations will most likely see a framing error, CRC error, or other such problem. Electrically, it is theoretically possible to detect the difference between a collision and an actual error by the receiver, but this is not commonly implemented. Therefore, to find the total number of collisions experienced on a segment, the network manager has to go to each network package on each system and find the number of collisions encountered in software counters. The problem is that only those packages that have been transmitting may demonstrate collisions, and depending on which station was transmitting at the time of collision, the network manager may need to correlate a great deal of collision information from many nodes.

Some vendors of protocol analyzers claim to be able to sense collisions on LANs by using their product on the network. In my experience, these products claim to have sensed collisions for a variety of error conditions that have little to do with collisions. When a collision occurs, in reality, some electrical signaling is detectable that is unique to a collision in progress. This signal could be detected by the vendor *if* they were to build specialized network hardware to detect the conditions and flag them to the analysis software in the protocol analyzer. Unfortunately, many times the protocol analyzer has nothing but standard, off-the-shelf hardware installed and lacks the ability to detect the rise in electrical disturbance associated with the network during the collision.

Of course, making remote hardware clairvoyant enough to detect what should have been sent and comparing that to what was actually on the cable will work best, but there have not been a great deal of clairvoyant-algorithm analyzers on the market of late.

How Many Collisions Is Too Many? (Part II)

Still, we have not answered the question of how many collisions is too many.

Many network software packages, such as DECnet, have collision counters that are basically derived from the Ethernet/802.3 controller attached to the system. Some nodes will show 10 collisions in a week, some 100 collisions in a second, others 10,000 collisions in a day. A customer of mine recently told me he had 50,000 collisions in his Ethernet collision counters. The problem, globally, with all of these counters is that they do not tell the network manager the time frame in which the collisions happened. More specifically, what is the time period(s) in which collisions were experienced?

I have long believed, and been proven correct, that although the number of collisions is important, more important is *when* the collisions occurred. This may sound a bit strange, but bear with me. First, if you don't know what is going on when the collision happened, how can you determine what caused it? Second, if you cannot correlate a collision to a given activity, it will be very difficult indeed to find out what is causing it.

There Are Few Collision-Free Ethernet/802.3 Networks

There are few collision-free Ethernets. Even the one in my house has collisions from time to time, and I have only 18 nodes on the network. Larger networks at some customer sites experience some collisions from time to time, but many may attribute them to propagation issues, the most common cause. Some collisions are bound to happen due to the 1-persistent nature of the Ethernet/802.3 transmission method.

By the way, beware of the theoretical studies on collisions. Many of them consider the issues of p-persistent or nonpersistent CSMA/CD. The metrics for these kinds of studies are very different from those of the 1-persistent Ethernet/802.3, and therefore many of the studies do not correlate with reality.

On some networks, due to ambient noise or the configuration, getting 10 to 20 collisions per hour is common. Some get only 20 collisions in a month. The number of nodes may have little to do with the collision amounts. One network I spend a lot of time on experiences an average of 200 collisions a day (all nodes)—it has 130 nodes on a main thickwire segment (via DELNIs) 234 meters in length. Another network I spend some time on has more than 500 collisions an hour—it has only 8 nodes on a 117-meter segment of thickwire.

Another network with a DELNI as the main network segment has more than 500 systems connected via repeaters in the building and has fewer than two collisions a day, for literally millions of packets. Traffic levels have little to do with collision rates on properly configured networks that are well within propagation tolerances.

What is important to note also is how the networks are being used. The 130-node network is a factory network with low traffic volume, but the nodes are somewhat spread out, so occasionally distant nodes will attempt to transmit at the same time and collisions occur. The systems on the 8-node network are on a highly active Local Area VAXCluster and experience collisions due to high traffic volume and some distance separation issues. Also, this site has two other systems that violate the 512 slot-time rule and tend to cause some collisions due to overzealous acquisition of the medium.

What is important is to know the network topology and the transmission distance between nodes that are communicating. Two active nodes a good distance from each other (500 meters apart causes about a 10-microsecond delay) may cause more collisions than the same two nodes 23.4 meters apart (which has almost a zero propagation delay). Which nodes are communicating with which nodes and where the nodes are located, physically, on the medium is critical to understanding whether collisions experienced are normal or not. Further, knowing the topology and the distances may allow the systems or network manager to correct the problem by putting the nodes closer together and reducing the number of collisions caused by propagation delay.

"When" a Collision Happens Is Important

Another issue in determining what level of collisions is normal for your Ethernet/802.3 network is to discover *when* the collisions are happening. Finding this out is not trivial, and an analyzer or other tool will be of little help. Basically, the systems or network manager must write a small command procedure for each networking package on each system that samples the counters on the system for collision statistics. The best sampling to start with is about once per hour, to get a feel for the general range of time when collisions are happening. For example, if DECnet were to be sampled, a simple batch command procedure might be useful, such as this one:

```
$ !
$ show_stats:
$ run sys$system:NCP
show known line counters
zero known line counters
$ counter = counter + 1
$ if (counter .eq. 24) then goto finished_for_24hours
$ wait 00:59
$ goto show_stats
$ finished_for_24hours:
$ reply/network "24 hour stat run now available in batch log file"
$ exit
```

This VMS command procedure shows the line statistics for all lines, clears them, waits 59 minutes, and then does it again. All the statistics will go to the batch log file, which will be kept in the default account that submits this command procedure. Since this procedure runs only once an hour, it creates low overhead. In this manner the number of collisions per hour may be determined. If the network has other software on it that can report collisions (such as a TCP/IP package or other communications package using the Ethernet), then those commands to show statistical output should be included before the line that increments the counter in the sample command procedure.

After the procedure runs for 24 hours, 24 samples will be available. They should be plotted for comparison of hour-to-hour statistics as well as comparison with other systems in the same time frames. This is the tedious part. Obviously, the clever manager could write a command procedure to extract and correlate all the batch files from all the systems. In any case, now a mapping method is available, to show when collisions happen on the segment throughout a period of time.

Compare Activities on the Network to Collision Occurrence

Once the previous step is complete, it is important to map overall activities to the times that collisions seem to occur. For instance, if there were many collisions between 3:00 and 4:00 p.m. on Thursday, was there any network activity that could be correlated to this? Was a node being installed, a new repeater being put on-line, a new server being placed on the segment? Were workmen messing with the segment? These all can cause collisions, and since they are one-time occurrences, the number of collisions is irrelevant. If, however, no significant events may be recognized and the count is escalating, there is something causing the count to escalate. A detailed investigation is in order.

Oddly enough, once the reason for collisions is identified, fixes are usually fairly straightforward. If the problem is due to propagation delay, it may be rectified by inserting a bridge or brouter unit in the right place and "shortening" the propagation between systems. Since the bridge or brouter unit regenerates the packet onto the adjacent network, the propagation is segmented by the bridge or brouter.

If the problem is a babbling transceiver, replacement is the solution. (Finding a bad transceiver can be interesting: you usually have to power down each transceiver until the offending hardware is found.) If the problem is noise, the segment in question will need to be isolated from the rest of the network via a bridge, or the segment of cable will need to be replaced with a more suitable, less noise-prone medium, such as thinwire coax or fiber.

Finding the source of the collision problem on your network may not be easy, but solving the collision problem is straightforward.

Some Collisions Are Not Collisions: SQE

Beware of software packages that mislead you into thinking that you have a problem that does not technically exist. Some systems require the signal quality error (SQE) signal from the transceiver to be generated after every packet has been completely sent to the network by the transceiver. At completion, the transceiver sends to the controller a pulse on the collision-detection check pair of wires on a 15-pin thickwire connection point, signifying that the packet-sending operation is complete.

If the SQE signal does not appear after a given time frame beyond the packet transmission, the controller typically sends an error message to the protocol suite using the network, which may result in a collision-detection check failure or be registered in some packages as a collision. In fact, the packet went out and there was no collision. Verify that the SQE setting on the system having problems is set correctly before chalking up the problem to collisions. A dead giveaway symptom of this problem is a collision per packet generated by the node and no or few collisions actually seen on the network.

On system interfaces such as the DEMPR and similar units, setting SQE incorrectly will cause actual collisions to appear on the network. Such simple devices have no way in which to signal that there is a problem, and the improper handling of SQE causes actual collisions on the network. Simply by setting SQE correctly, you can often fix the problem, and protocol performance increases.

Check with the vendor of your equipment to verify the requirement for SQE for the device being connected and make sure that it is set correctly for each device on the network. The user's manual for the device controller will usually have information on whether SQE is used or not.

Summary

Finding out that you have a collision problem on your Ethernet/802.3 network is much more involved than just looking at the counters. Correlating the activities on the network is critical to finding out what is causing the collision problem. Any number of collisions should be examined, but the ones that are really an issue are the unexplained occurrences that cannot be correlated to a network activity of some sort. If you are a victim of the "unexplained" collision or two, further in-depth investigation is in order.

Switching Bridges *7*

This chapter focuses on the technologies used in the design and implementation of switching bridges for Ethernet/802.3 networks. This technology is rapidly becoming the most important add-on to existing Ethernet/802.3 networks to increase performance and reduce errors on networks in high traffic-load environments.

Some Background

Performance on most networks is categorized as "bursty," because of the manner in which systems transmit data to a network. Although it is possible to estimate network traffic loading during a specific period of time, from second to second the traffic levels on the network usually change from very low to very high and back again. If the rate of activity is sustained for, say, five seconds or more, the network will start to suffer performance problems. Some of those problems include the following:

- **Frame deferrals.** When a system is ready to transmit a frame but the network is busy, a frame deferral occurs. The transmitting system must defer, or wait, until the network is quiet. If the average load is high (over 30%), then deferrals may be normal. If the network load is light, there are few errors, and frame deferrals are present, a high burst rate contention very likely exists on the network. Frame deferrals, as a rule, should never exceed 10% of the transmitted frames of a given system.
- **Collisions,** especially if the transmitting bursty nodes are, propagation-wise, far away. High traffic loads for short bursts of time on nodes that are "close" do not necessarily translate into collisions. High traffic loads from bursty nodes that are electrically distant do tend to cause serious collision problems on the network.

- **Session disconnects.** Nodes that cannot communicate effectively with each other eventually timeout their protocol sessions between the two nodes. Such a disconnect may be due to network congestion (because of the bursting of traffic), the inability of the network to send traffic back to the system in a prescribed time frame to keep the protocol happy, or other such problems. Bursting is an especially nasty problem for timing-sensitive protocols.
- **Congestion.** Node hardware controllers for Ethernet/802.3 devices have a finite amount of CPU power and a finite amount of memory on the cards. All devices that access the Ethernet/802.3 network have a controller. When a burst of traffic arrives, the controller must collect all data, whether or not the data is meant for that node, before the controller logic can determine if the data is valid for the node. So a high burst rate of traffic can cause all buffers on a node to fill quickly and can cause the controller to lose data destined for that node while collecting data destined for other systems. When a node cannot receive data because its buffers are full, the data is lost; eventually the data will be retransmitted by the software packages. As a result, both the traffic load on the network and the bursting rate increase. Overall, the problems get worse.
- **Retransmissions.** As nodes lose data destined for them, the data must be retransmitted. This causes additional bursts of traffic on the network and an artificially inflated traffic level on the network.

Sheer traffic loading on the network can cause a specific system to lose frames. All nodes must collect traffic as it appears on the cable, so that the controller can determine if each frame should be kept or discarded. As the load increases, the chances increase that a controller will miss data intended for its node. Thus, if the node does not have to see every piece of data on the network, it can collect only the data intended for itself more readily.

The traditional way to reduce the amount of traffic that a node must examine is to divide the network into smaller components that are isolated from one another via traffic restrictors such as bridges and routers. This approach also helps alleviate the network burst rate: as the traffic rate decreases, so does the incidence of collective bursting.

What Is a Switching Bridge?

A switching bridge is a very high speed multiport bridge with special hardware facilities that isolate traffic and provide forwarding of frames at near cable speed. One of the first companies to recognize the potential for intelligent segmenting of Ethernet was Kalpana, based in San Jose, California, which was founded in 1987 by executives from Excelan. The Kalpana EtherSwitch, introduced in 1990, used multiple application-specific integrated circuits (ASICs) to implement a crossbar switch that could switch Ethernet segments to guarantee certain subclasses a 10-Mbps throughput. Originally intended as a stand-alone system, EtherSwitch proved easy to incorporate into an intelligent hub and was made available to vendor hubs, such as those from Bay Networks. In 1994, Kalpana was acquired by Cisco Systems and now manufactures systems under the Cisco banner.

Most normal filter/forward bridges can move about 3000 to 6000 pps between connected networks (where the max is about 30,000 pps). Switching bridges can commonly handle well over 400,000 pps, and some can achieve throughput of more than 1,000,000 pps in lab tests. Considering that Ethernet/802.3 networks can generate 14,882 pps at 64 octets per frame, a switching bridge provides the required speed to keep up with a full-burst 10-Mbps network connection.

I expect that, eventually, 10BASET repeater modules will be replaced by switching bridge modules that configure cable identically but provide bridged connections to each port on the card. In other words, the trend is to be totally switch-connected from the user workstation to the hub unit.

A switching bridge unit usually offers the following features:

- Isolation of traffic between network segments or, possibly, between nodes, if the systems are individually cabled to ports on the bridge unit.
- Movement of data at very high speed with minimal latency between network segments connected to the bridge.
- Buffers and data flow from each bridge port (segment) to each bridge port at a rate commensurate with what the port can deal with.
- Data filtration on a port-by-port basis for all bridge connections.
- High port density: most switching bridges have at least eight ports for Ethernet/802.3 network connections; some units can accommodate up to 200 ports on one switch.
- Spanning-tree (IEEE 802.1) facilities, which allow a bridge to function as the root bridge or as a fail-over device in a loop configuration. This feature is critical in high-availability networks or in networks in which redundant facilities are required for reliability.

Latency is the biggest problem for any bridge unit. In most normal bridges, latency (per packet) is in the range of hundreds of milliseconds. When congestion builds up, the bridge may ignore arriving traffic, because the bridge has no storage capability. This causes retransmissions and timing problems, usually leading, over time, to frequent session failures and disconnection of applications.

On switching bridges, latency is managed by the ASICs and the speed of the CPU(s) on the switch. In some switch architectures, there is a separate processor for each port; others have one very fast RISC processor for the entire switch. While the architecture of the hardware can vary dramatically, the switch, as a rule, introduces minimal latency when forwarding frames from port to port. Latency is a function of the product's architecture and its type: cut-through or store-and-forward.

Cut-Through Switching Bridges

Cut-through switching bridges usually have the lowest latency. As a node transmits its frame to the bridge, the bridge scans the destination address and determines which port the frame should be forwarded to. Before the end of the frame arrives at the bridge, the beginning of the frame has already been forwarded to the bridge's destination port. The operation is analogous to a train entering a track switching area: the engine is diverted to a new path before the end of the train arrives. The benefit is speed: latency in a cut-through bridge is on the order of 20 to 40 microseconds. Considering that the total round-trip bit propagation speed of an Ethernet/802.3 network is on the order of 51.2 microseconds, the speed of a cut-through bridge approximates cable speed, even with the logical scanning of addresses.

On the downside, because of the way a cut-through bridge works, there is no opportunity for the bridge to do a checksum operation on the frame before the frame is forwarded to another port on the bridge. This means that if the frame is busted after the header (destination and source address), the broken frame will be forwarded to the destination port. As a result, error conditions on a specific port may be propagated to other ports on the bridge, depending on the destination address.

Store-and-Forward Switching Bridges

A store-and-forward bridge waits to receive the entire frame from a specific Ethernet/802.3 port before acting. Then it performs a cyclic redundancy check (CRC) checksum operation to make sure the frame is good. Next it checks the destination address and selects the proper port for forwarding. Finally it forwards the frame to the proper destination port.

Store-and-forward switching bridges provide not only traffic isolation, but also error immunity to any destination port. On the downside, the latency for store-and-forward bridges may be in milliseconds, not microseconds, which is a serious concern for some applications.

Hybrid Switching Bridges

A recent development in the switching bridge market is a combination cut-through and store-and-forward system that integrates the best features of both technologies. The first switching bridge to incorporate both technologies was the Kalpana EtherSwitch Pro16.

The EtherSwitch Pro16 can be configured on a per-port basis to automatically change from on-the-fly or cut-through packet switching to store-and-forward switching if error rates exceed a user-defined threshold. When the error rate falls below a certain level, the EtherSwitch Pro16 reverts back to cut-through switching. Additional capabilities include a "runt-free" mode, in which the switch discards packets smaller than 64 bytes. This ensures the filtering of collision fragments while maintaining the low-latency characteristics of cut-through switching.

Network Topology and Switching Bridges

Switching bridge technologies work best in a point-to-point or star topology. In such networks, all nodes are connected to a central point via dedicated cable runs from the central point to the workstation location. A typical wiring plant for a workstation-to-hub star topology is shown in Figure 7.1.

In this configuration, the user workstation is patched to either the hub or the switching bridge using patch cables at the closet location. In some situations, the switching bridge module may be integral to the hub unit and an external switching module is not required.

In some cases, a switching bridge offers isolation at the closet level and is subsequently connected to a master switching bridge in the building, as shown in Figure 7.2.

In this configuration, the timing problems of adding a new hub are eliminated. Further, it is possible to improve the traffic isolation by adding multiple network interface cards to the high-volume nodes and positioning the various ports on various bridge segments. Using the switching bridge does not impose a substantial latency delay on traffic, so the bridge not only solves the problem of dissimilar hub connections, but also allows better throughput by restricting traffic flow to improper destination segments. Bridge units may also be used in a closet, but doing so would underutilize the bridge and increase overall network cost at no appreciable gain in performance.

Figure 7.2 specifically illustrates a network configuration for hubs and switching technologies. In each closet, a switching bridge would interconnect with

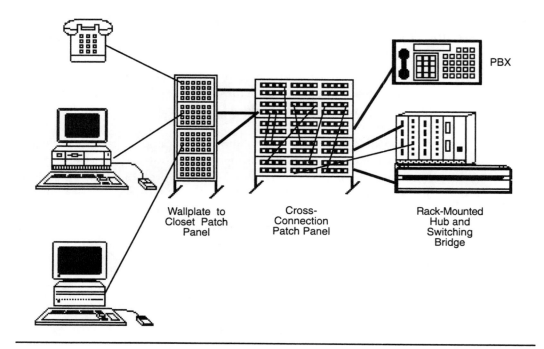

Figure 7.1
Sample Closet Configuration

the main computer room switching bridge via fiber optic connection. The hubs in all three locations would interconnect between the bridges. In locations with a very high density of application users (such as color printers and the nodes providing files to them), the nodes and devices should be placed on different ports of the same bridge rather than connected to a cabling hub and sent through to the destination system/output device.

Which Should I Choose: A Switching Bridge or a Router?

It is possible to use a classical multiport router (such as those made by Cisco, Wellfleet, and ACC) in place of a switching bridge, but this is not always a good idea. The traffic levels on many LANs are high enough to cause serious router congestion at most sites, and routers are substantially more expensive than switching bridges. In fact, a recent high-traffic-volume network configured by the author required more than 300 high-density nodes to be inter-

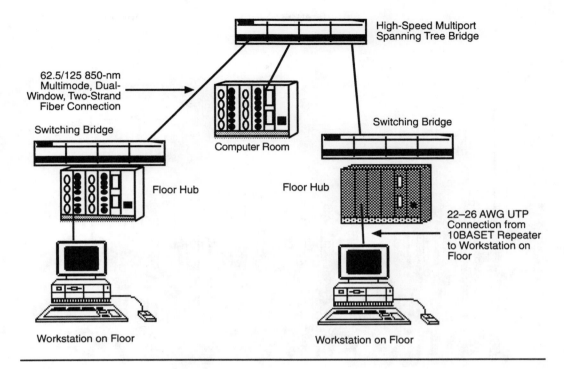

High-Speed Multiport
Spanning Tree Bridge

62.5/125 850-nm
Multimode, Dual-
Window, Two-Strand
Fiber Connection

Switching Bridge

Computer Room

Switching Bridge

Floor Hub

Floor Hub

22–26 AWG UTP
Connection from
10BASET Repeater
to Workstation on
Floor

Workstation on Floor

Workstation on Floor

Figure 7.2
Sample Configuration Using a Master Switching Bridge

connected. Figure 7.3 shows the traffic characteristics of only 50 of those nodes.

Of the 1000 samples taken (over a two-week period), the network shows very bursty behavior with some periods of activity being sustained at 100% of available bandwidth. This figure applies to eighteen protocols used on the network in a variety of transaction, terminal, and file-transfer activities.

A switching bridge was introduced into the network topology: each system was connected to its own port on the bridge. Figure 7.4 shows the composite loading of the network after installation of the switching bridge between systems on the network. The average load seen by each node has dropped from 5–15% to less than 0.1%. Peak loading has dropped from 10–70% to a worst-case peak of 0.62%. (The figure is a composite developed by measuring all ports on the switching bridge unit to give an equal comparison between situations.)

This reduction in traffic is dramatic considering that no software or system changes were made and no protocols were modified. The entire reduction in

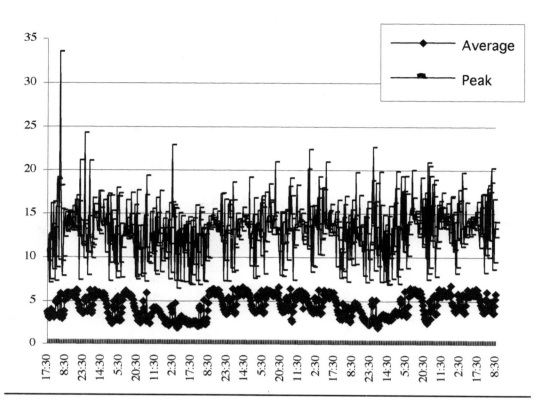

Figure 7.3
Traffic on a High-Volume Network

network traffic and increase in performance is directly due to installation and use of high-speed switching bridge technologies.

Note that a 3% collision rate and a 5% deferral rate were completely eliminated from the network after the bridge was installed.

Interconnecting Switching Bridges

Many vendors offer either proprietary network connections or specific high-speed network interconnection facilities between switching bridge units.

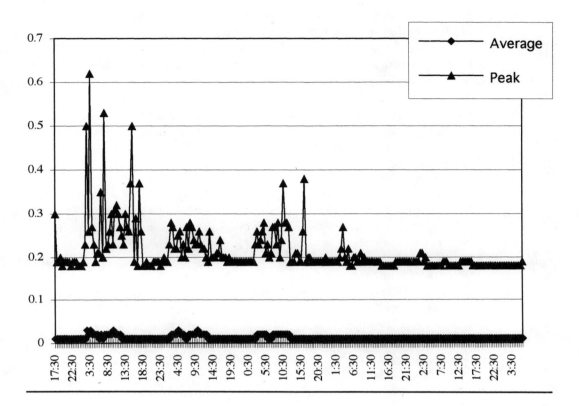

Figure 7.4
Composite Loading on a Network Using a Switching Bridge

The most popular interconnection is FDDI. In these interconnection facilities, the switching bridge allows an FDDI connection between bridge units on an FDDI ring. Traffic from one bridge port on a specific bridge is forwarded to another bridge port on another bridge via a backbone FDDI interconnection. Many vendors of switching bridges now have either an integral FDDI capability or an add-in module that allows FDDI access. In this situation, the originating Ethernet/802.3 frame is forwarded to the remote bridge unit in one of two ways:

- **Encapsulated in an FDDI frame.** In this situation, the Ethernet/802.3 frame is sent to the remote bridge unit over the FDDI without conversion. The frame is inserted within an FDDI frame and sent to the remote bridge. This method tends to be very proprietary to a specific vendor product set, because only a "knowledgeable" bridge will be able to understand the incoming frame and properly forward it to the right port. This type of technology is best when an FDDI is used to interconnect and the originating and destination nodes are Ethernet/802.3-based.

■ **Converted to an FDDI frame.** In this situation, the Ethernet/802.3 frame is actually converted to an FDDI native-mode frame and treated by other devices on the FDDI ring as if the originating Ethernet/802.3 network device were on the FDDI (that is, directly connected). This configuration is best when there are multiple bridges, switching bridges, and routers from multiple vendors interconnecting with each other and when the source node is on the switching bridge and the destination node is on the FDDI.

A secondary methodology for interconnecting switching bridges uses Asynchronous Transfer Mode (ATM) connectivity facilities. In the case of ATM, almost all vendors offer it as an add-in module only. There are no encapsulation capabilities, because the ATM format is much smaller than an Ethernet/802.3 frame, and the ATM switch matrix must do a great deal of work to get the traffic from node to node.

Another interconnection methodology between switching bridges is a vendor-proprietary link. Many vendors have 200-Mbps or better link facilities that interconnect the bridge units, via either twisted-pair or fiber connections. Although proprietary, these interconnections tend to offer the best speed between units and are useful if the source node and destination node are attached to the same vendor's bridge units. If the source or destination node is on a network other than the bridged Ethernet/802.3 networks, then additional hardware is required and reliability and performance are compromised.

100-Mbps Ethernet/802.3 Connectivity and Switching Bridges

There is a trend to offer speed-agile connection ports in a switching bridge that will allow 10-Mbps or 100-Mbps connection facilities per port. With chip vendors providing 10/100 chip sets on controller cards and system motherboards, this trend will continue for some time. It makes a lot of sense for growing networks and servers.

Due to the manner in which idle nodes on twisted-pair systems send pulses, a technology known as *auto-negotiation* can be used to identify what speed a port needs to configure to support the connected node.

The auto-negotiation function is an optional part of the 100-Mbps standard that enables devices to exchange information about their abilities over a link segment. This, in turn, allows the devices to perform automatic configuration to achieve the best possible mode of operation over a link. At a minimum, auto-negotiation provides automatic speed-matching for multispeed devices at each end of a link. Multispeed Ethernet interfaces can then take advantage of the highest speed offered by a multispeed hub port. The auto-negotiation protocol includes automatic sensing for other capabilities as well. For example, a hub that can support full-duplex operation on some or all of its ports can advertise that fact with the auto-negotiation protocol. Interfaces connected to the hub which also support full-duplex operation can then configure themselves to use the full-duplex mode in interaction with the hub.

Auto-negotiation takes place using Fast Link Pulse (FLP) signals. These signals are a modified version of the Normal Link Pulse (NLP) signals used for detecting link integrity and defined in the original 10BASET specifications. The FLP signals are generated automatically at power-up or may be selected manually through the management interface to a device. The FLP signals are designed to coexist with NLP signals, so that a 10BASET device that uses NLP signals will continue to detect the proper link integrity even when attached to an auto-negotiation hub that sends FLP signals. Like the original 10BASET link pulse, the FLP signals take place during idle times on the network link and do not interfere with normal traffic.

The FLP signals are used to send information about device capabilities, and the auto-negotiation protocol contains rules for device reconfiguration based on this information. This is how a hub and the device attached to that hub can automatically negotiate and reconfigure themselves to use the highest common denominator of their abilities. The auto-negotiation feature is *optional,* and the system is designed to work with older 10BASET interfaces as well as 100BASET interfaces that do not support Fast Link Pulses and auto-negotiation. The auto-negotiation standard also includes the ability to disable auto-negotiation from the management interface of a hub, or to manually force the negotiation process to take place.

At this writing, the 100-Mbps 100BASETX standard is still under development; the auto-negotiation function is part of the draft, so it is expected to be in the standard. Current vendors of switching bridges support a limited number of prestandard 100BASETX connections, which usually affects how many of the 100-Mbps and 10-Mbps connections are allowed on a switching bridge configuration. For instance, Cisco prescribes the following loading for the Kalpana ProSwitch-16 when using 10-Mbps or 100-Mbps connections to the switch:

Interface	Example A	Example B	Example C	Example D
10-Mbps switched Ethernet	192 ports	128 ports	128 ports	128 ports
100-Mbps Ethernet	—	16 ports	—	8 ports
155-Mbps ATM	—	—	16 ports	8 ports

In the case of 100BASETX, remember that there are three potential standard configurations that will emerge:

- 4-wire (2-pair) Category 5 connections (100BASETX)
- 8-wire (4-pair) Category 3, 4, or 5 connections (100BASET4)
- 2-fiber (1-pair) multimode graded-index fiber connection (100BASEF)

Whether a switching bridge vendor supports one or all three 100-Mbps interfaces is a function of module availability and market acceptance. At this writing, most vendors favor the 100BASETX (802.3U) component, but it is too early to tell what the final acceptance in the market will be.

Redundancy in Switching Bridges

A new development at this writing is the ability to provide redundancy in bridge units via the use of a cross-matrix and shadowed logic facility. This means that a switching bridge could be configured to provide not only traffic isolation, but also redundancy if a motherboard in the bridge unit fails.

The Cisco PROSTACK Matrix, using the ProSwitch-16 modules, is available with a redundant option. The standard chassis supports one crosspoint matrix module, with a slot, or bay, to add a second redundant module. Each module is self-contained with complete logic and power supply. In the redundant configuration, if the primary module fails, the secondary module detects the failure and resumes operation within 2 to 3 seconds. This feature is highly beneficial in situations where bridge outages are intolerable and where nodes require a very high up-time network.

I fully expect that many more vendors will provide an equivalent fail-over capability as time goes on.

Summary

The use of switching bridges to solve performance and connectivity problems is increasing and will eventually be one of the more popular interconnectivity options in a LAN environment. As speeds of Ethernet/802.3 networks increase to 100 Mbps and beyond, the need to isolate traffic and keep the network functioning at peak performance will be critical. At higher speeds, network inconsistencies and problems are exacerbated, and the need to keep the network healthy increases with traffic volume and speed.

Using Protocol Analyzers   8

Although the average systems or network manager does not need a complete breakout of a packet on the network, occasionally it can be very useful to be able to do so for popular protocols to find out what the protocol is doing. Many protocols do not provide retransmission statistics, and sometimes peeking into a packet to see which node name generated it helps the network manager resolve Ethernet/802.3 network addresses with node names for popular protocols. Protocol analysis tools help in this endeavor, and this chapter helps to shed some light on how to use the tool's output to manage the Ethernet/802.3 network, as well as what to look for in such a device.

What Is an Ethernet/802.3 Analyzer?

One of the most pervasive problems in managing any network is finding out what is happening on the network. This sounds easy, but depending on the network architecture, the effort can be substantial and very time-consuming.

Managing the network resource takes more than simply using some vendor-supplied host network control utility. Because many networks use many different network architectures, there is naturally some confusion as to how to control all the different network products from one place. Further, many network architectures are capable of sharing the same physical transmission resource, so the problem of management escalates fairly substantially as more and more systems find themselves using more than one network product on the same system attached to the same network resource.

For example, DECnet uses DDCMP protocol for normal DECnet activities (file transfer, task-to-task, and so on) plus other higher level protocols (such as NICE for network management functions, DAP for file transfer, NSP for session control, and others) for full network functionality. Further, DECnet also uses MOP for downline task and system loading, and it is treated as a separate data-link protocol when connected to the network. If a system has terminal servers connected to it, it will most likely use the LAT protocol, which has a completely different architecture and data-link protocol. To compound the problem, many systems also connect to UNIX systems, which may require usage of TCP/IP—again, more protocols and more network overhead.

If the aforementioned network architectures were all connected to an Ethernet/802.3, the problems would increase. Most likely, all the mentioned data-link protocols would be sharing the same Ethernet/802.3 controller and attempting to use the same Ethernet/802.3 cable. Of course, there is no "consolidated" network management and analysis tool available that can control all network packages from a single command utility—that is a difficult and tricky proposition to implement. Yet all packages would use the same hardware to connect to other systems. Unfortunately, the hardware and driver software that connects the hardware to the operating system are not "smart" enough to provide adequate network management and performance information.

Another way to collect the information is to use a network analysis tool, such as a protocol analyzer. Figure 8.1 shows the display of a protocol analyzer. Though protocol analyzers may collect network packets and provide some

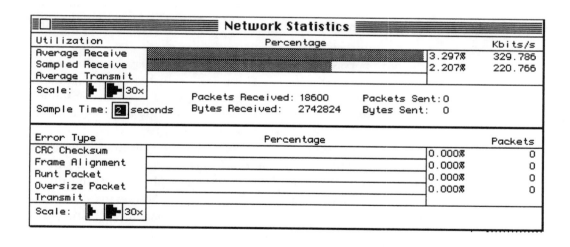

Figure 8.1

The Main Screen of a Protocol Analysis Tool

rough statistical information, the job of actual analysis is usually left to the tool's user. This is usually where the problems start.

Why Buy a Protocol Analyzer for Ethernet/802.3 Management?

Before we explore the necessary components of an analyzer, you need to know the answer to the first obvious question: "Why do I need one?"

You need one because your friendly neighborhood analyzer salesperson tells you that you do. Salespeople all have the same basic reasons, including the following:

- Network control
- Network monitoring
- Problem isolation
- Traffic loading analysis
- Packet content breakout

They are all good reasons, for sure. The problem is that they are all the wrong reasons for most system managers, because managers know little about what they would be looking at and the analyzer vendors presume that the user of the tool knows what to look for.

Most folks who need an analyzer usually don't know why they need one. The reasons for purchasing an analyzer vary from vendor to vendor and user to user. For the most part, however, unless you are willing to *learn* how to use and understand an analyzer's output, there is not much point in getting one. If, however, you *are* willing to learn how to use the analyzer properly, it can tell you a great deal about what is happening on the network and point out telltale problems—often before they get very serious.

For example, consider the following situation. You get a bright, shiny new analyzer. It's cute and fast. It has all the features that you could possibly want—and then some you were told you needed. You hook it up to your Ethernet/802.3 and, after collecting gross packet counts for two days, it tells you that the average load is 25%.

The loading-is-too-high figure will vary depending on who you talk to (some say 30% is too high, some say 10%), the phase of the lunar cycle, and how near is the end of the salesperson's quarter. In reality, various studies have shown that when an Ethernet/802.3 approaches a load average of 20-25%, connected machines have to wait too long to access the network and provide a reasonable response time to network operations. Remember, on an Ethernet/802.3, only one system at a time may have control of the actual cable. All other systems must wait until the sending station completes its message.

How Much Loading Is Too Much Loading?

So, is 25% loading high for an Ethernet? That depends on who you talk to. At 25% load, there is still bandwidth available 75% of the time. As far as I'm concerned, it's still not time to get hyperactive about it. Just getting a load metric figure is not enough to get concerned yet. Yes, it is too high when compared to most average loading on Ethernet/802.3 network cable plants. The real question is why.

Loading on an Ethernet/802.3 can be caused by a lot of things. Nodes sending out too many HELLO messages at too close an interval can cause a great deal of loading. Having many routing nodes on the network and frequent node failures can also contribute to the problem. Improperly tuned network software can cause a variety of problems also, as can improperly set network timers in network software (if links are always timing out, there are a lot of reconnection requests and retransmissions).

Improper Network Tuning

An improperly tuned system on an Ethernet/802.3 can cause a variety of problems as well.

Consider a 10-node Local Area VAXCluster (LAVC) with one system acting as BOOT system with the only disks on the cluster. In this situation, all disk I/O must go to/from the system with the disks on it. Worse, if the individual satellite LAVC members do not have their user account parameters set up correctly, the network can experience a severe degradation. For instance, what if a large image, say one that took 2500 pages to activate, were to be loaded from disk. That translates to 1.28 MB worth of data! If a user were to activate such an image from a terminal on one of the diskless machines, all 2500 pages would have to be transmitted across the Ethernet/802.3 from the disk server system to the diskless machine. Since the higher-speed Ethernet/802.3 controllers can handle only about 3.6 Mbps (about 450 KB per second) when running at best speed, this can translate into a long load time and much data on the network (about 900 full Ethernet/802.3 data packets). Of course, we are figuring raw data issues and not even beginning to consider processing overhead and other determinants.

Now that we have an idea of the volume of data, let's examine the problem. If a user has been given a working set size on the diskless VAX system that is large enough to allow the user's processor to allocate all possible memory necessary for the image being activated, then there will be 2500 pages worth of data, plus a small amount of pages for image activation and other system needs. If the user's working set were set to something smaller, say 512 pages, the diskless VAX system would be required to page-fault the pages in the diskless system's user's working set many times over to get all the necessary working set pages in to support the desired image activation. This does not translate into simple division of the expected working set usage by the actual working set allocation. No, the pages in the image would need to be faulted many times over and over to support the activation, sometimes as much as 10 times the amount of pages being stored. Taking a conservative factor of 5, this means that the actual data being transferred across the network would be the equivalent of 2500 pages times the paging factor of 5, or 12,500 pages that would need to be faulted for the singular process. This means that 6.4 MB of data would need to be faulted into the diskless machine to support the image activation! Since the controller can handle about 450 KB, it would take, at a minimum, 14.2 seconds for the image to activate on the diskless system. This is, of course, presuming that this is the only process activation on the diskless system, the node has exclusive and total access to the network, and there is no overhead other than the paging operation.

From a sheer data point of view, a single process activation data requirement was raised from 1.28 MB to 6.4 MB simply by having a working set that was too small on the diskless system. This could mean that the network load is falsely induced: an increase of working set size would increase throughput (activation time could be as low as 2.8 seconds) and reduce the network traffic by about a factor of 5. Obviously, more systems running the image and more users on each system would serve to compound the problem.

What does this exercise show? Simply that proper tuning of system resources, especially in the diskless environment, can reduce the network overhead substantially. It also shows that if the systems were tuned wrong, the network might very well show an inflated data load figure. A load of 25% on the Ethernet/802.3 is high, but it might be due to bad systems tuning. A simple adjustment to the user's account might substantially reduce network overhead.

Retransmission Issues

Another factor in excessive loading might be retransmission. While we have seen that bad adjustments to a system might induce serious network overhead, the load induced may cause other problems that would further contribute to the overhead. For example, if controllers and bridges in the communications path become congested due to inordinate traffic levels, the solution to congestion in many Ethernet/802.3 components is to start throwing away packets. If the number of Ethernet/802.3 packets being transmitted is large and the intermediate bridges or controllers in the path get congested, some packets may be lost (Ethernet/802.3 does *not* guarantee delivery of packets). Lost packets require retransmission, as requested by the destination, which causes the amount of traffic to increase. It becomes a vicious cycle: packets get lost because of congestion, retransmission happens and causes more congestion, which causes greater packet losses, even more retransmissions, and so on.

Analyzers Are Useful—If You Know What to Look For

What does an analyzer have to do with all of this? This example shows why one is very useful:

1. An analyzer can usually tell not only how many packets but also which protocol types are the most common. This can help pinpoint a particular network architecture that is causing problems.
2. Analyzers may be able to identify who is sending what to whom. While this is an advanced feature in most analyzers, it is very useful, because it identifies not only the protocol but also the volume of traffic, which tells the network manager what systems are the most useful to start looking toward "fixing."
3. An analyzer can provide the overall packet count for the Ethernet/802.3 segment. This information is useful because it identifies that there is a loading problem.
4. If the analyzer is capable of breaking out the protocol, the user can determine if the packets are original data or retransmissions. A high retransmission count means that the problems are more serious than simply high traffic volume.
5. If a bridge is being used, using an analyzer to compare traffic volumes with protocol types seen (and source/destination addresses) between segments can help identify if intermediate connectivity products are the source of problems.

So, an analyzer, properly configured and used, can allow the systems or network manager to identify problems properly on the network and isolate systems that need remedy. From the previous example, however, it is plain that the analyzer is simply a collection tool: the user of the analyzer must be able to understand the results of the collection to gain any benefit.

Vendors of analyzers offer as many combinations of them and collection "tools" as there are system configuration possibilities for all vendors on a network. Some vendors include all features in their package. Others require you to purchase collection tools and products as required. There are good and bad points about each method. If you get everything in one package, you may be paying for many things that you do not need. Conversely, module selling techniques may force you to purchase necessary modules at inflated prices and cause confusion and licensing problems.

Personally, I tend to favor the "all-together" approach, as I do not like to hassle with all the trash involved in module licensing or in finding out that something is missing. It also makes it easier for the vendor's support staff and salespeople. If all parts come with every system, people are not constantly asking "what is missing now?" and you can avoid the piecemeal approach to configuration. The all-in-one method simplifies ordering and maintenance, and lets salespeople set the customer's expectations (it saves the user from the somewhat disconcerting and disheartening scenario of first learning an analyzer's features and then finding that many of the capabilities are costly options).

Desirable Features in Protocol Analyzers

What features should you look for in an analyzer? All analyzers need to have a set of basic features, otherwise they will be less than productive in most environments. The basic set includes the following:

1. Packet identification of

   - Destination address
   - Source address
   - Protocol type
   - Total packet length
   - Errors in interpretation

2. Counters for

   - Total packet count
   - Protocol types
   - Size of packet ranges (how many are 50–100 bytes, 101–200 bytes, and so on)
   - Occurrences of destination or source addresses (how many packets are addressed to specific destinations and how many are generated from a particular source address)
   - Appearance of unknown protocol types
   - Frames out of format or "broken"
   - Oversized or undersized packets

3. Collection of entire packets and ability to display them to the user for analysis, in hex or ASCII.
4. Long-term statistical collection of counter information for accumulation over weeks, months, and possibly years.
5. Report generation capabilities to allow production of printed reports on collected information or statistical information generated over a period of time.
6. Generation of packets to test other components on the network. Such capabilities might include the ability to generate broadcast packet destinations (FF-FF-FF-FF-FF-FF) to load up the entire network for stress analysis, ability to capture and replay sessions to emulate live traffic, and ability to generate original packet protocol for testing of applications or new protocol types.

Although this list may not provide an all-inclusive shopping ticket, it does give an idea of some of the features that are absolutely necessary in a useful analyzer.

Unfortunately, many analyzer vendors forget one very critical item: most buyers of network analyzers do not necessarily understand what the analyzer is trying to tell them. More specifically, many of those who would use an Ethernet/802.3 analyzer are not qualified to understand what the analyzer is capable of producing. Worse, there are few places to go to learn the necessary information.

So you don't need an analyzer, right? No, it's still useful. In many situations, traffic load metrics and reasonable estimates as to which protocols are doing the most damage are good indicators of where to start looking at problems and whether possibly to consult a professional. A network analysis expert can glean much information from an analyzer's network traffic measurements. Traffic matrix, security risk levels, protocol violations, overall noise metrics, traffic throughput profile, network parameter adjustments, and many other useful items of information may be learned, thereby allowing adjustment of the network and increased throughput and performance.

The lesson is this: if an analyzer is to be useful, the network manager must know how to use it and understand what the information being collected is capable of showing. When the network breaks is not the time to be looking for the instruction manual—it's too late for that. Learn to use and understand an analyzer before that happens, so that it can be useful when the network does run into trouble or when an analysis is necessary.

Some forward-thinking analyzer vendors are in the process of developing additional analyzer functionality that will allow network managers to derive much more information from the network. Such information may be a re-iteration of collected data or, in some cases, interpretation tools that sift through the data being collected to provide a meaningful analysis. Real-time collection of data on an Ethernet/802.3 is a virtual impossibility for any analyzer—there are simply too many packets for most analyzers to handle, so a certain amount of loss is to be expected from all analyzers. True, some are more accurate than others and are capable of collecting almost all network information. Analysis of a network starts with regular sampling to identify possible problems and migration to a more refined sample as problems manifest themselves.

VMS VPA is a good example of this. The default collection value for data is once every 12 minutes. This collection interval is usually enough for a first pass to understand if there is a problem. Should an issue arise that is unfavorable, the collection interval may be shortened. Obviously, shortening the collection interval causes a greater accumulation of data, which means that while a more refined look at the analysis is possible, there is the problem of data storage and processing. More data equals longer processing time and more storage. So, in most cases, a network analyzer would be used to collect periodic data, followed by times of intense collection where detailed analysis may be performed.

Even if the analyzer is capable of collecting such data, it may signify that the skills of the network analyst may need to be greater. Collection of raw data means the ability to sort out what is valuable and what is not. Since most analyzers do not necessarily provide this feature without some knowledge of network architecture, packets, and operational features, it is difficult to expect network analyzers to improve much in analysis aids in the near future.

Expert Analysis

One possible hope on the horizon is the use of expert systems. One enterprising company is in the process of writing software for their analyzer to assist the network analyst in understanding not only what was collected but also what the collected data means. On the first pass, the software appears to be able to collect very long term data and provide a variety of "what-if" capabilities and analysis tools. Plans for the product include multisegment collection capability as well as incorporation of a frame-based expert system that will allow non-networking-oriented users to understand collected information from the analyzers on the various segments.

Developing an expert system is an ambitious project; it is not trivial and will require refinement. But this company is on the right track: it is impractical to expect an analyzer user to be able to use the analyzer effectively, so why not give the user the right tools to understand the collected data.

Some vendors have gone so far as to include an on-line time domain reflectometer (TDR) capability in their analyzer. A TDR allows the network manager to identify the location of a break or short in the Ethernet/802.3 network segment. (Of course, it's only useful if the cable has been properly marked, but that is another matter.) With the TDR capability, the location of breaks and shorts can be found, but the feature may be expanded to allow location of bad transceivers and other network components. This type of expansion is highly useful in rapidly identifying and resolving network problems.

Summary

Ethernet/802.3 analyzers are useful systems if the network manager or analyst is willing to spend the requisite time learning how to use it. Analyzers are not without expense: full-featured analyzers cost anywhere from $15,000 to more than $40,000. For that kind of expense, understanding the capabilities is essential for proper and full usage. To purchase an analyzer that is suitable for your network needs, you must understand the analyzer's capabilities, features that have been added, and new features that may be included. As with any system, proper analysis of capabilities and a commitment to usage are essential for best use.

Understanding SQE/Heartbeat

9

There is an enormous amount of confusion about the setting of the signal quality error (SQE) or "heartbeat" between controllers and transceivers on Ethernet/802.3 networks. Because improper settings of heartbeat, or SQE, can cause performance problems and phantom errors to occur on the network, it is important to set it correctly. This chapter explores what SQE/heartbeat is and how it should be set for the various types of network equipment to ensure proper network performance and functionality.

Understanding Heartbeat

It is absolutely amazing how many people are confused about the concept of heartbeat when configuring Ethernet/802.3 networks. Heartbeat, simply put, is a signal from an Ethernet/802.3 transceiver to the Ethernet/802.3 controller that is used for different reasons depending on whether the controller is compliant with IEEE 802.3 or Ethernet V2.0. Heartbeat may be used either to tell a controller that the transceiver is alive (a self-test) or to tell a controller that the signal quality on the cable has degraded.

Transceiver Cable

To send signals from the transceiver to the controller, a transceiver cable is required (see Figure 9.1). Obviously, this applies only to devices or systems with a 15-pin D-connector interface to the network. In the Digital environment, this would mean that a system, such as an Alpha AXP system, has a 15-pin connector on the bulkhead on the back of the system; a 15-wire transceiver cable is connected to the bulkhead and then to an Ethernet/802.3 transceiver such as an H4005 or a DESTA.

137

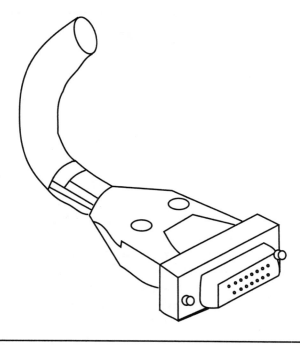

Figure 9.1
Transceiver Cable

The transceiver cable uses pairs of cables in the cable itself to transmit signals between the transceiver and the controller as well as to receive power from the controller (see Figure 9.2). These pairs are as follows:

Transmit Data (pins 3 and 10)

Receive Data (pins 5 and 12)

Power (pin 6: power return; pin 13: power)

Collision Presence (pins 2 and 9)

All other pairs are reserved. Pin 1 is the shield (which is connected to the connection shell). In the displayed list, the first pin of each pair for signaling is the positive value and the second pin in the pair is the negative value. Pairs of the transceiver cable are either the one power pair or the remaining signaling pairs.

Transmit Data is fairly obvious: it is the pair used by the controller to send data to the transceiver. Receive Data is the pair used by the transceiver to send

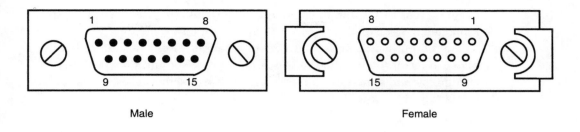

Figure 9.2
Transceiver Cable Connectors (Pinout)

incoming data to the controller. Power is also obvious—it gets the juice from the controller to the transceiver. Collision Presence is used by the transceiver to indicate the presence of a multiple transmission attempt on the main network cable. This signal becomes active, typically, when two or more nodes are transmitting simultaneously and the transceiver is connected to one of the transmitting nodes. Another reason for this signal pair to be active is when there are three or more stations transmitting simultaneously on the cable (regardless of whether the transceiver is connected to one of the transmitting nodes or not).

The Collision Presence Test

One not-so-obvious function of the Collision Presence pair is to transmit to the controller a self-test to indicate the operational status of the collision presence circuitry in the transceiver. This action is known to most as heartbeat, collision presence test (CPT), or sometimes Signal Quality Error Enabled (SQE) and is used *only* on Ethernet V2.0 nodes. This signal is sent up the pair from the transceiver to the controller after every transmission from the controller to the transceiver. Therefore, every time the controller pumps out a packet to the network, the transceiver responds with a signal on the Collision Presence pair that lets the controller know that everything is working in the collision presence circuitry.

In IEEE 802.3, the capabilities of the Collision Presence pair are basically the same, with one optional addition: the transceiver may, on a medium-dependent basis, transmit a signal back to the controller based on a variety of possible problems encountered on the network cable (such as improper signal or a break or short in the medium). When this capability is used, it is typically called signal quality error, or SQE, in IEEE terms.

Therefore, heartbeat, SQE, CPT—or whatever else it may be called this week—refers to the method in which the transceiver and the controller exchange discrete signals to keep each other informed of various events on the network or the status of the transceiver.

Vendor Inconsistency

In the early days of Ethernet/802.3 networks, the vendor had to provide the transceiver and controller hardware for things to work properly. Thus, the vendor decided how (and whether) to enable CPT/SQE. Most vendors implemented the V2.0 Digital-Intel-Xerox (DIX) standard, which sent a signal after every transmission to the transceiver so that the controller would know that the transceiver was functioning properly. As IEEE 802.3 has become better known, and especially after it was adopted by the ISO as an international standard, there has been a steady migration to the use of 802.3 as the preferred standard over the V2.0 definition.

To solve the problem, vendors began to provide transceivers with DIP switches on them that allow the installer of the network to select either SQE enabled or disabled. Although there is a technical difference between what SQE actually is and what it is generally called in the industry (it's a lot of the same nonsense as the difference bit rates and baud), in general, a controller is said to desire SQE enabled (heartbeat enabled for V2.0 devices) or SQE disabled (heartbeat turned off for 802.3 controllers that require no function similar to the V2.0 CPT function). From a purely technical point of view, the use of SQE as a differentiating term is inappropriate, but it is the norm.

Should I Enable or Disable Heartbeat/SQE?

The question then becomes this: When should heartbeat/CPT/SQE be enabled and when should it be disabled?

It's up to the vendor of the device or system being connected to the Ethernet/802.3 network. Each vendor implements their controller for the network as either V2.0-compliant or 802.3-compliant. Some controllers are quite capable of supporting both V2.0 and 802.3 frames and cable diameters but may still require SQE to be enabled due to the vendor's decision to provide a positive handshake mechanism between the controller and the transceiver.

Even 802.3-compliant systems may require SQE to be enabled. There is nothing that restricts an 802.3 device from using SQE in the same manner that V2.0 uses CPT. Usually, most vendors of IEEE 802.3-compliant equipment do not implement this feature, but it is important to check and make sure.

There are a couple of very general rules of thumb. As a rule, any V2.0-compliant device will require SQE (CPT or heartbeat) to be enabled. If the device being connected is an 802.3 controller card, check with the vendor to make sure that the DIP switches on the transceiver are set in the proper manner. If the device is an 802.3-compliant repeater or bridge unit with an 802.3 internal controller, SQE will typically be turned off to keep the units happy.

Not all vendors are consistent. For instance, most Digital Equipment Corporation devices are V2.0 compliant and require SQE/CPT/heartbeat to be *enabled* so that the unit and associated software will work properly. For instance, if heartbeat is disabled on a 6000-520, network software will experience framing errors and timing errors. This, of course, degrades not only the system but other systems on the network, as retransmissions may be required and general throughput between pairs of systems communicating with the affected one will suffer. Setting the switches in the transceiver to SQE mode will clear up the problem. It will still work, but the error counters will get quite high. Where the inconsistency arises is that newer devices made by Digital are 802.3 compliant and do not use the SQE feature, so they must be disabled. The Digital Ethernet Multi-Port Repeater (DEMPR) is a good example of this. If a DEMPR is connected to a backbone network with SQE enabled, the network will experience collisions and other problems. Changing the switch settings on the transceiver to SQE inhibit will cause the problems on the network to disappear.

Most transceivers that are switch selectable must be powered off and then on again *after* switch positions have been changed. To do so, disconnect the 15-pin cable from the host and reconnect the cable. This will power off the transceiver and all will be well.

Summary

Not all devices require SQE/CPT/heartbeat. Some do. Check the vendor documentation and then configure each and every transceiver properly for the equipment connected to it. Your error counts will go down, nodes will avoid processing errors, and performance will improve. In all cases, check first and you'll reduce your aggravation and stress.

Network Security 10

In this chapter, we discuss the types of network and system security problems on Ethernet/802.3 and related networks, with emphasis on the types of breaches that can occur. Although not every possible threat to network security is covered, this chapter provides guidance as to the more common problems you may encounter.

The Need for Security in Technology

In the computing sciences, the need for systems security has grown explosively. Most such growth has occurred due to isolated and highly publicized incidents of computer break-ins and the corporate paranoia that naturally has ensued. Though many vendors and research facilities are now offering both free and for-pay solutions to individual operating system and application security problems, there has long been the need to monitor and report on the status of network security and the problems involved in the protection of all information that is accessible to network resources.

To compound the problem of network security, the economic climate of the last few years has forced many companies to consider installing computer network components on existing computer systems rather than purchasing new computer systems to meet their corporate needs. This trend has translated into an enormous jump in the number of interconnected systems: between 1976 and 1988, fewer than 10 million total systems were installed; in 1991–92 alone, installation of more than 25 million total systems was estimated. Estimates for 1995 point to more than 35 million being installed. Even greater numbers are expected as more and more computational engines enter the mainstream of everyday life.

The Network as an Essential Business Instrument

As a network becomes more essential to a business, the network becomes a critical resource that must be protected from unwanted intrusions, runaway applications, "eavesdropping" operations, lax security in network protocol architecture(s), and many other potential security problems. Further, as network resources increase in size and as more users consume and abuse those resources, it becomes all-too-probable that viruses, worms, and other contaminants will infiltrate the network and spread, degrading the performance of the network and its individual systems.

Some computing sites, due to the classified nature of their business, require network monitoring, but there simply are no products that currently can do so. Other sites, though not engaged in classified activities, require network security monitoring due to information access reporting laws, audit requirements, guarantees of access (so that only the proper entity is accessing the proper items), protection of competitive information, laws requiring the guarantee of restricted access to personal information, general electronic security (such as electronic mail access and document transfer), electronic funds exchange, monitoring of exchange or transaction data volume between systems, and many other reasons.

Computer Crime

Computer crime is generally defined as any crime accomplished through special knowledge of computer technology. Increasing instances of white-collar crime involve computers, as more businesses automate and information becomes an important asset. Computers are objects of crime when they or their contents are damaged, such as when terrorists attack computer centers with explosives or gasoline, or when a computer virus—a program capable of altering or erasing computer memory—is introduced. As subjects of crime, computers represent the electronic environment in which frauds are programmed and executed, such as the transfer of money balances in accounts to perpetrators' accounts for withdrawal. Computers are instruments of crime when used to plan or control criminal acts, such as complex embezzlements that might occur over long periods of time, or when a computer operator uses a computer to steal valuable information from an employer.

Computer Crime Statistics

Since the first cases were reported in 1958, computers have been used for most kinds of crime, including fraud, theft, forgery, larceny, embezzlement, burglary, sabotage, espionage, and murder. One study of 1500 computer crimes established that most of them were committed by trusted computer users within businesses—persons with the requisite skills, knowledge, access, and resources. Much of known computer crime has consisted of entering false data into computers, which is simpler and safer than carrying out the complex process of writing a program to change data already in the computer. With the advent of personal computers, which allow people to manipulate information and access computers by telephone, increasing numbers of crimes—mostly simple but costly electronic trespassing, copyright piracy, and vandalism—have been perpetrated by computer hobbyists known as hackers, who display a high level of technical expertise. Organized professional criminals also have been attacking and using computer systems as they find their old activities and environments being automated.

There are no valid statistics about the extent of computer crime. One recent U.S. Government report stated that more than 86% of all computer break-ins happen from internal sources, mostly via the in-house communications network. Victims often resist reporting suspected cases because they can lose more from embarrassment, damaged reputation, litigation, and other consequential losses than from the acts themselves. Limited evidence indicates that the number of cases is rising each year, because of the increasing number of computers in business applications where crime has traditionally occurred. The largest recorded crimes involving insurance, banking, product inventories, and securities have resulted in losses of tens of millions to billions of dollars—all facilitated by computers.

Recent U.S. legislation, including laws concerning privacy, credit card fraud, and racketeering, provide criminal-justice agencies with tools to fight business crime. As of 1992, all but two states had specific computer-crime laws, and a federal computer-crime law (implemented in 1986) deals with certain crimes involving computers in different states and in government activities.

Network Security: A Potential Solution

It was immediately apparent, due to research done by the author with data relationships in biological neural networks, that the problems of overall network security could not be solved with a singular application of logic. Data relationships in biological neural networks are very similar in many ways to data relationships of computer nodes on computer networks. To monitor and detect changes in the states of neural activity requires serious real-time computational capabilities that are very compute-intensive and logic-intensive by nature. The result is that it is not economical to provide full analysis and coverage of network events related to security, due to the sheer cost of implementation and the bulk of analysis required. Further, neural network analysis shows that significant events often replicate themselves, allowing for the possibility of using a sampled approach rather than an exhaustive collection-and-analysis effort for all data on the computer network.

Another problem was guaranteeing that the network security monitoring mechanism itself was secure. It does no good to install a monitoring system only to find out that the system itself is tainted. Further, any security feature is immediately subject to attack by the unscrupulous few who view others' network security not as a right but as a challenge.

Analyzing and monitoring the performance of the security monitoring mechanism is a problem for all security tool sets. Security on any system is possible, but the amount of CPU time and resources required for proper monitoring reduces system performance rapidly, and the overhead of the security-related function usually far exceeds the desired capital outlay for such resources.

Security Features That Cause Security Problems

Vendor-supplied security features in applications and network product architectures are problematic. Most network applications and architectures leave virtually no provisions whatsoever for security features and require that operating system security be stable to provide what minimal network security features are available. The problem is further compounded by the fact that most network security features in practically all architectures are easily bypassed with simple effort or via "node spoofing." In node spoofing, a third system is configured to look like the original system or a dyadic communications link. The second system of the dyad "thinks" that it is communicating with the original system, but it is really talking to the third, masquerading system.

This problem is illustrated by the use of proxy connections to "spoof" a destination node. The originating node changes its node address and user ID to reflect a valid one (or a valid guess) at the destination node. Since most popular networking protocols do not provide for authentication of sessions, the connection from the spoofer to the destination will appear valid to the destination, and the connection will be allowed. At this point, the spoofer obtains the privileges associated with the user ID being spoofed. In many networks, this method may allow spoofing of the systems manager's account ID on other, less-protected nodes, and the spoofer may gain access to valuable data or information that is useful for breaking into other systems.

Another example of this technique is the use of network proxy connections. A proxy connection, available in many of the more popular commercial network protocols, allows a user on a particular system to be connected to another system on the network without the need to send a password to the remote system. The concept is similar to placing a vote by proxy: the vote is filed on behalf of the voter when the voter is not physically present.

The network software issues a special type of connection request to the destination system. The destination system identifies the special connection as a proxy connection. In a proxy connection, information on the network object (the program) requesting connection, user ID, and system ID is passed in a connection request. The destination system is previously informed, via network or system management software, that a particular user ID from a particular system will be logged on to the system in a specific account without the need for a password. In this manner, any system on the network "eavesdropping" on the session will see a connection request by a user but will never see the password in the connection negotiation. The effect is that passwords are not propagated on the network, which is supposed to increase security.

In fact, most systems originating the connection request are easily modified. For example, a microcomputer using a commercial protocol may change its node address and default user name without any requirement for privileges on the microcomputer. So a microcomputer may "look" like a node, which it is not, and may change the default user ID to a valid, but inappropriate, user ID on the microcomputer system. If a connection to a remote system is then made after the fairly trivial changes to the microcomputer (some protocol suites may allow the required network software changes with a single command), the remote system will identify the changed microcomputer as being a different system with a different user ID. Obviously, this is not the intent of proxy connections, but it is, in fact, what can and has happened on many networks. Therefore, through misuse, a security feature becomes a security liability.

Packet-Content Security

Packet-content security, another major issue in network security, is very, very difficult to monitor and report on. In this situation, individual packets on the network are analyzed independently for security violations. Although collecting the packets is not difficult—and neither, necessarily, is scanning the packets for content—analyzing packet content is very difficult, because there is no way of knowing what packet means what to which application. For instance, an electronic mail message from one VAX/VMS system to another may contain a true mail message, the source code of a program, or a binary file suitable for execution on another node (for example, the MAIL/FOREIGN command in VMS allows transfer of programs and binary files via the standard VAX MAIL utility, available on all VAX/VMS systems). The connection between two systems, the message transfer between accounts, and the amount of data and time of day may all be 100% legitimate, but unless the actual contents are analyzed, there is no way to know what kind of buffer was sent between the systems and whether that exchange was detrimental to the overall network security effort.

Finally, it would be far too burdensome to analyze every packet on a network. On 802.3-class LANs, with peak loads of almost 15,000 packets per second, attempting to perform packet breakout in real time would far exceed the maximum network loading capabilities of most supercomputers.

Session Security

Session security between cooperating nodes is a likely target for security monitoring, except that for a particular system to monitor all sessions of all protocols is virtually impossible. As with breaking out protocol packets, session security would require serious CPU capabilities and memory requirements that far exceed the expense that most facilities would be inclined to part with.

In the case of node spoofing, another node can "look" like the real node being accessed, and sessions can be controlled and accessed in a nonsecure way. The connecting program does not know that the remote system is anything other than the real target system.

To help with session security, there is session authentication or verification. The idea is that each node has a key that is changed periodically and used to encrypt a data item that is known to both systems. The originating system on the connection issues a connection request with a verification request embedded in the packet. The destination system breaks this out and sends a specially encrypted message back to the original node. The originating node breaks this out with the key and reencrypts the information and sends it back to the target node. The target node, after successfully decrypting the packet contents and scanning for proper components, sends a connection acceptance message back to the originating system and the session is up and running.

By using the authentication mechanism, the session between the two systems is verified as being between the proper systems and not a remote system or originating system that is spoofing a valid node. Most nodes attempting to spoof other nodes would not have the proper keys to provide the encryption/decryption function required to successfully negotiate the link connection request.

Encryption

Although encryption is always high on the list of solutions to network security problems, it shouldn't be. For one thing, distribution of keys is a problem for any site, especially if there is a geographic distribution problem. Another major issue is the selection of the cryptosystem and the mechanism in which the cryptosystem is implemented.

Then there is the issue of exportation from the United States. U.S. law is very unforgiving in this matter: there are strict and complex rules regarding the export of encipherment systems and encryption algorithms. The penalties for improperly handling encipherment systems are very serious, so many companies do not engage in the development or export of such systems. To compound the issue, the U.S. Government strictly regulates which companies may create government-certified encipherment systems, what specifications those systems must meet, and for what networking technologies they may be developed.

Experienced and knowledgeable cryptologists agree that a number of cryptographic systems are unsolvable by analytic techniques. Cryptographic systems in which a key is used only once, known as holocryptic systems, can be mathematically proven to be analytically unsolvable. Other cryptographic systems, especially those using electrical devices, can often be highly secure from a practical viewpoint against cryptanalytic attack. Nonetheless, the most theoretically secure cryptographic system can be vulnerable if the system is incorrectly used or if there is a partial or complete physical compromise of the system. This is especially important in network security, where any system connected to the common network is physically attached and may violate physical security by listening to traffic on the network medium.

Cryptographic systems invented by amateurs or nonexperts will almost always be either impractical or cryptographically weak. The amateur usually overlooks the problems inherent in electrical or telegraphic transmission, such as whether messages received with many erroneous letters, or even with missing letters, can still be read by recipients. With any new cryptographic system, it must be assumed that the enemy, or adversary cryptanalyst, knows everything about the general system. Only specific keys can be presumed unknown.

As cryptographic systems become more complicated, however, sophisticated cryptanalytic techniques are required. Today, the computer's ability to store millions of pieces of information is both an invaluable aid in cryptanalysis and itself an incentive to develop highly complex cryptographic systems, because of the wide range of sensitive information that now exists in computer databanks and is transmitted through computer networks. Such data is stored in ciphers so complex that only other computers can decipher them. Governments, banks, and manufacturers make use of encryption systems that are primarily based on the difficulty involved in factoring large numbers, as compared with the difficulty in finding out whether those numbers are primes. Primes are used in coding systems by computer networks, which encrypt their data so that only those authorized users who have the proper key can decode the transmitted information. A key, which determines the relationship between the plaintext and the ciphertext, is made up of a certain number of binary digits.

The reality of encryption is that it is not magical, mystical, or even exciting. Encryption simply involves the use of an encipherment algorithm with a key (like a password) to take normal network data and scramble it into bits that only a system with the encryption algorithm and the proper key can understand. The problem is that most people tend to look at encryption in the mystical sense—few people understand what it really is.

To facilitate the use of encryption by the public sector, the National Bureau of Standards (NBS—now called the National Institute of Standards and Technology, or NIST) published a Federal Information Processing Standard (FIPS PUB 46) on January 15, 1977, called the Data Encryption Standard (DES). The DES uses a 64-bit key structure implemented with a defined permutation (change mechanism) method. Of the 64 bits, 56 are used for the actual key and 8 are used for error control. If you compute the various combinations of a 56-bit key, you will find that there are more than 70 quadrillion different bit combinations. So the chances of breaking a properly enciphered DES data stream are pretty slim, unless, of course, someone has access to the key.

Understanding DES takes a little patience. First, the 64-bit block data undergoes a permutation that arranges the data according to a specific matrix. Then the 64-bit block is split in half. The right half is permuted to a 48-bit value (the matrix that specifies the order of data happens to duplicate 16 bits of the data). The generated 48-bit value is the "exclusive-OR," with a 48-bit key value that is obtained from the original 56-bit DES key. The exclusive-OR operation reduces the 48-bit value to a 32 bits by splitting the 48-bit value into 8 groups of 6 bits each. The 6-bit values are then converted to 4-bit values using a 6-bit-to-4-bit selection table. Following the conversion of the 48-bit data to 32-bit data, the 32-bit data is permutated again to a new 32-bit value. Now, as if this was not complicated enough, when the data on the right is reduced to 32 bits, this value is exclusive-ORed to the unaltered left 32 bits. This completes the first level of iteration of the encryption computation.

The result generated from the previous computation now becomes the right half and the unaltered right half becomes the left half. The data then is permuted 16 different times in a specific fashion, using 16 different keys (one new key per permutation). Following the 16 permutations, the data is permuted one last time, but now in the reverse order of the very first time. The data is now encrypted and ready for transmission.

DES has been implemented in a wide variety of products other than networking and communications products. File encryption, password encryption, and other traditional computing components have been given the benefit of the DES encryption algorithm to secure access to sensitive system components.

Another encryption method that is gaining some notoriety is known as the RSA (for Rivest-Shamir-Adelman) Public Key Scheme. The RSA scheme is simple yet very secure. The idea revolves around the fact that it is much easier to multiply prime numbers together than it is to factor the result. This means that the result could be used as part of the enciphering key without compromising the necessary factors required for the deciphering operation. If the result generated were, say, more than 100 digits long, it would take billions of years to factor out the result on a high-speed computer using the best algorithms possible. All in all, RSA is an elegant, high-speed method of encrypting data and keeping it secure. For you folks using X.25 communications, you should be aware that the RSA algorithm is being used as the authentication mechanism for the X.32 subset. RSA is also being used in many of the system card-ID systems that require magnetic or optical cards for specific personnel to access systems.

Actually, encryption could be implemented anywhere in the network architecture, but the fastest way is within the communications hardware. This is further justified when one considers that DES is already on a chip (the Motorola MC6859; the Burroughs MC884; Western Digital WD2001E/F, WD2002A/B, and WD2003; Advanced Micro Devices AmZ8068; Intel 8294; TI TMS9940; American Microsystems S6894; and other multichip sets and board products) and the RSA mechanism is math computation-intensive (making it ideal for something like an 8087 arithmetic coprocessor or other such chips). But while encryption at the communications interface level is the simplest, it does not keep the node secure. From a system management point of view, encryption of data *before* it hits the network architecture is usually preferable, as it precludes network software and hardware from performing data encryption. Should the network be compromised, the data is already encrypted on the node. It is also reasonable to perform encryption at the session control layer (and below) of the network architecture. This ensures that outgoing data is secure before it hits the network communications hardware.

While this looks good on paper, it can also cause a great deal of computational overhead, due to encryption of seemingly innocuous transactions such as ACKs and NACKs, as well as other problems such as when to encrypt data and when not to (as in the case of downline loading). Encryption of data prior to hitting the network architecture or encryption in the hardware precludes the network software from having to make all kinds of decisions about when and where to encrypt data.

Finally, the big question: Why bother with network encryption?

First, the old adage "An ounce of prevention is worth a pound of cure" definitely applies to networks. In areas where line tapping is possible, the cost of implementing network encryption equipment can be far less than the loss of data or market edge caused by network intrusion. Line tapping involves more than someone tapping a telephone connection. Line tapping is the term also used on public data networks when a node on the network intercepts an in-progress communications session. It is also useful to get a bit paranoid about LANs, especially nonintrusively tapped networks (such as Ethernet), as nodes could easily be added without the network software recognizing the new node as a node on the network (this is common on networks that support different protocols). Software encryption in the network architecture prevents "session" tapping by nodes. For instance, while node A is establishing a connection to node B, a different node X may make A think that it is node B. By the use of a network encryption algorithm, X would *have* to know the encryption key, which is highly unlikely, to simulate node B.

Is Encryption Really Useful?

Encryption, strategically placed within the node, can be a very useful thing. Many embarrassing moments have happened at many companies due to unauthorized users reading files or electronic mail messages. With encryption, such encounters become rare, and business relationships can be salvaged. Encryption can take place at the file level, file system level, or even at the image level. Some companies offer programs that allow the encryption of executable images such that a key has to be supplied for the image to run. While this approach may be somewhat troublesome, it does minimize circumvention of the normal system protection mechanisms and allows control over who has the key(s).

One problem to keep in mind is access to the encryption mechanism. If the mechanism used is hardware, then the components need to be kept physically secure from tampering—and if they are tampered with, there needs to be some sort of notification that tampering has happened. If the method used involves software encryption, it becomes much more difficult to keep tampering from happening. But, just as with monitoring hardware tampering, it is critical that some sort of mechanism be placed in the encryption software to keep tampering from happening.

Encryption of data in networks will become a necessity in the modern corporate environment as a matter of course. How you decide to implement encryption in your situation will depend on the tradeoffs in performance you can accept. In any case, it would be a good thing to start looking into. Who knows? Your network may be the next "statistic."

Before we leave encryption, there is one product on the market that can help with Ethernet/802.3 security from an encryption point of view. Digital Equipment Corporation makes a product named the Key Distribution Facility (called KDC), which works with special encryption transceivers that are connected to the systems on the network. By using public key cryptographic techniques, the nodes on the network connected via the encryption transceivers and KDC unit may exchange information on the Ethernet/802.3 network in a secure and encrypted manner. The product is not inexpensive and does have its limitations, but it is a powerful tool in encryption technologies to help cope with the need to exchange information in a secure manner on an "open" network.

Promiscuous Mode

Problems with network architectures that cannot be solved are a major issue in network security. Practically all LAN technologies allow any node to collect all data seen on the LAN. Also, since most LANs broadcast all packets to the LAN media, any node in data-collection mode may see all packets at will. Some network LAN technologies, such as Ethernet/802.3, token ring/802.5, and others such as FDDI, have inherent capabilities to facilitate network packet collection from the cable media. When a programmer issues the proper software instructions (usually minimal), the network controller card will collect all packets and forward them to the collection program. This feature, called "promiscuous mode," is a serious network security problem that cannot be solved in most LAN architectures—because it is available in most network controller architectures for LANs.

Promiscuous mode is the state in which many LAN controllers may be placed to allow the system using the controller to see all packets that appear on a LAN. Practically all Ethernet/802.3 controllers for all systems have promiscuous mode capability, as do many token ring/802.5 and other LAN and metropolitan area network (MAN) technology controllers.

Promiscuous mode is enabled by a programmer setting certain register values in a controller and forcing the controller to collect all packets from the network and forward them to the host system's software. The software may then either capture the packets to a file, display them, or do whatever the program is designed to allow. The number of packets that may be collected and the ability of the system to deal with the volume of traffic is a function of controller buffering, system speed, bus speed, and many other issues. It is also a function of the ability of the software written for promiscuous mode to be fast enough and intelligent enough to provide useful information as it arrives from the network.

Since practically all protocols do not encrypt data in the packet, the contents of captured packets are easily examined. In most situations, viewing the packet in ASCII is sufficient to capture user IDs and passwords, as well as other types of valuable corporate information. In some cases, known compression algorithms or data encoding (such as Radix-50, TASCII, ASCII, or EBCDIC) are used, which are easily broken out by the program collecting packet data from the network. This ability, plus the fact that most specifications of networking protocols are publicly known via vendor-published information or via public domain information available from a variety of sources, allows easy packet breakout for almost any programmer.

Probably the worst problem with promiscuous mode is that there are plenty of public domain programs on the various bulletin boards and freeware distribution centers that will allow PC, Macintosh, UNIX, VMS, and other operating system environments to exploit the network resource. Although the authors of such programs never had the primary intent of network intrusion, the programs do allow it nonetheless. If packets may be captured and viewed, they may be exploited. After one Network-1 customer site was informed about this during an Ethernet course we were teaching, the programmer at the site decided that he would verify for himself how hard it was to create a program that would place a PC controller into promiscuous mode and capture data. He used Microsoft Fortran on a 386-based PC clone with a Micom 4010 Ethernet/802.3 controller on a standard thickwire Ethernet installation. It took the programmer about 45 minutes to craft an original program from the Micom documentation on promiscuous mode. He did this during lunch.

Obviously, the code aspect of promiscuous mode is not difficult for the average programmer. Most of the code required is in the setup for promiscuous mode and the setup for the capture and display of data following collection from the network. It is even easier for the average user, as there are plenty of programs for promiscuous mode available. While some LANs, like token ring, do not have promiscuous mode in all controllers, some micro-programmable LAN controllers do have promiscuous mode and can be enabled with the right code. There are examples of this on various popular bulletin boards and public Videotex systems.

The biggest problem with promiscuous mode is that it cannot be detected on the network when it is enabled on any particular system. It is analogous to someone listening to a phone conversation on an extension phone with the mouthpiece on the extension disabled—no one knows there is anyone on the extension and the entire conversation may be heard.

Promiscuous mode, in addition to being a dangerous feature, is also a very desirable one. All network analyzers and network monitors use promiscuous mode in one way or another. Unfortunately, in many respects, promiscuous mode is a necessary evil if certain aspects of network management are to be achieved.

Companies with a lot of microcomputers or workstations are the primary targets for intrusive attack via promiscuous mode. The best countermeasure is a regular audit of microcomputer programs and usage as well as network activity audits between systems for traffic pathing (who is going where). Using a checksum utility to identify certain programs may help detect promiscuous mode programs. Remember that file names may be changed, so searching for offending programs by file name is not enough.

Wireless Local Area Networks

The promotion of wireless LANs increases the problems of network security, simply due to the LANs' architecture. Popular wireless networks achieve speeds up to 10 Mbps (at this writing) using CSMA/CD technologies; much higher bit rates are possible in the next few years. Since these networks, by nature, are public broadcast over airwaves, all an intruder needs is the proper reception and transmission equipment to breach the network resource.

Fiber and Network Security

Some network hardware technologies, such as fiber, that have been traditionally secure from explicit intrusion are now susceptible to access due to new connectivity technologies. Some of the larger fiber vendors recently demonstrated nonintrusive fiber connections and radiated photon transmission subsystems. Both technologies allow a "clamp-on" type of network connection to fiber networks, provide the ability to nonintrusively tap existing fiber, and provide full duplex communications facilities without fiber cable disruption. While this is a great step in the usage and planning of fiber networks, it is also a very large problem for network security in fiber optic plants.

The Misuse of Protocols

Network security issues arise when nodes use protocols they should not be using for communications or when unlicensed protocol architectures appear on systems on the network. This is especially important in these days of packages for microcomputers that include a formidable set of differing network protocols (such as DEC's PathWorks) that allow systems to communicate with each other in methods previously impossible due to lack of protocols on the microcomputers.

From a pure business point of view, there are also copyright restrictions the network manager must worry about when using network packages. Just like word processing and other types of software, nodes require a software license to run most network packages. Since few network packages impose a software protection mechanism, it is usually easy to install the same network software package on many nodes and simply change the node address on each to allow the software to function. In most countries, this is an illegal act, as the software is licensed for that particular node, not every node. For instance, if a node all of a sudden started to run TCP/IP and was not licensed to do so, this would constitute a copyright violation. Such a violation can be more serious in some countries, such as the United Kingdom, where there are very specific laws and penalties for such activities, including heavy fines and jail time in extreme situations.

Node Interaction as a Security Problem

Interaction of traffic between nodes may introduce security issues not readily apparent on a computer network. Two nodes that normally interact with each other on a network have a normal traffic profile that indicates not only which other nodes the systems communicate with but also the protocols, packet counts, times of day of activities between nodes, frequency of traffic appearance, and volume of traffic in each transaction, as well as cumulative traffic volumes. When any one item is analyzed, it may seem normal or irrelevant to network security. When pairs of nodes on the network begin to exceed their normal operating environment with either lower amounts of all of the above activities or greater amounts, this may indicate a serious anomaly in network activity and may be tied to network security issues and problems.

Network Topology Security

Network topology can have a dramatic effect on network security. Not only which nodes are communicating with which other nodes is important, but the locations and functions of the nodes are inherently critical to network security. For instance, a packet from node A to node B might not mean a lot to a protocol analyzer or other management tool, but if the packet is destined to node B on the financial transaction token ring/802.5 network and originated from a programmer's workstation on the Ethernet/802.3 network at node A, a flag should be raised, declaring that this is not a normal transaction on the network and may represent a violation of overall path security. There are legitimate needs to cross-communicate between hardware architectures, but these paths and nodes are usually well defined in advance of any network installation, and any other transactions should be identified and investigated for possible intrusions.

New and Mysterious Protocols or Nodes

New and unidentified nodes or destination systems and protocols are always a source of concern to network and systems managers. New systems may be legitimate nodes but the interaction between the new and existing systems must be established to identify potential intrusions. Some systems should be accessed only by a finite number of specific nodes due to their inherent application mix; other systems must be carefully monitored for new connection requests to ensure that only the allowed systems are trying to connect.

While this may seem obvious, there is no package or operating system that monitors for this. If a terminal server port on a terminal server were to attempt to connect to a specific node on the network with the LAT protocol, after three attempts on most VAX/VMS systems the connection would be rejected. The terminal server, however, could try three more times, as the default on many systems is to defeat exhaustive break-ins by storing information about retry connection requests in the Unit Control Block (UCB) of the port connection (this is stored in the device driver). Since most LAT connections create a new port for each subsequent connection attempt, the scenario is to try three times, disconnect, connect, and try three more times. If this situation were being monitored, an alarm could sound, informing the network manager of a potential intrusion. Since LAT is not the only protocol nor VMS the only operating system to allow this condition, monitoring connectivity between nodes is the only way to detect this type of intrusion.

Virus and Worm Propagation

Virus and worm propagation on a network is difficult to monitor and detect. In most cases, nodes on a network communicate with two to eight other nodes in a typical work period in most peer-to-peer network technologies (certain nodes are exceptional, such as those that poll other nodes for information). Should a node, spontaneously and without prior setup, begin to communicate to a variety of new nodes with either the same protocol or a brand-new protocol, this may be the beginnings of a virus spreading through to other nodes on the network. Of course, there are technical details that allow a more refined definition of whether such activity is a virus, but in general, to isolate the origin of network viruses and worms, it is very important to collect data showing which node started the trend and which nodes were connected.

"Trap Door" Insertions from Network Components

Some products on the network are vulnerable to attack by "trap door" mechanisms. A trap door is a technique used by some types of security infiltration code that inserts what appears to be a normal bit of code, batch file, command procedure, shell script, or other component into a valid existing component, so that when the existing component runs, the trap door is also activated and may run.

For instance, DECnet task objects on VAX/VMS systems are actually activated, most of the time, by a command procedure. If a worm or a virus were to insert trap door commands into the files used by DECnet to access the network-executable objects, the trap door components would be run each time the command files were run to activate the network task objects. In this manner, a disreputable piece of code would be able to disrupt object activity, at a minimum, or gain user ID information and other security information to cause a much more serious breach of system and network security.

Piggybacking

Packet or session "piggybacking" is another possible avenue of computer network infiltration. A node watches a session connection in progress and then sneaks a valid packet into the stream of communications between the two nodes that causes disruption in the session or the destination (or source) of the session to dump useful information to further connect into either node. While this may seem difficult, it's really not and has been a problem for some protocols already. Also, as protocol suites become standardized, how a suite works is more available and easier for intruders to learn and exploit.

PBX Security

Increasing use of private branch exchange (PBX) equipment causes network security problems, as many PBX systems are migrating to an all-digital transmission technological base. This infers that PBX equipment will be a normal routed connection onto most data networks in the near future. Since digital voice at 64 Kbps is the standard in most digital PBX systems, the chances of interception and capture of voice packets on a network is very real, as this type of technology becomes more popular in the next few years. This also means that voice-only connections now are able to handle voice and data, simultaneously, and that both transmission types are now vulnerable to attack.

Cableless Telephone Systems

To compound the problem of network security, there is the emerging CT3 digital voice standard in Europe. CT3 allows cordless telephony equipment to be used in a premises or local geographic distribution facility with connections between the cordless equipment and locally placed repeater/router base stations. In this manner, personal telephone equipment may be used in a building or, eventually, in public, as CT3 base station installation proliferates. Obviously, any packet of voice or data on the airways is subject to interception and exploitation. CT3 makes this all the more likely, because its basic function is to transmit such data and voice over common airways.

In Europe, the predecessor to CT3, CT2, is very active and inexpensive to use. While CT2 can only originate phone calls, CT3 can originate or receive calls, as well as allow a data connection with the proper hardware. In the United States and other countries, this type of technology will allow everyone portable phone access, in a manner similar to handheld cellular phones. It will also allow access to airwave-oriented network data—and open the doors to spoofing calls, intercepting calls, and other despicable violations of network security.

Cluster Security

Some networking technologies, such as VAXClusters and Windows NT clusters, enhance the opportunity for disreputable network users to infiltrate and harm the network resource. Personnel on a VAXCluster, familiar with cluster setup and operations, may cause the cluster to react in unpredictable ways and, under proper circumstances, may actually take over the base root directories of a cluster. This allows total access to items such as common system images between cluster members, common user authorization files, Access Control List rights databases, and many other files and routines that would allow quick infiltration of a VAXCluster. Since, in recent years, Digital Equipment Corporation has allowed more and more nodes to be placed on VAXClusters (at this writing the maximum allowed is more than 100 nodes and rising, with an increase planned for the near future), there have already been reported incidents of usage of the network to break into a VAXCluster and extract valuable data.

Distributed Database Access

Dissemination technologies, such as distributed database products, distributed bulletin boards and notes conferences (such as Lotus Notes and VAX Notes), distributed directory services (X.500) and authentication services, and other types of decentralized information-sharing facilities are highly vulnerable to attack via the network resource. Because nodes on the network can masquerade as other nodes, and programmers on the network may create network sessions that appear legitimate, there is a high degree of probability that as decentralized access to distributed resources increases, network security will become more essential to business.

Some newer network architectural facilities, such as remote procedure calls, when embedded in applications or in operating systems, effectively neutralize the effect of operating system security, especially when embedded in operating systems. If the security monitor for an operating system is subjected to the operational security of the operating system, then distribution of the operating system over popular high-speed, broadcast-oriented LAN technologies with no security features whatsoever renders the entire security structure useless. If any packet may be collected and analyzed by any node on the network, the distributed operating system or distributed application is at risk.

Fax Infiltration

Older, but increasingly popular, technologies such as facsimile machines are starting to become the norm due to the dramatic price drop in fax equipment technologies and the ability to send and receive fax transmissions over common computer equipment. In a recent incident, a teenage hacker in California intercepted a stream of telephone transmissions between two fax machines, easily created his own printouts, and mailed them to the recipients in an attempt at extortion. As fax technologies yield to localized fax transmissions between nodes on a network, the opportunity to retrieve entire documents simply by being connected to the network allows a wholly new area of network security exploitation.

Before you tell me that fax security should be outside the scope of a book on Ethernet/802.3 network performance and management, stop and think again. Many of the more popular "fax server" technologies in the world are based on Ethernet/802.3 technology and can allow cooperative nodes on the network to use fax technology from their microcomputer or workstation. This means that the ability to send, receive, and view other people's fax transmissions is a real problem on larger Ethernet/802.3 networks.

System Security Packages That Cause Network Security Problems

Some mainframe security packages, to be able to work properly, send down parameter files with security information in them to subordinate workstations on the LAN. The effect is that any node which can get hold of these parameter files and change the node information to spoof the original may gain access to the mainframe as the legitimate workstation. Further, many of the required mainframe interrogatives are included in the parameter file-passing mechanism, and many times these files are stored on file servers that are not properly protected. This allows exchange of data, very easily, to other nodes, which may then use the files to access the mainframe without detection. This condition exists in such packages because the mainframe must connect to the network. On the other hand, terminals must access the mainframe but are not tied to the network in the same manner as a workstation and therefore do not require the same access and control information to be exchanged in the same way.

Common Wire Plant Infiltration

In businesses today, there is a thrust to cable new and existing office and personnel access areas with common twisted-pair copper wiring that can handle medium-rate data communications speeds (up to about 12 Mbps in the United States). Since most of these cable plants are set up for many more systems than will actually be connected, and since many of the plants also let any node connect to any available port in any location in the cable plant, the opportunity to infiltrate a communications network is easier than ever before in many facilities.

Although the intent of cabling so many of the facilities is pure, in fact it complicates connectivity issues and allows explicit intrusion onto the computer network. For instance, anyone armed with a personal laptop computer could easily wander into an unused office, connect to the network, extract data, shut down, and leave. There would be no trace of entry or sign of what was taken. Because many network analyzers are based on Macintosh or PC technologies and because there are so many laptop connection devices for LANs, the opportunity to perform just such an operation is clear and immediate in many corporate environments.

This threat may be further compounded by the introduction of "palmtop" (or personal digital assistant) technologies, such as the Sharp OZ-8200 Super Wizard personal organizer, which may be connected to a PC or Macintosh and exchange data. Although this use in itself is not a security problem, someone can connect the OZ-8200 to a battery-powered modem and connect to practically any dial-up connection on any other system at a very modest price. Such devices allow for the distributed access to networked systems, which increases the vulnerability of systems on a network by a substantial factor.

Multiple Cooperative System Security—On a Network

Finally, there is the security risk in networks that does not exist with singular systems—where the usage of the network itself is a threat. In a recent example, an aging electrical power control system was being replaced by dual hot-backup systems that were connected to three separate LAN segments. Since each of the hot-backup systems was connected to the same LANs, any disruption on any one LAN that caused one system to fail would also cause the hot-backup to fail. For instance, if a burst of traffic or a virus should overload or cause harm to software on the primary system, the same exact packets, delayed only by propagation time on the LAN, would arrive at the backup and cause the same problem, effectively disabling the primary and the backup systems.

In short, because both systems are connected to the same networks and receive the same data, both the primary and the backup are subjected to the same security problems. Further, if one system received an infiltration from the network, chances are extremely good that both systems would receive the same data and be affected in the same way. On singular or even dual systems that were on totally isolated network paths, this event might still be possible, but very difficult to achieve. When both systems are attached to the identical network resource, the chances of infiltration increase exponentially. The network, by virtue of its being in place and used, causes a security issue to arise.

Summary

While there are other potential network security issues, these topics represent the bulk of the major issues in attempting to define and solve the problems of monitoring network security and to identify potential intrusion and other hazards on the network. Some of the problems are well bounded and provide a finite set of potential solutions. This factor makes this set of problems well placed for the application of rule-based security systems. Other, less bounded problems (those with a large range of potential solutions) are not well suited for a rule-based approach, but certain aspects of the problems may be suited, or there may be more classical software solutions to the problems that would be superior to the rule-based approach.

Server Performance   11

As more and more Ethernet/802.3 networks are being used as backbones for computing, people tend to place everything (including the kitchen sink) on the network. So, it's natural that network users want to add servers (file, disk, printer, terminal, database, and others) on an Ethernet/802.3 network. It may not be a good idea (for many reasons), but it does happen. This chapter focuses on the issues that arise with servers on Ethernet/802.3 networks, as well as their performance management.

Useful, Sure, But . . .

As I write this chapter, I am using a couple of different servers. Of course, I am writing this on my Power Macintosh, but I am hooked up to my laser printer via a printer server and I am accessing one of my VAX systems via an X Window session and functioning as a display server for X Windows on the Mac. All on the Ethernet/802.3 network, of course.

And in the background, I am transferring a large file from another VAX on my Ethernet to my Mac, which I plan on dissecting with HyperCard when I am done with this chapter. Even with this light a load, the VAXes are groaning a little and the Mac gets a bit sluggish from time to time. And I am the only one doing anything on the network.

Servers do make the previously impossible (or at least extremely difficult) now possible, with the right hardware and software. Though there are many definitions of server—the word "server" is grossly overused for practically anything that moves on a network—the concept of some other system providing services that are not available on your system is now a big deal. Everyone is doing it.

Server Configuration and Management

The only problem with servers is configuring them and managing them. More often than not, servers are configured incorrectly or are incredibly under-powered for the work they must perform. This can be a real problem, because improperly configured distributed servers can not only cause the user a high degree of anxiety, but can also cause serious network overhead and cause other systems on the network to suffer undue wear and tear.

One of the most common mistakes people make with servers is the way they configure the system that will function as the main server. In most cases, vendors of hardware treat server systems like other systems and configure them based on how many users will be simultaneously accessing the system that is performing the server function. This in itself is harmful, because the vendor most likely does not have the foggiest idea which applications will be running on the system and the amount of load the applications will place on it. Worse, the server must implement server software, protocols, and overhead that would not normally be incurred on a single or multiuser system that has no server code.

An Example

Consider the use of Novell NetWare. Many sites will configure, properly, MS-DOS-based systems with Intel 80386 processors as the user systems and then configure an identical system with slightly more memory and disk as the server for the other systems. One site I deal with regularly had this problem. They placed nine 80386 PSs on a network with 2 MB of memory each and some local disk storage. Not a bad configuration. They then placed another 80386 system with 4 MB of memory and 200 MB of disk space on the network and used it as the server. Everything was all right for a while, until the users figured out that they could place their database files on the server (it looked like drive G:). That's when all hell broke loose.

The number of packets traveling between the nine satellites and the one server caused the server to become heavily congested and it was unable to keep up with the actual packet flow between systems. The result was that the server could not receive all packets transmitted from the users and many retransmissions occurred. This caused a higher-than-necessary traffic rate on the network, which made the server miss even more packets, resulting in even more retransmissions. The solution was not a faster network or even a faster controller in the server system. No, the solution was an 80486 system with 8 MB of memory, tuned to the nines. All was very well afterward.

If users are complaining about performance on their own systems, how can a server possibly perform better than the local system? It is impractical to configure a server system to have the same or lower power than the systems it will be servicing, and it is ludicrous to expect people to use the configuration just as it is installed. It is, however, highly practical to overconfigure the capabilities of a server, because most users will take advantage of them much more quickly than expected.

Sometimes the system used as a server incurs problems that neither the vendor nor the customer could have foreseen—perhaps due to system architectural problems, application mix, and desired configuration. One of my customers configured two 6000-class VAX systems to provide an application server system and a database server system. The application system would accept connections from PCs and Macs, and then the application on the application server (a 6000-320—a two-processor VAX 6300) system would then issue two connections per application user to the database system to allow a full-duplex connection to the database from the application. The customer was told that the system configurations given would provide application server support for 400 users and database connection server support for the same amount of users from the application server.

To illustrate what can go wrong if the server is not properly configured, let's study the configuration of this setup.

The Too-Many-Interrupts-from-the-Network Problem

In the V5.x VMS environment, a new concept of computing called Symmetrical Multi-Processing (SMP) was introduced as a part of VMS. In SMP, multiple CPU cards may be included in the same physical system. In this manner, as additional computing power is required, additional CPU cards may be added to certain models of VAX systems to provide the additional power.

In the SMP environment, a primary processor is used to bootstrap the system and to configure the other CPUs on-line. Further, the primary CPU has a VMS facility called the Primary CPU Affinity function, which means that all device I/O and console access must go through the primary CPU. In this manner, device I/O can be properly synchronized with all CPUs in the system. The penalty is that all direct device I/O must go through the primary processor, which limits the amount of device I/O an SMP system is capable of handling per second. The limit of I/O varies by SMP processor type and is due to the speed of the primary processor, caches, and other hardware capabilities of the primary processor as related to its I/O handling capability. Although sources at DEC claim that some of this overhead of I/O processing will be moved to other system processors in V5.6 and later versions of VMS, the system was configured for server access during VMS V5.1, and such facilities (multiple-processor I/O) were not available.

For example, the 6300 class of VAX machine allows multiple processors to be configured into the system. A 6310 system has one processor, a 6320 has two, and so on. If there is a single processor, it must provide all computing functions throughout all modes of the processor. In the case of a multiprocessor system, the primary has certain required responsibilities, such as device I/O, but other functions are shared throughout the other processors. This means that in computationally bound environments, a multiprocessor VAX system performs well, and as additional processors are added, performance for most activities may increase.

If, however, the primary processor has a limited I/O interrupt-handling capability, the entire system is subjected to the throughput allowed by the I/O handling capability. No matter how many processors are added to the system, the amount of I/O that may be placed through the primary processor is fixed on a processor-by-processor basis (based on the model type of the processor), as well as the amount of code required to service I/O at the initial device interrupt level. None of these features of SMP may be adjusted, as they are architectural issues in V5.0 of VMS that only DEC has any control over. The issue of primary CPU affinity for I/O does, however, heavily affect throughput considerations and the capability of a multiprocessor system to handle required I/O for the entire system.

In the May 1989 issue of *Quorum* (Volume 4, Number 4), a DEC publication, there is an article by a talented engineer from the VMS Performance Analysis Group on VAXCluster performance. Although the primary thrust of the article regards mixed interconnect VAXClusters, there is also some substantial information concerning SMP performance and I/O. On p. 28, in the second paragraph, he states that SMP systems "process remote [device] I/O requests on a single CPU." The engineer goes on to state that an SMP system "does not provide more disk-serving I/O capacity than the equivalent uniprocessor system. In fact, the SMP systems actually support about 5% to 10% fewer I/O's than the uniprocessor systems because of the added cost of synchronizing CPUs in an SMP system."

Although future releases of VMS and modifications to existing VAX hardware are expected to spread the primary CPU affinity for I/O to other CPUs in the system, it won't happen in the immediate future. And it doesn't help the current situation. In other operating SMP environments, the problem exists as well.

Protocol Overhead via Broadcast Messaging

Some existing applications on the Ethernet network at the site require various network protocols to be implemented and used. One method of connectivity on the network is the connection of Apple Macintosh systems to inexpensive LocalTalk twisted-pair networks. These networks are in turn connected to the Ethernet through Kinetics FastPath LocalTalk-to-Ethernet bridge units. The Kinetics units utilize TCP/IP to provide various network services on the LocalTalk and Ethernet networks. The problem with using TCP/IP is that it requires TCP/IP routing nodes (within which the Kinetics units function) to periodically broadcast to the entire network certain classes of network information to notify other nodes of availability, among other things. These messages are sent via the Ethernet broadcast DESTINATION message type (FF-FF-FF-FF-FF-FF) and are propagated throughout all cable segments on the entire network.

When a broadcast message is sent on the Ethernet, the message is accepted as valid on each Ethernet controller on all systems on the entire network and then propagated to each host system protocol as a separate interrupt. For instance, if a VAX system were running eight protocols, there would be one device interrupt for the packet into the system and then a separate software interrupt to each individual protocol on the system. There may be many more interrupts if the protocols have more than one driver associated with them. In any case, the protocols will be interrupted with the packet and will be required to examine it before determining that it should be discarded. This takes CPU time in KERNEL mode to happen, and the system may be heavily burdened.

On a multiprocessing system, the primary is required to service the actual device interrupt and not necessarily the software interrupts (the secondary processors may help with this facet of interrupt handling). But the fact that there are unnecessary interrupts coming in that must be serviced causes the primary to be tied up with work that is counterproductive to required application usage. On tests run on the Ethernet at the site, collected data showed that there were more than 500 broadcast packets per second on the network. Each broadcast packet represents a required device interrupt and possibly many other secondary software interrupts being serviced by the primary and secondary processors on the 6320 and the single processor on the 6310. This means that many interrupts will interfere with the systems even though the interrupts have nothing to do with the application running on the system, causing system overhead and degradation.

In addition, there are a number of Local Area VAXCluster (LAVC) systems on the site Ethernet as well. These nodes will send a message (called a HELLO message) to the boot node of the cluster which will help identify active nodes and detect nodes that have failed. While these messages are multicast, DEC nodes are typically configured to receive the messages and discard them, in software, if LAVC is not active.

According to DEC documentation, the broadcast message type is automatically disabled unless it is explicitly enabled as a multicast address (this violates all Ethernet and 802.3 standards). As it happens, the AppleTalk protocols and other protocols used on the systems connecting to the servers automatically enable broadcast messages, requiring the VAX system to service the interrupts experienced.

Because of the high amount of expected application load on the 6320 system and the already high load of traffic on the existing Ethernet network, the 6320 system being used for the applications will most surely reach maximum I/O capability before being able to support the total amount of user sessions required (more than 400 simultaneous users). Further, even if the total amount of logged-in sessions is achieved, the predictive response time will be very high and may make the system unusable from the user's perspective, due to the delay in response.

Ethernet/802.3, Interrupts, and You

Using a sophisticated system performance monitor with performance-specific system code testing on an off-site VAX 6320 system (VMS V6.x with a DEBNA), a test was done to isolate the amount of time required to service an interrupt on an SMP system with Ethernet/802.3 and other peripherals. Further, the test was isolated to test the interrupt service time to get a device interrupt from the SCB into a device driver from an IPL 22 interrupt. This required a special patch to ETDRIVER.EXE and a segment of code running at IPL 29 and "hooked" to the system clock interrupts at IPL 24. The test was performed on a nonproduction system to preclude problems with a production system and ran highly fragile test software. The system used, in practically all ways, mirrored the 6320 system configuration proposed as the application server.

The results showed that an average interrupt received from a DEBNA Ethernet/802.3 controller requires approximately 2200 instructions per interrupt total processing at IPL 22. Since the 6310 CPU allows approximately 3.8 mips (DEC Publication ED-32965-46/89-03-43-74.0, p. XIII), there would be a maximum of approximately 1727 interrupts per second allowed per CPU. Assuming a 50% cache hit ratio on instruction cache, the number of interrupts per second could reach as high as 2600 per second at IPL 22 on a 6310.

These figures are also substantiated by multiple papers on SMP by a DEC senior consulting engineer presented at the DECUS symposium in Cannes,

France, in September 1988. His figures on SMP overhead are actually greater than those arrived at in our test, so our figures on interrupts per second should be considered very optimistic.

A 6320 system, while rated at "up to 7.5 mips" (again, DEC Publication ED-32965-46/89-03-43-74.0, p. XIII), is two 6310 CPUs in the same cabinet running as tightly coupled processors (SMP). The mips rating, however, does not point out the fact that the primary CPU, still a 6310, must perform all device interrupt, clock interrupt, and console servicing functions, as well as any interprocessor coordination functions. As such, a 6320 may be rated at 7.5 mips, under optimal conditions, but it is incapable of servicing device interrupts at that rate, due to the method in which SMP forces interrupt servicing.

The amount of interrupts does not necessarily reflect the amount of data involved, because the data could be transferred into memory via direct memory access (DMA), and the interrupt is issued after the data has been transferred into memory.

What is important in these numbers, however, is the fact that there is a finite amount of interrupts that can be handled per second on each CPU. Because the primary processor can process only the number of interrupts per second allowed at elevated IPL, and because the primary must service all interrupts to and from devices, the total predictive amount of interrupts allowed—2600 per second at IPL 22—reflects that the primary could easily reach maximum interrupt processing capability long before the entire processing capability of the SMP system is reached.

This factor shows that interrupts which reach the CPU from any device source affect the primary CPU, and that there are a finite amount of interrupts per second allowed. Because there are many other products that will generate interrupts on the system from the network and other sources, the application's required interrupts and CPU power will be heavily interfered with, and the primary CPU will not be able to handle its own application's interrupts efficiently.

In summary, it is highly probable that the 6320 system being used as the applications processor will not be able to handle the device interrupt load required for 400 concurrent user sessions. Additionally, it is highly probable that the system will reach maximum interrupt capability (based on current network metrics and known user I/O with 62 users on the system and current applications at this writing) at about 100–120 user sessions. After that point, additional load may be placed on the system but response times will be very poor, and overall performance will be bad enough as to be unusable for interactive applications.

Another item to consider is that the application server system would require one network connection from each user to the server and then two network connections from each user application being served to the database system.

Because both systems are accessible only via DECnet between the two systems, 400 users would generate 400 incoming connections to the application server system plus an additional 800 connections between the systems to service the 400 users wishing database connections. This translates to 1200 connections (sessions) on the Ethernet controller in the application system and 800 on the database system. The chances of DECnet or any other protocol being able to handle such a load on the configured system and still provide an adequate level of user response is doubtful.

As additional justification for this conclusion, in the September 1987 issue of the *Digital Technical Journal on VAXCluster Systems,* there is a detailed technical article covering VAXCluster performance with differing system loads (pp. 80–92). In the article, there is a demonstration of various application loads on various VAXCluster systems (no DECnet or Ethernet activity) utilizing different types of products and applications to simulate various environments. One of the systems tested was the VAX 8700 system, which is reasonably comparable in capabilities with a single-processor 6300 (that is, a 6310) system. An 8700 system, now reclassified as an 8810 system, has a single CPU, a 6-mips rating, cache per CPU of 64 KB, cache cycle time of 45 nanoseconds, and can be configured with up to four CPUs, for a maximum of up to 22 mips for the entire system. A 6310 has a single CPU, a 3.8-mips rating, cache per CPU of 1 KB but an additional cache of 256 KB per processor board, and a cache cycle time of 60 nanoseconds for the CPU cache and 120 nanoseconds for the board cache.

All things being equal, the 8810 is a faster machine than the 6310 and can support more user sessions with the identical software applications. Because of the superior caching of the 6310, it is not quite as slow as the mips difference would have the reader believe, but it is not as fast as the 8810. This factor is very important, as the following sections will illustrate.

In the testing, it was demonstrated that the single 8700 (8810) system running a typical commercial transaction application could not support more than 10.5 transactions per second for 280 users and no more than 60 I/Os per second for all disks attached to the system. Considering that most of the RA series of drives will not support more than 25–30 I/Os per second, there is the limiting factor of disk I/O throughput on the drives and how fast I/O can be placed on the bus. Additional information shows that at the rate of 280 users, there are approximately 130 transactions per user per hour (the maximum possible), but at the 50-user level, there are approximately 155 user transactions per hour (the maximum possible). The difference has to do with additional overhead to manage more users and other cluster issues. It was also shown that at 280 users, a typical user transaction would take over a second per average transaction. Since a user may require many transactions per screen display, the user performance can be intolerable for many applications when the maximum amount of users is reached.

Although one could argue that the 6300-class machine as a server is superior in cache performance, memory performance, and interrupt handling to the 8700-class machine, they have a lot more in common than they have differences. The situation described in the journal includes cluster overhead, but not DECnet, Pacer, Rdb, or other products on the system. If the applications being demonstrated in the journal and the application being used on the 6320 server are considered a 1:1 tradeoff, and considering the additional overhead of communications products (DECnet and other protocols) and additional interrupt processing caused by other networking products, then the figure of 280 users is most likely optimistic. The actual supportable amount of users in the applications on the application server VAX system will be substantially lower. In fact, by using scaled performance figures, it is possible that a 6320 system could not support more than 240 users with the same applications as delineated. And if primary CPU affinity is considered, there may be even worse user session values (estimates range from 150 to 188).

This article serves to justify the figures we gathered for 6300 interrupt performance and to set the expectation that 400-user sessions on the application server system are desirable but not realistic, due to interrupt processing on the primary processor and other overhead that cannot be controlled by the 6320 system.

The purpose of this entire discussion is to illustrate the level of detail required before settling on a server configuration. Most "out of the box" configurations are seriously flawed for live environments and usually require some very serious upgrades before proper performance of a server may be achieved.

Suggestions for Handling Server Performance

So, what can a company do to get ready to provide proper server performance for systems wishing to use one? Some of the following suggestions may help:

1. Almost all servers require a substantial amount of CPU and I/O bandwidth—anywhere from two to three times the amount of the most active user of the server. For instance, if an 80486 running at 30 MHz is connected via PathWorks-OS/2 to a VAX system, the VAX configuration would have to be, at a minimum, a 3100-048 (3.8 VUPs) or better yet a 4000-class system. In some situations, a larger-class system may be called for, if the applications being served are very compute-bound and require a good amount of server time to provide the desired response time.

2. The louder the users scream into the right ears, the greater is the need for a high-performance server. Noisy users can get management's attention in ways that defy gravity, so be prepared and configure accordingly.

3. Every new protocol suite introduced into the server should be considered a duplicate copy of the worst-performing suite on the server. Most networking protocol suites provide equivalent basic services (file transfer, electronic mail, program-to-program, and virtual terminal), and because of various nuances in each protocol, they all have their own brand of inadequacies of performance. By taking the worst suite and considering all protocols on the system to perform at that level, a best guess at overhead can be made and the server's needs properly identified. This may seem a little strange at first, but you'd be surprised how close it comes in live systems. It defies all logic and lab tests, but users do not use the systems in the lab; between user access methods, improper configuration, and lack of proper tuning, such estimates work well in reality networking.

4. All servers will be tied to a network of some sort. They all have strange overhead metrics and should be carefully watched. In almost all situations, the network controller (the hardware to access the network) is the most predominant bottleneck. Be sure that you understand the maximum performance metrics of a controller (such as RAM buffering, I/Os per second, and CPU type in the controller) before pronouncing performance expectations and metrics. Many controllers, especially on smaller systems, cannot hope to keep up with larger system I/Os; retransmissions will happen, degrading all nodes due to network tie-up.

5. Networking protocol suites and server software processes tend to be in memory at all times and, as a result, horribly compute-bound. Some sites will tend to use available, but underpowered, systems as servers when the need arises. Remember that the server should be more powerful than any of the systems being served, so using underpowered systems as server nodes is disaster looking for a place to happen. Being compute-bound due to being memory-resident also implies that a large amount of memory will be required to serve connected nodes.

6. Place nodes and servers for a workgroup on the same network cable segment and do not divide them by bridges and repeaters, where possible. This allows the workgroup to continue to work even if there is a bridge or repeater failure. Further, in the future, when segmentation of the network via bridges becomes a necessity, the bridge can be inserted between the workgroup's segment and the rest of the network—the network does not have to be totally reconfigured.

7. Beware of fault-tolerant servers. If the host operating system is not fault-tolerant, the system will still fail. The hardware and software must both be fault-tolerant before a reasonable level of satisfaction may be achieved by a fault-tolerant system as a server.

8. Systems that are marginal in performance now will be even worse than before when server or client software is added. Adding any software to most

systems is an invitation to performance problems, but servers and networking protocols tend to run at higher priorities and generate ample interrupts, so server systems and systems that previously did not run client and server software can suffer, big time. For instance, my VAXStation 3100 with 9 MB of memory easily handled the 5 to 10 user processes I had on it before I installed OSF/Motif (X Windows) client and server on it. Now I am lucky to get four processes running before swapping starts. The only change? OSF/Motif. Further, it can take 2 to 3 minutes just to get a terminal emulation window up and running.

9. Some systems are simply not suited to be a server of any kind, ever. This may be due to system architecture, memory constraints, bus I/O issues, allowed disk types, network interconnects, and many other reasons. Don't expect any system to be able to be a server and don't expect the vendor to always know better.

Servers are not easy to configure if things are done properly and configured in a logical and performance-oriented manner. Servers are also expensive and take time to properly activate and manage. Take care and consideration in configuration of servers and the network, and users will appreciate it and enjoy the server experience. Beware of so-called network experts who claim knowledge of network server configurations; many are single-protocol people and do not understand the issues of system architecture, applications, and other levels of knowledge that are required for proper server configuration.

A very good friend who I consider one of the best in the networking business often sends customers to me for server configurations because I know a lot more about operating systems and applications than he does, and he claims to be in over his head when it comes to servers. He could easily do it, but he does not feel comfortable with it, because he does not keep up on operating system developments as closely as I. When the professionals get itchy about server configurations, those who do not do it very often better pay heed and be wary of prepackaged configurations and instant server mixes (just add software and users).

Summary

Properly configured servers offer serious networking and shared resource capabilities. Improperly configured systems, as illustrated, may cause some contention and performance problems that are difficult and costly to correct. Spend some time carefully configuring servers, and match applications and workgroups to achieve good traffic mix and server performance.

Microcomputer Performance 12

There's always a lot of concern about performance when microcomputer networks are mentioned or contemplated for installation on an Ethernet/802.3 network. There exists the mania that the network is horrible to micros and that they will perform badly when connected. Then there is the other mania: that the network will solve all the problems of the universe and the microcomputers connected will be happy and all corporate problems will be solved. This chapter attempts to clear up what performance problems can be expected and managed on Ethernet/802.3 networks.

Doing It Right

Implementation of a sound microcomputer network that performs well and stands up to use and misuse is totally dependent on sound technical design. Unfortunately, most of the folks who have to make the "buy/no-buy" decisions are individuals who are either totally nontechnical or who were technical once upon a time and have not kept up with the latest and greatest goings on. The technical folks who design a network would prefer to place file servers where it makes the best technical sense, not where someone tells them to put them, to avoid making certain people angry. (Figure 12.1 shows an example of a microcomputer network.)

Technical designers should not have to deal with the routing overhead problems of multiple DECnet areas, TCP/IP networks, IPX domains, SNA domains, and the such, just because some corporate yahoo decided that Chicago will be one group and Dallas another group. Software does *not* understand geography, and you can bet your horse's horseshoes that no one bothered to ask the routing software's opinion about having four DECnet areas for 10 computers. The routing overhead imposed is blamed on the protocol suite when, in reality, some political decision was made to use different area designators for

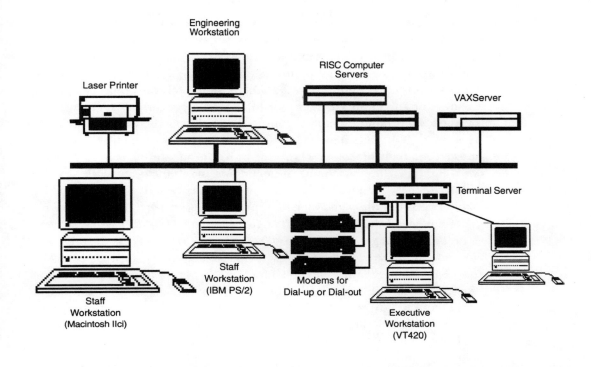

Figure 12.1

A Typical Microcomputer Network

geographic or political boundaries as opposed to what was best for the network topological implementation and traffic matrix.

The biggest problem in microcomputer networking on Ethernet/802.3 networks is upper management. Yes, those fine folks who have decided that "everything shall talk to everything." While this is fine for PBXs and other voice activities, it's the pits for data networking, where there are serious incompatibilities in data formats, protocols, applications, security, and many other problems that most managers have no concept of when they pronounce the need for global connectivity in the firm. The reason voice systems can provide "all-to-all" connections is because there are solid voice interconnection standards, as well as certain industry-standard connection methods that are well defined and available to all. On the data side, much of these types of standards are still under development, and it will be some time (read: years) before data systems can connect with the ease of voice systems.

The need to connect everything to everything introduces, by nature, performance problems. Two identical microcomputers with identical hardware and software configurations and different word processing systems immediately introduce storage and performance problems. For instance, if one system uses word processor A and the other system uses word processor B and the two word processors have incompatible file-storage formats, an immediate overhead is introduced simply to convert the file formats between the two word processors. If A wants B to see the file created on A, the file must be resaved into a format suitable for direct reading by B or in an intermediate file format, such as RTF, ODA, or CDA, that B can understand. If the original file was 500 KB in size on A and saved in RTF, the intermediate noneditable file would be about 1 MB. The file would then be copied with some network stack to the remote node, and word processor B would read the RTF 1-MB file and convert it to local B storage format of about 500 KB. The result is that the same file with an original storage requirement of 500 KB ends up taking a total of 3 MB (500 KB for the original, plus 1 MB for the RTF version on A, plus 1 MB for the RTF version on B, plus 500K for the result on B equals 3 MB) of actual disk space. And in fact, the 1-MB file had to be transferred to the remote system when a 500-KB file should have been shared instead.

This type of problem usually manifests itself when the political entities have allowed anyone to purchase his or her favorite applications and have not standardized on data file formats. This causes conversions (overhead), larger files (storage and transfer overhead), lack of sharing, and other problems that could have been solved if common file storage formats were established and products selected that could read and edit the common formats. For technology to compensate for the political decision, additional software and storage are required and performance takes a hit.

Some sites have chosen to use noncommon hardware for interconnection purposes. For instance, Apple Macintosh systems used two forks (resource and data) to store information about a file. Because these two forks are stored in separate locations on disk on a Macintosh, and because the Finder on the Macintosh knows all about these things, performance is fine on the home system. Impose the Macintosh file system on a unary file system such as ODS-2 on VMS and the problems of performance start to come up. To properly compensate for the dual-fork file storage on a VAX/VMS system, the file-serving software on VMS must store the data fork and resource fork in differing areas so as not to confuse the VMS side and the Macintosh side. In most implementations, the different forks are stored in different directory structures on the VMS side, and the Macintosh sees no difference in how a VAX/VMS disk looks as opposed to an AppleShare volume on the network. While this method works fine, there is overhead in the management of the dual-fork file structure on the VMS side that is not normally included in typical ODS-2 with RMS overhead access methods. Further, since VMS is a multiprocessing, multiuser operating system, the chances of other jobs or activities slowing access are good, and this will degrade file operations. While this particular issue can be argued even on UNIX and other similar operating systems, there is no denying the fact that the VMS side of the file access operation must do more work than the Macintosh side, which introduces overhead not normally required for file access.

Ethernet/802.3 Is "Too Slow"

Another myth is that Ethernet/802.3 is too slow for today's network traffic volumes and corporate needs. In fact, the real problem is controller speed, followed by bus speed, CPU speed, driver speed, and then protocol overhead in memory, in that order. Most communications controllers for LAN access do not possess the full-speed capability that most network cables can deliver, especially in extended bursts of traffic on the cable. For instance, many PC controllers can deal with only about 50 to 100 packets in a burst before their buffers are full and cannot accept any more data. In a particular second, most PC controllers cannot handle more than about 200 to 300 packets per second (peak). In a peak burst on an Ethernet/802.3 network, more than 14,800 packets may be delivered in one second. Although this is not the norm, it is quite normal for more than 100 packets to be delivered in a second, and even more normal for the number to be in the range of 1400 to 2800 pps on most normal Ethernet/802.3 networks (that is, 10–20% of full load capacity).

Since all controllers on a LAN must scan all packet headers to see if the packet captured is supposed to be processed by the controller, few PC controllers can keep up with a heavily loaded network. This results in retransmissions, which further increases the load on the PC and the network. Therefore, the myth that cable speed is not fast enough is not true: the problem starts with the bottleneck in PC controller capabilities to receive, buffer, and process network packets.

Some newer PC controllers have powerful CPU chips in them to compensate for previous performance problems. These new controllers can achieve up to 8000–12,000 pps, but then the problem of controller-to-bus-to-CPU path becomes an issue. Many PCs still use the old 8-bit transfer paths on the bus. This means that while the controller may be perfectly capable of transferring data at a very high rate of speed to and from the network, because the bus transfer is slow, the controller cannot shovel the data out of the buffers and onto the system bus fast enough to keep up with the incoming data. The result is loss of data on the network and the need for retransmissions.

Micros based on Intel processors which use MCA and EISA bus structures, as well as some proprietary bus structures, can compensate for the bus performance issues—now the problem becomes CPU processing speed. Obviously, the faster the CPU, the better the processing capabilities. The next problem is driver buffering and interrupt-processing capabilities. The problem after that is the protocol-buffering capabilities (if TCP/IP is initialized for only six buffers, when they are full the software stops accepting data from the controller).

The bottom line is that in most cases, faster network cables do not increase the speed of network throughput. There are exceptions, of course, but these are not usually in the microcomputer area and are reserved for very high speed super-minicomputers or mini-supercomputers. Even then, the chances are good that the network is "too" fast for the systems; most systems, when *all* overhead is considered, cannot keep up with the speed offerings of networks like FDDI and T3 interconnects. In fact, in many cases, the improper implementation of microcomputers on faster networks may actually slow down throughput, because the systems cannot keep up with the faster network technology, will lose packets, and will need retransmissions. As a result, what should be faster is not, and money has been spent on a faster network that yields worse results than before.

Traffic directional flow is another major contributor to microcomputer network performance problems. If an 80286-based PC is sending a file to a VAX 6000-520, all is well, because the 6000-520's DEBNI Ethernet/802.3 controller far exceeds the micro's controller capabilities. The slower system is sending to the faster system, so the performance is adequate for the access. Reverse the situation and the 80286 system will require quite a few retransmissions for data that is missed due to the inability of the 80286 system to keep up with the 6000-520 transmission rate.

These are just some of the myths in microcomputer network performance that surface when problems in transfer rates occur. There are still the problems of competing software products, excessive memory usage of existing products, server overhead, storage overhead, and many other issues that would take reams of paper to explain. Microcomputer network performance is rife with potholes and problems, but, properly implemented, microcomputer networks can provide reasonable performance at reasonable cost.

Problems in Configuring Micro-Based Ethernet/802.3 Networks

Recently one of my customers desired to add more systems and install an Ethernet/802.3 network at the same time.

Normally such expansion is not a big hassle, but this customer had extenuating circumstances: they had some UNIX-based workstations and were connected to an existing token ring network. Because UNIX systems usually (98% of the time) come with TCP/IP and because the token ring network was running TCP/IP as well, it seemed infinitely logical to run TCP/IP on the soon-to-be-installed workstations and PCs on the soon-to-be-existent Ethernet.

The installation of the cable was not a problem. The UNIX workstations installed fine and came up in good order. The PCs, however, were a different story. To start with, the customer decided to arbitrarily buy an Ethernet controller for the PCs without talking to the TCP/IP vendor first to ensure that their software would work with the purchased controller. PCs, theoretically, should be able to support various makes and types of network controller interfaces, and usually they do. The problems surface in three major areas:

- Hardware and driver compatibility
- The problems with MS-NET and NETBIOS
- Proper option configuration in software protocol package

The hardware and driver problems are well known and have been around for years with no relief in sight. Basically, the software device driver must be coded for each particular brand of hardware. To compound the problem, some vendors originally released their network hardware to support 8-bit bus transfers (for PC and XT models) and later introduced 16-bit controllers that could emulate the 8-bit controllers and still utilize 8-bit drivers. In other words, if the driver was coded for 8-bit transfers, then a 16-bit controller still only transfers 8 bits at a time. Many vendors still have this feature because they do not want to change the driver and reissue software; other, less-known vendors may have subcontracted their driver, and the person who wrote it is nowhere to be found, so an upgrade is impossible without some serious work and money.

Another problem with PC network Ethernet/802.3 controllers and drivers is the issue of MS-NET and NETBIOS. Theoretically, network applications coded to the MS-NET interface should be compatible with any vendor's network hardware controller. This is because, in theory, MS-NET provides a well-documented, standardized data-link interface that is supposed to be universal on all PCs.

In reality, MS-NET (and NETBIOS) has problems and lacks certain types of features required for proper protocol handling with certain protocol stacks. As a result, most vendors start out by trying to be MS-NET-compliant, only to soon find that this is an unsupportable situation and end up bypassing the facilities. This leads to the drivers and hardware configuration being very specific and also requires the vendor of protocol suites to code their applications to specific drivers and their commensurate routines. The result is that application packages for the network require certain brands of vendor hardware and drivers or the package will simply not work.

Want proof? Simple enough. Until *very* recently, the DEPCA (and the DEPCA Turbo and DEMCA) from DEC would work only with DEC products, and it has been on the market for a good while. A couple of third-party vendors have now produced new drivers for the DEPCA that allow it to work with selected TCP/IP packages and Novell NetWare implementations. For this reason, I have often told customers to shy away from the DEC-proprietary controller technologies for PCs, especially if they plan on supporting more than the DEC protocols or if they plan on migrating the PC in question to environments where DEC protocols and network solutions would not be used. This is no reflection on the quality of the DEPCA, by the way—it's a great card. The problem has to do with software compatibility and the lack of production of a compatible Novell, 3Com, or Banyan driver for the DEC product.

In theory, this should all get straightened out with the use of NDIS-compliant software packages and drivers. I, however, am not holding my breath.

In the PC networking environment, PCs tend to get moved around a lot and require reconfiguration from time to time. While the Ethernet/802.3 card may stay in the newly reconfigured-for-the-nth-time PC, the protocols used most likely will not be the same. For this reason, selection of a network controller capable of supporting multiple protocols is smart planning, because you may not need the other protocols now, but you most certainly will in the future.

Moral 1: Check with the vendor of the protocol suite that you are going to use on a PC to ensure that the vendor supports the selected hardware type. There is no such thing as global compatibility in the PC environment.

Moral 2: NETBIOS and MS-NET are not necessarily your friends.

Some Vendors Think Ahead

For those Macintosh users out there, you don't have to worry as much. Why? Apple system architecture on the Macintosh provides a data-link layer that is pretty rigid in adherence requirements. This means that any protocol that knows how to connect to Apple's data-link layer interface (DDP) and any device driver that adheres to the data-link layer specification will most likely be able to connect without a problem. I rarely have trouble with most Macintosh network components, from a configuration point of view. You do want to check, however, and make sure that the protocol vendor supports the hardware selected.

One last thing about hardware and driver compatibilities: Some of the more popular PC clone vendors have a hard time with networking software and drivers due to bus interrupt problems as well as incompatibilities with NETBIOS. Be careful: not all clones and BIOS/NETBIOS like networking software; there have been many a site disappointed with their network experience using these products.

Package Configuration and Network Installation

The next problem with PC setups has to do with package configuration. Assuming that the network controller and driver are compatible with the selected package, one would think that all would be well. Not so! Many packaged suites, such as TCP/IP, have configuration files that cause the package to produce the proper frame protocol (in the case of Ethernet/802.3, there are three frame possibilities), address type (TCP/IP uses three classes of address types—A, B, and C), link negotiation options, buffer allocation, and a myriad of other items that are configured, typically, at installation time. The problem is that two similarly configured PCs, with the same controllers, drivers, and software packages from the same vendors, may not be able to converse with each other due to configuration differences in the initialization of the vendor software package.

Ethernet/802.3-to-Token Ring/802.5 Interconnections

This problem is compounded if a particular framing protocol is selected and is incompatible with already established nodes on the network. Remember that token ring network I mentioned earlier? Well, they had TCP/IP hooked up on the PCs and were configured to frame the TCP/IP as an 802.5-compliant frame on the token ring, an IEEE standard. This network had been in place for some time and was working very well. The token ring was to be hooked up to the new Ethernet/802.3 network via a special bridge unit that knows how to move packets back and forth between the networks.

This connection is not as easy as it seems. On 802.5, the framing protocol at first looks suspiciously like 802.3 (CSMA/CD, like Ethernet), except for a few minor field changes. The big gotcha, however, is the DATA field length on 802.5: it is allowed to be almost infinitely long. In 802.3 networks, the DATA field is allowed to be up to 1500 octets in length, a length substantially less than infinity. To transfer packets between token ring networks and 802.3 networks, the bridge unit has to be very smart and know that the 802.5 packets must be chopped up and passed in 1500-octet chunks to the appropriate node on the 802.3 side.

Since the IEEE is aware of this problem, a logical link control (LLC) protocol called 802.2 was created to provide, among many other things, a way for the various 802-class standards to interconnect. If the source node of a frame uses the 802.2 LLC protocol in the 802.5 frame, the bridge between the 802.5

and 802.3 networks may properly split up the 802.5 frame (if it exceeds 1500 DATA octets) into multiple 802.3 frames and deliver them to the proper node. The catch to the whole deal is that the source node must know about 802.5 and 802.2. The bridge must know about 802.5, 802.2, and 802.3. The destination 802.3 node must know about 802.3 and 802.2. If any of the participants does not have knowledge of the proper sequence of events and proper frame protocols for each side of the transaction, nothing works at all.

At my customer's site, they were using straight 802.5 on the token ring nodes, with *no* 802.2. That configuration will work fine unless there is a need to connect to other types of 802-class networks. The bridge the customer selected knew 802.5, but it was configured for IBM source routing, and the customer was improperly told by the vendor that it would connect without problem to an Ethernet. Further, they had configured the PCs on the Ethernet side to use a straight V2.0 Ethernet frame protocol and none of the 802 protocols. PCs on the Ethernet side worked with each other just fine. PCs on the token ring side worked with each other just fine. Crossing over, though . . . . Needless to say, the attempt at interconnection was a disaster of biblical proportions.

The solution? Multiple problems had to be solved. First, the Ethernet nodes had to be reconfigured in their parameter files to generate and accept 802.3 with 802.2. The token ring nodes also had to be reconfigured to generate and accept 802.5 and 802.2. The bridge had to be replaced with a proper 802-class MAC-layer bridge that understood all the various frames on each network. To reduce the possibility of problems, it was also advised to make the TCP-generated buffers less than 1400 in size on the token ring and 802.3 networks to preclude the bridge's needing to segment traffic (this reduces bridge overhead big time, as it will not be required to segment long 802.5 packets traveling to the 802.3 side of the network). When all was said and done, magic happened: the network has worked fine to this day.

The funny part about the whole situation is that the TCP/IP packages being used on the token ring and 802.3 sides are identical.

Moral 3: Never assume that the software protocol suite, though it may come from the same vendor on all nodes, is configured properly for traversing network connections, especially where dissimilar network technologies are involved. Also, even if the nodes are on the same physical hardware path (all on 802.5 or all on 802.3), the setup for framing on each node may be different enough to cause major connection problems. Everyone may be on the same cable, but only certain nodes may connect with other nodes.

Configuring PC network nodes properly for connection is not a slap-it-together ordeal anymore. With the proliferation of dissimilar types of network hardware technologies, such as token ring, Ethernet/802.3, and FDDI, in the same site environment, the need to support multiple types of framing protocols in the same networking environment will be essential in the coming months (notice I used "months," not "years"). Also, as OSI matures and becomes commonplace in the network arena, many systems will be connected to various types of network technologies and will need to be properly configured to communicate.

Summary

The next time you consider microcomputer networking, remember to scope things out carefully in advance and avoid problems. Be flexible: someone will most likely require some configuration modifications for things to work properly. Above all, be methodical, be patient, and remember that you were not the first person with the problems you face, just the latest.

Fiber Optics

13

To fiber or not to fiber—that is the question. There is no doubt that using fiber *as* the Ethernet/802.3 medium of choice is coming. In fact, some vendors have decided not to wait on the IEEE and have developed their own fiber optic solutions. This chapter is designed to help you get ready for fiber with your Ethernet/802.3 and understand the problems and issues in the installation and management of fiber optic segments on your network.

Ample Reasons for Fiber Optics

Lately I have spent a considerable amount of time researching the issues of fiber cabling for networks, mostly because my customers have wanted to run fiber to expand or increase the speed of their networks. (Figure 13.1 shows one kind of fiber network.)

In any case, there are many reasons to run fiber, preferably more fiber than required, in many sites. First there are the speed reasons: fiber bandwidth, easily in the range of more than 375 terahertz (THz), allows a great deal of speed options and growth when broadband fiber transmission technologies become economical (practically all fiber these days is baseband). Second is the recognized need to provide an error-controlled (not "error-free") transmission environment that allows good throughput without major error-control facilities. Another is that properly installed and certified fiber plants can be used for not only data but also voice communications (on different strands of fiber, please). Of course, there is the need to support new network technologies, many of which are fiber-based.

Fiber, however, is not inexpensive. Sure, the cost of the cable itself is not too nasty, but there are splices, terminations (the most expensive part of the installation), expensive diagnostic tools (fiber optic TDRs), and so on. Then there is noise testing of fiber, an expensive operation that gives the fiber plant

184

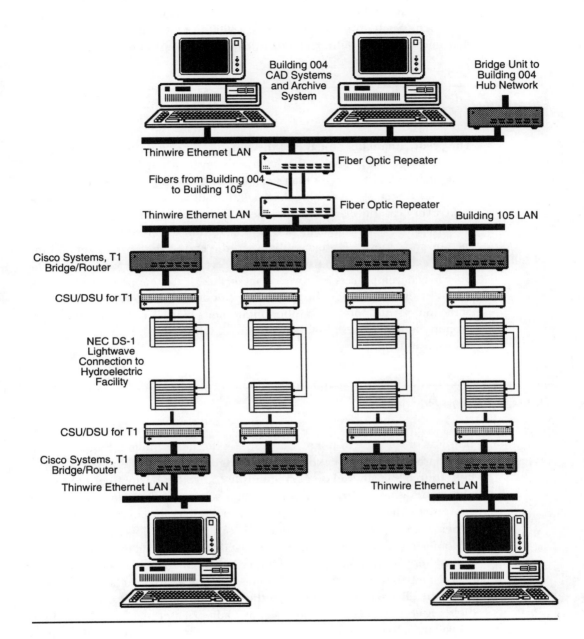

Building 004
CAD Systems
and Archive
System

Bridge Unit to
Building 004
Hub Network

Thinwire Ethernet LAN

Fiber Optic Repeater

Fibers from Building 004
to Building 105

Fiber Optic Repeater

Thinwire Ethernet LAN

Building 105 LAN

Cisco Systems, T1
Bridge/Router

CSU/DSU for T1

NEC DS-1
Lightwave
Connection to
Hydroelectric
Facility

CSU/DSU for T1

Cisco Systems, T1
Bridge/Router

Thinwire Ethernet LAN

Thinwire Ethernet LAN

Figure 13.1
An Example of a Single-Mode Fiber Interconnection

Ample Reasons for Fiber Optics

owner the peace of mind of knowing what the noise levels are on each tested fiber and what light bandwidth the individual fibers will support in a live environment. Such testing easily can cost $3000 to $4000 and is required to understand what bandwidth and data rate the fiber can support.

EtherFiber

The predominant fiber today on Ethernet/802.3 networks (or between them) is composed of a type of glass that has a high tensile strength. When it is pulled, straight, it is almost stronger than steel. But tie it in a knot and press on it lightly with your finger, and it will break in half. For all of its strength, fiber must be pulled very carefully, and under a specially watched load "pull." This means that when the fiber is actually pulled in a conduit or wire tray, a foot-pounds measurement device is attached between the end of the fiber jacket and the pulling cable. If the pull tension exceeds a certain amount of foot-pounds, the fiber may develop stress fractures on its surface. If this happens, the fractures may, over time, cause light "leakage" in or out of the fiber and cause distortion of the waveform, "noise," and other phenomena that will cause the fiber to improperly transmit the light from the source. Obviously, this can cause overall failure over time.

Fiber and Noise Budgets

Another problem with fiber installation is the noise budget. Simply put (it takes a while to properly explain noise budgets), there is a certain amount of light source loss allowed on a fiber, mostly controlled by the fiber light module's generation and reception components at each end. Many vendors of equipment that use fiber to interconnect their components provide customers with a "loss budget," or allowable optical quality loss metrics that the customer must adhere to during the installation, testing, and usage of the fiber. These are usually expressed in decibels (dB) and can range from as little as 1 to 2 dB to as much as 30 dB, depending on a variety of factors. In most cases, the allowed decibel loss is in the range of 10 to 20 dB range, with 13 dB being very popular. Any loss of signal quality greater than the allowed budget will most likely result in an inoperative fiber linkup between the vendor's components.

Noise can be caused by fiber anomalies, splices, external light sources, fiber stress, improper terminations, bends in the fiber, and many other things. It is important to test the fiber for the amount of signal noise after installation, so that you can gauge the noise levels at the installation. For instance, suppose the fiber gets extracted from a conduit the hard way—something rips the conduit from the wall and the fiber is severed. A splice may be required, but most likely, due to space limitations and available fiber "loop," a section of fiber may need to be spliced into the cable to repair the problem. This results in not one splice but two and, therefore, more potential noise. If the fiber was originally certified and tested for noise, you can estimate what noise the additional splices will cause and decide whether to splice or replace. Why? Because splicing is expensive (it can cost up to $240 per fiber per end, which gets very costly with 24 pairs of fibers!), and if the splice is not going to do any good, why bother?

Who should be splicing fiber? Qualified technicians, of course. I usually opt for personnel who have been through the AT&T fiber courses. Such courses are intense, are well prepared and delivered, and let the technician learn about all the problems of fiber splicing. Splicing is not easily done, and experience counts a lot. It took me a good three or four times before I got my first splice to work properly. Learning the correct ways to cut, polish, inspect, test, and fuse fiber is not trivial, so find someone who knows the business.

Fiber and FDDI

There are many types of fiber transmission technologies and many types of vendor equipment that use fibers. Then there are standards. ANSI released a networking standard called the Fiber Distributed Data Interface (FDDI) that prescribes very specific fiber types. (Figure 13.2 shows one kind of FDDI topology.) A primary fiber is recommended and then alternates are suggested—but there are reasons galore for the recommended type. Rather than get into a religious argument about which is better, suffice it to say that most fiber optic devices transmit in one of three different ranges: 850 nanometers (nm), 1300 nm, or 1550 nm. Most of today's vendors use the 850-nm fiber for their connections, although while FDDI recommends, primarily but not exclusively, 1300 nm. The 1500-nm fiber is intended for high-end transmission systems and is not seen very much in commercial applications yet—but it is coming along. For most sites, however, it is usually a good idea to get your fiber certified for at least 1300 nm, so that an orderly migration to FDDI or other high-speed technology is possible with minimum hassle. Some vendors claim, already, that they will support FDDI on 850 nm. The standard still recommends 1300 nm. Get a copy. Read. Understand why.

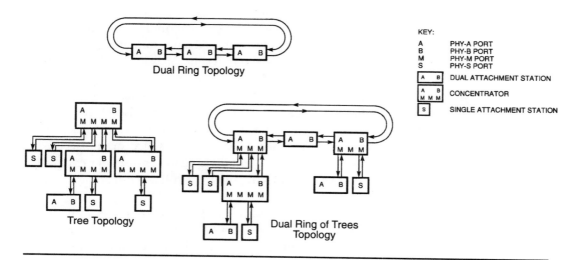

Figure 13.2
FDDI General Topological Diagram

How Many Fibers?

How many fibers should be run from one facility to another depends on who you believe. The Electronic Industries Association (EIA) and the Telecommunications Industries Association (TIA) have published recommended numbers of fiber pairs (always run fiber in pairs—it takes two to transmit and receive full duplex) between various facilities (the standard is called EIA/TIA 568). Digital has published their recommendations, IBM has theirs, and so on. What is best depends on your needs, but the following guidelines may help:

Building to building	24 to 48 pairs
Closet to closet	12 to 24 pairs
Closet to desk	8 to 16 pairs

Though these amounts may seem like overkill, they're not. They are overkill, however, right now—but probably too low for later. Later, however, you will be using broadband fiber and the numbers of fibers will be able to handle much greater connection capabilities.

When running your pairs of fiber, remember that most fiber connection facilities will require fiber repeaters at intervals throughout the network. Some connection technologies need no more than 2 kilometers between repeaters; others allow up to 10 kilometers between repeaters. Check with your vendor for proper guidance as to how many and where repeaters are required.

Plastic Fiber

Plastic fiber is not new. As early as 1979, I was involved in the use of plastic fiber to solve some fairly specific communications requirements. The media used had to be flexible, lightweight, easy to install, EMI and RFI resistant, and so on—no different from today's glass fiber requirements. The main reason for the need for plastic in that project was resiliency: the fiber was going to be placed in an area that could easily be mashed down, which would crush glass fiber. The media had to "bounce back."

So we used plastic instead of glass. It was rude, crude, and socially unacceptable, but it did work and has to this day. Plastic, as a communications medium, works well, but has manufacturing difficulties that affect the quality of the fiber, tensile strength, flexibility, noise metrics, light diffusion and refraction, and other anomalies that make it difficult to configure properly.

Plastic's Advantages over Glass

Plastic fiber has three major advantages over glass fiber: flexibility, ease of splicing and tapping, and price.

Plastic fiber is flexible and does not have all the bend and run restrictions of glass fiber (although it does tend to have a lower allowable level of maximum ambient temperature), because it is more pliable and less susceptible to breakage. Since it is, by nature, less brittle, it may be used in areas where it may be subjected to pressure that would crush a glass fiber. For instance, if an office chair runs over plastic fiber, the fiber springs back to its original cast shape; glass fiber breaks and must be cut out and spliced.

Because the materials that compose plastic fiber are nonrigid, polishing a plastic fiber for connection mechanisms is not advisable. Better, most plastic fiber runs may be cut by specially-constructed plastic fiber cutting and stripping tools. Once the fiber is stripped back and cut, the remaining fiber is cut away and heat-fused to the destination fiber. The whole operation, when done by a qualified technician, takes about 10 minutes (start to end) per fiber—compared to at least 40 minutes per glass fiber. So plastic offers substantial time savings in installation as well as splicing operations.

Price is always a concern in any network. Plastic is less expensive than glass, but not by much on a cable-foot basis. Where plastic shines is in the installation environment. Because installing plastic does not require nearly as much expertise nor connectivity splicing hardware, it is much less expensive to install and to reconnect after a fiber disruption. Comparing plastic to glass in terms of cost will require comparison of not only cable costs but also ancillary costs.

There are a few drawbacks, however. First, although plastic fiber has the potential for great speed, most vendor implementations at this writing will not allow speeds greater than 10 Mbps, due to fiber transfer limitations. Further, there will be limitations on how far a plastic fiber may be run without intermediate repeaters (most vendors allow about 100 meters total run length). Then there is the problem of plastic fiber expertise, vendor availability, development of standards for plastic fiber, and many other issues that are just now starting to emerge.

Most limitations on plastic fiber speed and configuration rules have to do with the ability of vendors to manufacture plastic fiber properly within strenuous specifications that will allow communications capability on the fiber. Because producing plastic fiber is not similar to producing glass fiber, there are a great many anomalies in plastic fiber that cause production problems as well as light path problems in the fiber. It also takes longer to certify plastic fiber for optical transmissions, which adds to the cost of manufacturing and distribution.

Fiber cable to the workstation is already a reality in some sites. I know of many locations that currently have such facilities installed. Plastic fiber will allow many other facilities to install and benefit from fiber to the workstation, but it will be some time before this is a reality. How soon? Probably two to five years, depending on demand and plastic fiber production facilities. There is currently no standard for plastic; some will need to be developed before it can be a viable, global medium. And higher speeds will need to be certified for plastic fiber, as well as better distance metrics.

Fiber Splicing and Network Configuration Issues

I configure a lot of fiber on Ethernet/802.3 networks. In some cases, it's because of speed. In others, the reasons vary, but they usually have to do with RFI and EMI. I recently had to pause, however, and consider whether fiber is for all applications and the ramifications of the decision to use fiber for more mundane applications.

The most recent revelation came when I was configuring an Ethernet/802.3 network for a process control environment. Because I am used to configuring fiber to defeat the problems of electrical noise with heavy equipment and motors, as well as the nature of many process environments to be distributed between various buildings with ground potential differences, fiber was my logical choice. I was asked to verify the cable plant for a network that was being installed to solve the needs of the process network. I am normally very hesitant to have only one data access path when industrial networks are involved, having seen cables torn asunder whenever the whim suits nearby equipment, construction crews, accidental explosions, and a host of other problems common to the industrial environment. This network was no different: a redundant cable path made infinite sense to ensure that control stations could do what control stations do—control the operation.

Subconsciously I kept thinking that there was another reason that there should be a redundant fiber path, and then it hit me why: fiber splicing. When a coaxial cable "bites the big one," it is not a biggie to fix the situation. Cut out the offending section of cable with cable cutters, strip the cable back properly with cable strippers, attach ferrules, crimp ferrules, put on connectors, crimp connectors, and seat and crimp outside ferrules to connector. Do the same to the other cable segment, attach a barrel connector in the middle, and voila! patched cable segment. Time to fix: about 20 minutes for anyone marginally skilled in such activities, and I have seen it done completely from start to end in less than five minutes by someone who can "do" cable faster than I thought possible. In short, at worst case, coaxial resegmentation of cable is not difficult, can be done by those with minimal skills, and does not require specialized knowledge or equipment; the tools are low-tech and readily available and there is little effort involved to get things rectified.

Although resplicing a bunch of coaxial cables after a backhoe has run amok is not trivial, it is still not terribly difficult to do. It is low risk and requires a little patience for a short time.

Twisted pair is even easier, since crimping and stripping tools are much more readily available and easy to use, for speed purposes. One tool can strip, cut excess, and crimp all connectors onto the twisted pair in at most two operations, and one new tool can do it in one. No rocket science here.

Actually, I said that once at NASA's Kennedy Space Flight Center and they took exception.

Which leads back to my fibrous dilemma. The main cable path back to the main control center from the outlying buildings was up the middle of a grassy knoll that was constantly the butt of trenching and dirt-moving tools. As a result, the chances of the various 24-pair fiber bundles being removed from their subterranean repose were much better than average. The field superintendent of the facility pointed out that they are always digging something up—including dinosaur bones in a low-water area!

Splicing Fiber Is Not Like Splicing Copper

Splicing fiber is not at all like splicing coaxial cable or twisted pair or any other copper cable. To splice or terminate fiber, properly, involves careful scoring of the fiber (under a magnifying glass or microscope), cutting the fiber, polishing the end with a fiber polishing machine, inspecting the end that was polished, and fusion-splicing it to an equivalently prepared end of another fiber—or gluing it to a connector for attachment to a device. While this seems simple enough, it is not. I had to go to a school for six days to find out the proper ways to do it (different fibers, different techniques) and then spend about $50,000 on polishing, inspection, and testing hardware. Once the fiber is spliced, a spectrum analysis should be done to measure signal loss and to ensure that the signal is adequate for data transmission. This involves the use of a spectrum analysis system and a fiber optic time-domain reflectometer (FOTDR) to ensure continuity and proper light levels for data transmission.

Correctly done, it takes about 20 to 40 minutes per fiber end. Since a typical fiber splice after the backhoe has come and gone involves a minimum of two fibers per path (this means four fiber ends to be cut and polished), it will take anywhere from an hour and a half to three hours to get everything back to normal for one pair of fibers. It will cost anywhere from $100 to $240 per fiber for a specialist to splice them together (they have to pay for that equipment somehow), and the specialist may take some time before he shows up to correct the problem. In short, fiber splicing is a pain in the right posterior cheek.

Since the original plan for this network was to run all the cables down a common wire path that was typically exposed to all items that walk, crawl, and dig, there was a good chance that the fiber bundles would be uprooted either now or in the future. With 24 pairs of fibers to reconnect after such an event, the fiber paths, if everything went correctly, would take over 75 hours to reconnect—and that would be working straight through until completion. Figure the odds on that. Not at all the repair scenario described for coaxial or other types of copper cable.

Even to get an emergency connection up and running properly, at least two fibers (four ends) must be spliced to provide continuity for one fiber path. This means that the network would be down for a minimum of 1 to 2 hours—if there is a repair team on site. If a team has to be fetched from afar, the delay goes up two to four more hours, and if there are any problems, the time delay is increased even more.

In short, although fiber offers a great many attractive options, such as noise immunity and very high speed, there is the dark side of repair that causes concern.

This condition may not necessarily last forever. As plastic fiber starts to make the scene over the next few years, there will be more and more implementations of it in communications networks. Plastic fiber is not at all spliced in a manner similar to glass fiber. In fact, a very sharp cutting device is used, and no polishing is required. By using reflective ceramic connections, the splicing of plastic fiber takes only a few minutes, as opposed to the hours of oppression of glass fiber.

Nonintrusive Fiber Taps

New (glass) fiber tapping devices are starting to make their appearance. Recently, a nonintrusive fiber tap was demonstrated as a possible tool to allow quicker and more reliable connectivity to fiber optic networks. New splicing tools are being developed as well.

For the near term (12 to 24 months or more), the penalties of fiber splicing are here to stay. While there are some solutions on the horizon, they will be the exception rather than the norm for some time. In the meantime, be wary of where fiber is used and how it is run and remember that the required amount of time to splice is nontrivial and needs to be considered in proper network design and implementation.

The "Right" Kind of Fiber for Ethernet/802.3

Here is a list of fiber requirements that may be of use to those sites contemplating fiber installation. Though not comprehensive, it will be sufficient for most sites to help your vendor install the proper fiber that will last a long time.

Fiber Conformance Requirements

1. All fibers will be 62.5/125, graded index, dual-window. Additionally, fibers will provide a minimum of 1300 nanometers wavelength capability.
2. All fibers will be terminated and tested via light spectrum analyzer and fiber optic time-domain reflectometer prior to sign-off to ensure proper functionality. Fibers not used for initial connections will be terminated properly and sealed from access except for when warranted in the future.
3. All fibers will meet or exceed the following standards:

   ■ ANSI X3T9.5 PMD
   ■ UL 1581 (OFN)

- UL 1666 (OFNR)
- UL 910 (OFNP)
- NEC Article 770 (1987)
- EIA 455

4. All fibers will possess the following minimum qualities:

- Fiber shall be graded index, glass on glass fibers.
- Core diameter shall be 62.5 microns, plus or minus 3 microns. This shall be measured via one of the following methods:

    a. EIA 455-29 (transverse interference)
    b. EIA 455-43 (near field)
    c. EIA 455-44 (refracted ray)

- Fiber cladding shall be 125 microns, plus or minus 3 microns, per EIA 455-55 or 455-48.
- Fiber shall have a mechanically strippable coating, per EIA 455-55:

    a. Loose-tube construction shall have a diameter of 250 μm plus or minus 15.
    b. Tight buffer construction shall have a diameter of 500 μm plus or minus 25.

- Core noncircularity shall be less than or equal to 6%, per EIA 455-45.
- Cladding noncircularity shall be less than 2%, per EIA 455-45.
- Core-to-cladding concentricity error shall be less than 6%, per EIA 455-45.
- Coating/cladding concentricity error shall be less than or equal to 20 microns, per EIA 455-45.
- Tensile load minimums shall be:

    a. 50 Kpsi (0.35 Gpa) for 250-μm coated fibers
    b. 100 Kpsi (0.7 Gpa) for 500-μm coated fibers

- The fiber attenuation coefficient shall be within the range of:

    a. 2.8 to 3.5 dB/km at 850 nm
    b. 0.8 to 1.5 dB/km at 1300 nm

- All attenuation will be tested per EIA 455-46 (cutback method).
- No localized attenuation will be greater than 0.2 dB, per EIA 455-59.
- Bandwidth shall be 160 MHz-km at 850 nm and 500 MHz-km at 1300 nm, per EIA 455-51 (pulse distortion) or EIA 455-30 (baseband frequency response).
- Numerical aperture shall be 0.275 plus or minus 0.015 at 850 nm (EIA 455-47).

■ Chromatic dispersion shall be zero wavelength between 1332 nm and 1354 nm. Zero dispersion slope shall be less than 0.097 ps/nm-km and tested per EIA 455-168.

■ All terminations on the fiber shall be of the industry standard type ST (unless specific FDDI conformance is required, in which case the ANSI X3T9.5 connectors must be used).

■ All connections that are metallic in nature shall be corrosion proof and shall withstand a minimum of 0.75 microns of corrosion per year (mill-wide average is 0.4, but many areas the network will be run into are much higher).

5. Fibers run underground between facilities will be of the gel-packed variety to preclude moisture penetration and seepage.

6. Any fiber run in any wire tray will be aerial conformant and may also be required to possess armor-interlocked shield fiber with interconnect fire blocks in the armor to preclude fire travel through the armor shield.

7. Interlocked armored fiber is required in some sites, especially those with open wire trays, as maintenance personnel are frequently observed walking in the actual wiretrays (especially the wider ones in industrial installations). This activity cannot be stopped due to the necessity of access to wire trays and cable in most industrial or plant sites. Further, an unarmored fiber would easily be crushed by maintenance personnel and would require expensive and time-consuming fiber splices to repair. The splices would also need to be placed in hard-to-get-to locations. For these reasons, armored cable will be required for all fiber runs in the facility.

8. Interlocked armored cable will meet or exceed NEC Article 333 and/or 334.

Summary

There is no question that fiber will be a major part of any network diet now and in the future. To properly prepare for fiber optic connectivity in the Ethernet/802.3 environment, management starts with proper planning and putting in the exactly "right" type of fiber for long-term applicability. This chapter includes a specification for fiber that is very durable and compliant with the ANSI FDDI standard. This will allow a smooth transition and upgrade in the future, when the fiber usage for your Ethernet/802.3 network is done and it's time to evolve to a new type of network—but not necessarily a new type of fiber.

Interconnecting with T1 Links   14

More and more Ethernet/802.3 networks are being interconnected with T1 communications links. The problem with such links is that very few people even understand what T1 is and why they would want to use it. This chapter focuses on using T1 for interconnection between Ethernet/802.3 networks and the problems involved with configuration and selection of T1 vendor products.

A Little History

The history of T1 is rife with intrigue and mystery (not really, but it reads better). You can tell it is not even a typical vendor-approved abbreviation, since it is only two characters long. Every site wants it, the phone companies tell us we need it, and we are told that it is the latest technology and, therefore, the best. (Figure 14.1 shows one kind of T1 topology.)

Sound a little like the snake oil sales pitch?

T1, unfortunately, is widely misunderstood and lumped into the general area of high-speed interconnects that few people seem to understand. To compound the problem, T1 lines, with the advent of fiber carriers, have become fairly cost-competitive with other serial link network technologies (such as the workhorse 56-Kbps leased lines and permanent virtual circuit X.25 links). Recently, a customer placing a leased line between Manhattan and North Carolina was quoted $5048 a month for 56-Kbps service from the local (N.C.) phone carrier. I called MCI and a few other vendors and was quoted $5120 a month for T1. For $72 a month more, we eliminated the other 64-Kbps voice service (at $4900 a month) and increased phone and network capacity fivefold at half the overall price. Sound too good to be true? It's not. A little careful shopping can go a long way. Always remember that a local phone company service will sell the service that they support and maintain and have the greatest margin on. They are not interested in lining anyone else's pockets but their own.

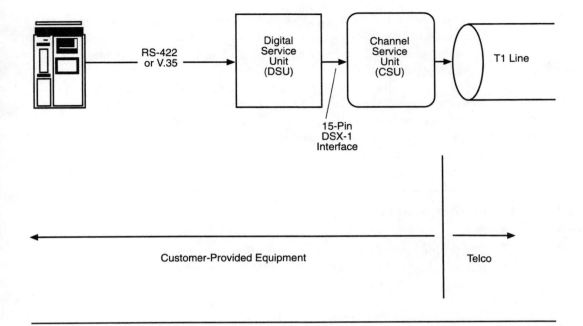

Figure 14.1
T1 (DS-1) Connection Path Topology

T1 provides 1.544-Mbps digital service in the United States in a manner similar to leased line access. By multiplexing the link, a T1 circuit may provide 24 subchannels of 64 Kbps each or combine the rates of various channels to provide specific speed service for various applications.

T1 is usually referred to as a data rate, but in historical fact, it refers to the type of cable method used to transfer voice signals in underground cable. Although T1 became available to the public in 1983 as a carrier service, in reality the concept and speeds of T1 had been around for more than 20 years. When the first digital data networks were installed, it was found that a reliable digital signal data rate needed to be identified that could be used between digital signal regenerators. Through experimentation and the need to support the existing wiring hierarchy, it was found that 1.5 Mbps could be reliably supported between large city manhole locations (about a mile apart). Since a digitized voice signal generates about 64 Kbps of data (this is called Data Signaling Rate 0, or DS-0), 24 simultaneous voice signals could be multiplexed over the 1.5-Mbps link in a frequency-division multiplexed (FDM) manner. This generated 1.536 Kbps of data. By adding 8 Kbps for synchronization of the two multiplexers (one at each end of the link), the rate jumped to 1.544 Mbps and became known as Data Signaling Rate 1, or DS-1. Since the cable system that supported the signaling rate was particular to this type of multiplexing installation for some years, the cable type, called T1, also commonly referred to the signaling type DS-1.

Other countries also have T1, but there it has a different definition. T1 in those areas involves a data rate of 2.048 Mbps (30 voice channels and two signaling channels) and is also called DS-1. To help avoid some confusion, organizations such as British Telecom refer to T1 service in the United Kingdom as "megastream" service.

There Is More Than Just T1

Lest ye think that T1 or DS-1 is the end of the road, think again. Currently, the following signaling rates are used in telephone systems throughout the world:

DS-0	64 Kbps	1 digital voice circuit
DS-1	1.544 Mbps	24 digital voice circuits
DS-1C	3.152 Mbps	48 digital voice circuits
DS-2	6.312 Mbps	96 digital voice circuits
DS-3	44.736 Mbps	672 digital voice circuits
DS-4	274.176 Mbps	4032 digital voice circuits

Even as you read this, some companies are already introducing T3 (DS-3) services and controllers for systems. IBM recently demonstrated a T3 controller for its new RISC system, the RS6000. Companies that make bridges and routers, such as Cisco Systems, have shown the T3 technology up and running. In short, about the time most of us get to understand and implement T1, T3 will be widely available for the higher speed networks.

Over the longer term, even T3 will be too slow. Soon-to-emerge technologies such as Frame Relay, Switched Multimegabit Data Service, and Synchronous Optical Network (SONET) promise data rates of 50 Mbps and greater (SONET tests have been run to rates over DS-4 and greater). While all these speeds seem far-fetched at this time, many companies with multiple Ethernet/802.3 networks will need to incorporate these technologies to support node-to-node speed of delivery requirements.

T1 Data Frames

Data sent on a T1 circuit is encoded in a frame format known as D4 (AT&T calls it M24, but it is the same thing). A D4 frame consists of one sample from each of the 24 channels in the T1 path. Each sample is 8 bits and occupies a time slot in the frame (8 bit times). Since the input voice analog signal is sampled 8000 times per second (once every 125 microseconds), one time slot per frame represents 8×8000, or 64 Kbps per channel (24 channels = 1.536 Mbps). By adding a framing bit, an additional 8000 bits are added to the total, yielding 1.544 Mbps, or DS-1. The bits are separated in the D4 frame format by taking 24 channels' 8-bit sample and placing it in a specific 192-bit format. The 193rd bit in the frame is used to mark the end of the frame (framing bit). To ensure that the receiver can detect the proper framing offsets, at the completion of every 12th frame a specific data pattern is transmitted (100011011100).

Why T1 on an Ethernet/802.3 Interconnect?

What's the point of all of this? Simple. These days we need to provide better high-speed services between networks and voice communications facilities. With the advent of fiber trunks and the cost drop of the components for modems and digital multiplexers such as T1 units, the cost to provide high-speed networking interconnection has dropped dramatically. A T1 service drop in 1985 for a link between New York and Los Angeles was about $70,000 a month. The same service in 1990, depending on where you shop, can be had for much less than $10,000 a month. In the next few years, as higher speed interconnects become de rigueur at the telcos, the cost for T1 connections will drop even more. Since many companies are distributing personnel, services, and facilities, the need to interconnect not only data but also voice is essential, and T1 offers a cost-effective, high-speed method to do it all.

T1 Is Good for Timing-Sensitive Protocols

A further point is the interconnection of timing-sensitive protocols that are appearing on LANs and other types of networks. Traditionally, network connections between routing nodes were accomplished via traffic analysis and estimation of expected load. Proper line speeds were provided and lines installed. In the case of LANs, some protocols these days expect the turnaround time for protocol packets to be in the order of milliseconds and do not expect the network cable speed to drop below the expected norm (10 Mbps for Ethernet/802.3, 16 Mbps for token ring, and so on). As a result, low-speed connections between LANs frequently cause timing-sensitive protocols (like LAT) to go nuts and produce worse performance than protocols that are less sensitive to turnaround timing issues. In these cases, the volume of traffic between LANs is not the issue—the issue is the speed of turnaround.

With more and more LAN bridges and interconnect systems supporting ISDN and T1 as interconnects, the need to connect high-speed systems is becoming, rapidly, the norm. T1 will not stand up to very high speed applications or high-density applications such as distributed image processing or interactive video. To provide these facilities, speeds higher than T1 will be required—speeds like T3 and T4. In any installation of any component, it is essential to know what to install on the next round of upgrades.

Summary

T1 is here now and will be around for some time. Until technologies such as SONET get established and become affordable, T1 is a speed to consider for Ethernet/802.3 interconnects. Many times T1 is preferred for data rate, but sometimes it is preferred for protocol timing issues alone. You don't have to have a lot of data to require a fast link between networks.

Fiber Distributed Data Interface 15

With many Ethernet/802.3 networks having mid-life crises today, deciding when to upgrade an Ethernet/802.3 network to Fiber Distributed Data Interface (FDDI) is increasingly problematic. Furthermore, there is the proposed Copper Data Distributed Interface (CDDI), which would allow FDDI speeds and protocols over unshielded and shielded twisted pair in a manner similar to services currently provided over fiber. Because many Ethernet/802.3 networks are implemented over fiber or STP, it would be a natural progression from 802.3 networking technologies to FDDI or CDDI, as speed requirements necessitate. This chapter covers the basic definitions of FDDI, how it works, and the services it provides. The chapter also addresses the problems of choosing the right time to migrate to FDDI from Ethernet/802.3 networks—and how to do it properly.

Why Fiber on Your Network?

It seems that the ultimate network is one that is the fastest, cheapest, and easiest to install, and one that promotes harmony in the office, causes good feelings toward the network manager, and helps save the whales.

Theoretically, that is.

In fact, the overwhelming issue these days is that faster networks are critical to business and industry, and unless network and systems managers plan for "megadata" to hit in the next six months, they will land on the high-tech junkpile for lack of vision and forethought.

To compound the issue of network selection criteria, practically every vendor I know of is pushing customers to install fiber optic cable—even if the customers are not going to use it for "a while" ("a while" translates to "at least 12 months" and probably longer).

Facts before Fiber

Let's get some preliminary facts straight:

1. There is nothing wrong with a copper-wire network. The word "copper" does not mean "inferior" or "slow."
2. Most LAN cable speeds far outclass anything most of today's communications controllers can generate, datawise (most cables can handle much more data than a single or multiple controllers can generate).
3. At the same time that we huddled network masses are given fiber communications technologies, we are also provided with twisted-pair communications technologies at the rate of 10 Mbps or better. Many of the current fiber technologies have the same speed as the equivalent copper speed, to provide compatibility with existing equipment.

In short, fiber currently does not necessarily provide the speed boost some claim it does, at least in the short term. It is true that fiber can handle much greater speeds than copper, but for now most vendors seem content to provide the same rated speeds of copper networks over fiber media. There are those few applications, true enough, that may benefit from fiber connectivity (imaging systems immediately come to mind). But by and large the good ol' copper connection is not fully utilized now (most 10-Mbps Ethernet/802.3 networks average less than 10% of potential load), and it will be a while before communication controller technologies evolve to be cost-effective enough to uproot existing networking techniques that provide network speeds of 4 Mbps or greater constant capacity on the cable.

There is a raging argument about the use of fiber to help diskless workstations communicate more quickly. Some articles I have read state that the big use for fiber is to increase throughput for workstations. Obviously, some of these writers do not understand the whole problem. Diskless systems, such as LAVC nodes, diskless PCs, diskless NFS systems, and many other types, suffer from multiple problems: from the type of network protocol being used to tuning of network parameters, activity levels and available CPU/network resources on primary access systems, queuing delay issues, network controller buffering, system buffering, protocol timeouts, retransmissions, system CPU time available (most network protocols are generated and received by system-level software, which requires host CPU power), and many other just-as-serious issues.

I have found that, with the rare exception, I have been quite successful in clearing up network performance problems on token ring and Ethernet/802.3 networks without having to resort to faster network cable access. Most diskless workstation networks are not configured properly to start with, and many are misused or badly configured for the application at hand. There are many fixes to these problems; a faster network is rarely one of them.

Where Fiber Fits

So where does fiber fit in? In those areas where speed is an issue, or as a backbone network. Yes, some networks, today, could benefit from a higher-speed fiber as a backbone. These are networks with a few hundred nodes that have the ability to effectively utilize a fiber backbone network and have connection devices to the fiber network that would allow the connection to such technologies as FDDI to be cost-effective and useful.

These type of networks are few today. With corporate networks growing at an astronomical rate, however, the need for high-speed backbones will be on us easily within five years for larger companies, and within ten years for the rest of us. With voice-annotated documents, large data repositories (such as CD-ROM, CD/I, WORM, and erasable optical disks), higher-resolution color graphic displays (1–2 megapixel 24-bit or 32-bit color), integrated retrieval systems, graphical system access methods, and other data-intensive and compute-intensive systems—all fully distributed of course—a very high speed data "bus" will be required.

Eventually, years from now in the late 1990s, there will be a need for fiber to the desktop, but that is still a while off. Currently, most of us have enough trouble deciding whether to use coax or twisted pair.

Fiber to the Desk or to the Backbone?

Honestly, are you going to need fiber connection to the desktop five years from now? In most shops, the answer is a resounding *No!* Will you need fiber in the next five years for backbone interconnection? Probably, *Yes!*

Why a fiber backbone? Well, the standard reasons are as follows:

- High speed (obvious, but what if the controllers cannot keep up?)
- Noise immunity (obvious and not so obvious: optical communications may have "noise" as well)
- Security (misconception: fiber may be nonintrusively tapped by new connection hardware coming to the market very soon)
- Ease of future upgrades (not obvious, but the signal-generating equipment and attachments may be upgraded to a new speed without changing the fiber itself)
- Electrically isolated environment (obvious)

A more important reason, frankly, has to do with the rapid interconnection of networks (no one wants the interconnect technology slowing down a link between systems) and the conversion from one network technology to another. Now that various shops have gone Ethernet/802.3-happy or token ring-happy, there is the problem of tying it all together into one useful, cohesive network.

Also, there are the issues of speed matching between network types, protocol matching between data-link protocols (let the OSI stuff handle the upper-layer goodies), medium (cable) differences, data generation/reception techniques, and many others.

Fibrous Interconnections

To provide for rapid interconnection, the interconnecting network should be faster than the networks it interconnects or the direct systems connected to it. Further, the network should encompass the needs of data-link encapsulation and forwarding between dissimilar LAN types (such as 802.3-to-802.5 connections), reliable connectivity (no one wants the backbone to fail), expansion (it should be able to handle many nodes or network connections), and, these days, the ability to connect many systems over a fairly wide geographical area. Yes, the word "local" in local area network is supposed to generally mean a network that is 1 to 2 kilometers in total length. These days, with the connecting of existing LANs in offices throughout a city or a geographic region, there is a real need for high-speed connections between LANs that are within a distance of 50 to 100 kilometers.

Currently, this connectivity is handled with T1 leased lines between dedicated LAN bridges or specialized LAN protocol routers. In the near future, however, this type of connectivity will wear thin and will not provide the capabilities required for the access of data on remote network segments. Here is a good opportunity for a networking technology that

- Provides high-speed interconnectivity between nodes and networks that are farther apart than 1 kilometer but closer than 100 kilometers
- Allows many nodes or networks (250 or more connections)
- Provides reliability (some sort of backup or fail-safe)
- Allows dissimilar network connectivity
- Could be incorporated into OSI physical and data-link layers
- Allows a variety of interconnect capabilities

What's an FDDI?

Well, fear no more, fellow campers. Here is Fiber Distributed Data Interface, from the American National Standards Institute (ANSI) Accredited Standards Committee (ASC) X3T9.5. ANSI saw the need in the early 1980s for a network to provide the services just listed and eventually provide such services to the desktop as networks evolved.

The idea of FDDI is based on a token ring model. To better understand FDDI, let's review how a token ring network operates.

Token Ring Theory and Operations

Each station wishing to access the network is connected to the token ring network and is granted access when a data element called a token is available. A token is present on the network when the network is idle. A sending station grabs the token and modifies a bit in the token that changes the token from a token bit pattern to a start-of-frame (SOF) bit pattern. The sending node then appends the network frame information to the SOF and sends the data on the wire. The frame is sent from node to node, with each node inspecting the destination address field to ensure that the frame being passed is not destined for the current examining node. When the current node decides that the token message is not for it, the node forwards the message to the next station in the path. When the message reaches the remote station listed in the address destination field, the message is examined, and then up to two additional actions may take place.

First, many token ring networks have an "address recognized" field, which is used by the destination node to inform the sending node that the destination saw the message and recognized the message as being for itself. A second field in the frame, "data copied," is used by the receiver to inform the sender that the frame was actually copied into the destination. This is a very useful feature, because it allows the sending station to identify one of three conditions: (1) the destination address is not active (there are no modifications to the frame sent), (2) the destination node is active but was unable to copy the frame into the node (there may be a lack of buffers, and so on), or (3) the frame was copied properly into the destination node.

Once the destination has taken its actions on the frame, it is then passed on to the next station and eventually makes its way back to the originating station. When that station sees the frame marked as read by the receiving station, the sender deletes the message and generates a new token to show that the network is ready for the next node that has data to send. In this manner, only one station at a time may transmit data. The amount of transmitted data varies among token ring network types, but it may range from 20 bytes to as much as 4 kilobytes or more, depending on the ring architecture.

Types of Token Ring Networks

In the token ring world, there are three popular variations on the scenario just described:

- IBM's Token Ring with source routing
- IEEE 802.5 token ring network
- Cambridge "slotted" ring network

IBM's Token Ring and the 802.5 token ring work very much like the ring I just described, but they are slightly different in implementation. The Cambridge ring concept uses multiple "tokens" on a ring at the same time and allows more than one message to be "in-progress" from a host system to a destination or various destinations at the same time. In all three cases, generally, a token is used to identify the availability of the network to sending nodes.

The Deterministic Argument

Token rings are not without problems. Among vendors of token ring networks, a very popular argument is whether the networks are "deterministic" in nature. In networking terms, a network is deterministic if a network analyst may determine, pretty exactly, when a network packet will hit a destination after being generated from a source. This determination is possible because the network has quantifiable values that may be used to compute the various stages of packet creation and delivery and the amount of time before a particular station could create a packet. This type of networking technology lends itself well to applications where absolute timing of network activity is required to provide adequate network support. Examples are chemical reaction control networks, factory control, and other types of networks where timing is critical between events.

The argument is that token ring networks provide better throughput because of their deterministic nature. This is somewhat self-serving, because the companies that make such claims are usually the token ring network vendors. Ethernet/802.3 vendors pull the same thing. In fact, both networks have strengths and both have weaknesses; which network is required depends heavily on actual need. Although a token ring network is deterministic at the cable level, it is virtually impossible, especially on a multiprotocol, multitasking system, to determine when a process on the system is going to generate a packet for the network controller. Since this is a statistical function, it tends to blow the doors off of the argument of determinism and the token ring. Determinism is great if it can be used, but this is usually not the case: the network hardware may be deterministic till the cows come home, but the software is highly statistical in nature.

For example, assume that you decide to take the form of data. Imagine yourself, data, walking to a bus stop to catch a bus to the city. If you arrive at the bus stop just as a bus is arriving and you are able to step right on, your experience is highly efficient and you will not have to wait. You have matched the known determinism of the bus (it will always arrive at a certain time) to your arrival (remember, you are data) and all is well. Imagine, however, that you arrive just as the bus is pulling away. How long will you have to wait and how many more people (data) will arrive in the meantime? Worse, the more stops the bus has to make, the longer it will take before you get the chance to get on the bus. What if the bus has a wreck and never returns?

Token rings usually work very much like this. So although the cable is deterministic, these types of networks tend to be called node-based networks, because their performance is highly dependent on the number of nodes on the network, not necessarily the amount of data (which is just one of many factors). Networks such as Ethernet are called statistical because when a station wishes to send data, there is a certain statistical average that allows the fact that the network will be open and available to anyone who wishes to send a message to another system. There could be thousands of systems, but if no one is using the network, it is 100% available and ready for use; the sender does not have to wait for a network entity to become available.

Needless to say, the arguments for and against token rings reach religious proportions sometimes. I frequently liken the situation to arguments over which vendor provides the best computing solution. You know how those arguments can go.

What does all this have to do with FDDI? Well, FDDI is a token ring and, technically, deterministic. The difference is that FDDI does not act like a totally "classic" token ring network. Tokens on an FDDI react differently than those on most token ring networks, and FDDI accommodates statistical network interconnections better than classic token ring architectures do.

The FDDI Token-Passing Scheme

FDDI uses a token-passing scheme similar to those used on token ring networks. The difference is that the token is a series of specially defined bits that are sent from node to node. If the bits do not match a specific pattern, the receiving station knows that the token is used and that this is a data message and should be examined to see if the receiving station needs to keep the data being passed along. If the data is not for the station with the packet, it is regenerated to the next station in the path. If the data is for the current station, the station "snapshots" the data, passes it up to the host system, and marks the bit pattern at the beginning of the packet to signify that the message has been received and read into the receiving node. The token is then passed along to the next node and eventually to the sending station.

Differences between FDDI and Token Rings

There are some serious differences between FDDI and other token ring architectures, such as 802.5. These include the following:

1. FDDI networks may have one or two counterrotating fiber rings. This allows configuration of redundant topologies for highly reliable networks.
2. FDDI does not use standard encoding techniques like the Manchester encoding that is used in Ethernet/802.3 and in 802.5 token rings. FDDI

uses a group encoding technique that essentially allows 4 bits to be encoded in 5 bauds. In Manchester encoding, each bit to be sent requires at least 2 signal transitions, or bauds. This means that a 16-Mbps token ring network would require a signaling rate of 32 MHz. Ethernet/802.3 running at 10 Mbps would require 20 MHz. Using Manchester encoding on FDDI would mean that the fiber used would require more than 200 MHz to provide the FDDI-rated speed of 100 Mbps. Through the use of group encoding (also known as the 4B/5B method in FDDI, for 4 bits, 5 baud), the FDDI runs at a rate of 125 MHz and provides a data rate of 100 Mbps. With this scheme, the FDDI provides high-speed capability over less optimal media and provides data symmetry that allows for easier architecture of analog capture circuitry for receiving nodes. The FDDI group codes are shown in Table 15.1.

Table 15.1

FDDI code	Bit encoding
0	1 1 1 1 0
1	0 1 0 0 1
2	1 0 1 0 0
3	1 0 1 0 1
4	0 1 0 1 0
5	0 1 0 1 1
6	0 1 1 1 0
7	0 1 1 1 1
8	1 0 0 1 0
9	1 0 0 1 1
A	1 0 1 1 0
B	1 0 1 1 1
C	1 1 0 1 0
D	1 1 0 1 1
E	1 1 1 0 0
F	1 1 1 0 1
S (set)	1 1 0 0 1
R (reset)	0 0 1 1 1
Q (quiet)	0 0 0 0 0
I (idle)	1 1 1 1 1
H (halt)	0 0 1 0 0
T (terminate)	0 1 1 0 1
J (start 1)	1 1 0 0 0
K (start 2)	1 0 0 0 1

3. FDDI does not use bit definitions for various fields. All FDDI fields are defined by at least 4 bits and may be defined by a byte of information. As a result, the various fields may easily be modified or replaced by the nodes on the network as the frames and token travel throughout the ring(s).

4. An optional technique in token ring networks, but implemented as a feature on FDDI, is the concept of early token release (ETR). ETR is used to place a token on the network *before* the generated frame has had the opportunity to circulate throughout the entire network.

5. On 802.5-type token rings, it is possible for stations to implement a priority scheme whereby token ring nodes may "reserve" a token for access (AC—the access control field). This scheme does not exist on FDDI, as it would not work properly in the FDDI environment. FDDI nodes will usually send a token at the end of a data transfer, which means that reservation techniques do not work. This is called "new token after send," which is different from 802.5's "new token after receive."

6. There is an explicit maximum data size of 4500 bytes per frame on FDDI. On 802.5, there is no explicit data frame size. Specification of an explicit frame size keeps a node from "hogging" the cable.

7. Tokens on FDDI are not modified to an SOF as they are on other token ring networks. Tokens are absorbed and regenerated after a message has been sent.

8. FDDI implements a capacity allocation capability that allows the network to provide critical service to certain types of transactions and a priority-oriented service for other traffic types. This is implemented through a service called the Timed Token Protocol (TTP). Basically, the protocol separates traffic types into synchronous traffic and asynchronous traffic. Synchronous traffic would encompass traffic such as disk access data. Asynchronous traffic might encompass virtual terminal data and other types of bursty, aperiodic data. By measuring token arrival and departure times and following specific rules of the TTP, a node may compute how many of each type of frame may be sent and the next time such transmissions will be available to the node. In this manner, nodes on the FDDI balance data throughput and provide a pseudo-priority scheme for various types of data.

9. FDDI provides the capacity to support a distributed recovery capability in case of ring failure. This means that the ring could be cut, and between physical and FDDI frame components, nodes on the network would automatically isolate the fault and actively reconfigure the network to provide maximum availability.

10. On token ring networks, there is one clock on the network responsible for providing clocking signals for all nodes on the cable. The main clock node also provides an "elastic" buffer capability that slides to compensate for

speed differentials that appear on the network (jitter). In a 100-Mbps environment, this type of clocking mechanism is impractical and difficult to
maintain. At 4 Mbps, the bit time is 250 ns, as compared to 10 ns per bit
time at 100 Mbps. As a result, FDDI nodes each provide their own clock
(hence a "distributed" clocking scheme) and correct for timing jitter via
each node's own internal elastic buffer.

Configuring an FDDI Network

Configuring an FDDI is not simple (see Figure 15.1). The primary purpose of
FDDI, according to the original scope of the project, was to provide high-speed
networking for the following types of networks:

- Networks that connect workstations to file servers
- Networks that connect peripherals to systems
- Networks that act as backbones for other networks

To provide for these situations with FDDI, an FDDI interface controller is
an obvious need. But because the product is new, prices for such devices are
hefty; the cost is prohibitive except for those with the need and those with the
budget (some controllers cost in the range of $1000 to $3000, but the price

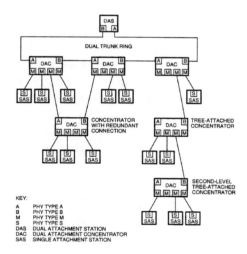

Figure 15.1
FDDI Topology

has been dropping slowly). With ASIC technologies and volume, the price will drop.

When considering implementation of FDDI, there are some rules to follow (as there are with any network).

FDDI and Fiber Standards

First off, there is the problem of the physical cable plant. FDDI uses either 62.5/125- or 85/125-micron multimode fiber. Alternatives of 50/125 micron and 100/140 micron are also specified. Smaller fibers allow higher speeds but also cause higher connector loss. Further, the fiber must be attenuated for light transmission at the 1300-nm wavelength (as opposed to some products, such as various Ethernet/802.3 bridges, that may work in the 850-nm range). Because most fiber plants transmit at 850, 1300, or 1550 nm, finding compliant fiber is usually not a problem for the network manager. Usually, in networks less than 1 kilometer long, 850 nm is usually adequate; however, as the need for performance of the medium increases, the 850-nm light source becomes inadequate. Light transmission above 1550 nm usually requires a sophisticated and expensive light source, such as a laser system. Fiber runs may not be longer than 2 kilometers between stations, and there is a total allowable distance of 100 kilometers per FDDI ring (two rings are allowed). Each ring consists of two fibers (two rings, obviously, would have four fibers). A total of 500 nodes are allowed on an FDDI.

Types of FDDI Nodes (Classes A and B)

Within FDDI, there are two types of nodes: Class A and Class B. Class A nodes (called dual-attachment stations, or DAS) are connected to two rings and have the ability to reconfigure the network between the primary and secondary rings to form a valid network in case of a failure. Class B nodes (called single-attachment stations, or SAS) only connect to the primary and could be isolated from the network in the case of some classes of failure. Of these nodes, some will be equipped with bypass connections, which allow light source continuation even if the node connection has failed, helping to ensure the uptime of the network.

In most wiring configurations with FDDI, the network designer will configure a main backbone to be set up as Class A nodes for reliability purposes. The length of the backbone is a function of how distributed a network is. In a building environment, the backbone may be located in a single room, with all segments connecting to it. The backbone may be located vertically throughout telephone closets in the building. There may be other variations as well. In all these cases, the backbone FDDI is contained within the building. In a campus environment, the backbone could also be in a single room in a single building, but most likely it will be running from building to building on the campus. In this type of configuration, it is assumed that each building may have a main network control closet, so there is only one tap on the network backbone at each building location. In any case, the backbone network may vary in size and number of taps, depending heavily on where the network is located.

Once an FDDI has been used as the network backbone, it may appear as a backbone within a building that is connected to the main backbone FDDI. In this example, there are two FDDI network levels: the main backbone and a separate FDDI per building. This may further be expanded to an FDDI on a floor and then connected to the building hub, which is connected to the main backbone in a campus building environment. In this configuration, the fiber is run to the actual machine(s) on the network, and other networks may or may not be bridged onto the FDDI.

FDDI and Fiber Count

Many vendors have come up with general fiber count (numbers of fibers) configuration rules that will allow customers to install fiber required for FDDI connectivity now and in the future. General recommendations usually include the following fiber counts to be included in fiber installation. Please remember that each FDDI requires a minimum of two fibers, and for a Class A node, there will be a requirement for at least four fibers:

- **Campus network interconnecting other buildings or networks:** 24 to 48 pairs of fibers (48 to 96 fibers) in an aerial sheath. This would usually be armored as well as configured for indoor/outdoor use.
- **Vertical run within a building (for example, in telephone closets or floor to floor):** 12 to 24 pairs of fibers (24 to 48 fibers) in a tight-buffer cable certified for air plenum use within the building.
- **Horizontal floor run for connection between closets on a floor:** 4 to 8 pairs of fibers (8 to 16 fibers) in a tight-buffer cable certified for air plenum use within the building.
- **Horizontal run from a local closet to an office:** 2 to 4 pairs of fibers (4 to 8 fibers) in a tight-buffer cable certified for air plenum use within the building.

Fiber Jackets for FDDI

While the selected fiber for FDDI is either 62.5/125 or 85/125, the correct fiber jacket is important also, to keep the fiber safe and also to meet most local electrical and cabling codes (if any). Typically, fiber is enclosed in a fiber jacket, called a buffer, that is used to separate the fiber itself from any external contact and also to protect the fiber from damage. Buffers range from standard dielectric foam to, in the case of fibers that may be submerged in water or other liquids, gel packing. Gel packing is useful because when water gets into a cable, it can expand and contract (based upon pressure and temperature) and damage the fiber(s). Buffers for indoor FDDI should normally be of the "tight" variety to allow maximum protection for the fiber. "Loose"-buffered cables are useful in those locations where the fiber or the "tube" around the fiber will expand and contract (usually outdoors). A loose buffer (tube) around the fiber allows the buffer to expand and contract independent of the fiber itself.

Cables may be jacketed with a variety of materials, ranging from aluminium and Kevlar to PVC. Which jacket is used depends on local fire codes and electrical codes, as well as where the cable is being placed in the structure. Some materials, such as PVC, give off noxious fumes when burned and are not allowed in areas where there is a return air plenum. Each jacket type has a variety of cable "stiffeners" inserted in between the fibers to give the cable some rigidity and add some strength when it is pulled or suspended. How many stiffeners and the type used (some have aluminum rods inserted in the jacket) vary from vendor to vendor.

FDDI Can Crack Up

Fibers, after a period of time, may develop microfractures (cracks), or strain fractures on suspended fibers. Besides the stress fractures that can appear on fibers that have been pulled, many other nasty things can happen to perfectly good fiber. Fiber used on networks such as FDDI is made of glass, but it has very high tensile strength. The problem is that if a crack develops on the surface of the fiber, it may, in the long term, cause the fiber to break or, in the short term, cause optical dispersion problems. In this respect the fiber is like a pane of glass. Unscribed, the glass is fairly strong. When scribed, the glass is easily broken. Further, when scribed and placed under strain, the glass may also cause the scribe to continue and weaken the pane, causing eventual breakage.

Another problem with fiber is bend radius. Although fiber cable is much more flexible than copper cable and can be bent in much smaller radii than equivalent copper, microbends may appear in fiber that has been bent too tight or "kinked." Microbends can cause light-path disruption and increase the loss on the cable. Areas subject to chemical exposure, radical temperature changes, nuclear radiation, and other disruptive effects require special consideration in cable jacketing and the type of fiber used. Check with a local installation specialist to find out which fiber type is best for your environment and where your fiber will be installed.

FDDI Splicing

Because uninterrupted runs of fiber are somewhat impossible in most fiber plants, splices will be required for many networks. Each splice introduces a signal-loss problem on the fiber (anywhere from 0.2 dB to 1.1 dB per splice) and must be carefully considered. Connectors, too, introduce loss problems. Other loss figures might include field service issues and cable length. All items to be considered in the loss accumulation are charged against the cable "power" budget to ensure that the connections and splices to the cable are not such that they will override the ability of the light source to deliver the signal to the destination. Fiber at 850 nm will usually allow 3.0 to 4.0 dB attenuation per kilometer. Fiber at 1300 nm allows only 1.0 to 2.0 dB maximum attenuation per kilometer.

The Costs of FDDI

FDDI is not cheap. As mentioned before, the controllers alone range from $1000 to $3000 at this writing and will most likely come down in price. Considering, however, that Ethernet/802.3 controllers range from $150 (for PCs) to about $4000 at worst, FDDI is not cost-competitive with Ethernet and other LAN technologies at this time. To compound the misery, the fiber, which is not terribly expensive to purchase and pull, has some unique problems that do increase, markedly, the cost per connection to FDDI.

Terminating Fibers for FDDI Use

For a node to be connected to a fiber network, the network must have a fiber coupler (tap) attached to it. These couplers will typically require that the cable be cut and terminated properly with approved connectors (these are typically the ST variety of fiber terminators). Splices in fiber may be made via a "score-and-break" technique, in which the fiber is scored, it is broken with special tools, and the end of the two fibers that will be connected are joined with epoxy. A secondary way is to use a fusion splicer, which may use an electrical arc to connect the ends of two fibers.

Splices are pretty straightforward and reasonable to implement. Termination of cable, however, requires that the end(s) be cut and polished before insertion into a terminating hood. Polishing is typically done coarsely with a hand tool and completed with a polishing machine. This allows a smooth, imperfectionless end that will properly pass the light source through to the optical receiver in the destination transceiver or repeater. This polishing effort may take up to 40 minutes per fiber (imagine this on a 48-fiber run), which is the reason for the cost of fiber installation. Improper polishing and connection of the termination points on a fiber will render the fiber useless for connection purposes and will, at a minimum, result in poor network performance. Termination is required for proper testing of the fiber (which may be done with an optical time-domain reflectometer), which is necessary to verify proper installation. In short, installing fiber properly for FDDI is painful, time-consuming, and expensive.

Cable Plants for Ethernet/802.3 and FDDI

In the midlife, Baby Boomer crisis of Ethernet/802.3 networks, there is the need to upgrade speed to be as fast as the Jones's network. So far, there is little reason in many networks to upgrade to a faster cable rate, as most sites are not using what they have to an efficient degree. Eventually, though, the cable rate will need to be faster to handle the loading that will surely come when we get all the spiffy graphics and "visualization" systems being cooked up in some dark recess of vendors' development facilities.

The so-called crisis I keep running into, which I don't view as a crisis but which network managers seem to, is what kind of cable plant is a safe bet for Ethernet/802.3 today and faster networks tomorrow that may not be Ethernet/802.3? Obviously, these are people who are worried about whether they should lay down some serious cash for fiber to the desktop or whether unshielded twisted pair is the way to go. There are others with IBM Type 1 plants that want to go faster as well and need to know what to do about their cable futures. And, almost universally, everyone is worried about how to use FDDI when the need arrives without having to rip out the lungs of the building to get FDDI speed.

Shielded Twisted Pair Is Your Friend

My answer to all of these issues is the same as it has been for nine years—the first time I was asked about cabling buildings to support an emerging standard for 100 Mbps transmission. Shielded twisted pair is the safe answer to the desktop; glass fiber is good for connecting closets and buildings. I've modified my opinion a bit to include plastic fiber to the desktop when the technology is stable, but that is still a ways away from here.

At this writing, the only "legal" twisted pair for copper-based FDDI (CDDI) is STP. Like it or not.

By now, the unshielded twisted pair folks of the world are coming unglued on me and calling me terrible things. Well, I have been called terrible things for years, so please get in line and take a number for better service.

Unshielded Twisted Pair and Long-Term Cabling Futures

First off, why not UTP for FDDI capability over copper? It has to do with two issues: noise and emission regulations. Noise is noise. The physics of what generates noise does not change radically when the same physical wire is used at a higher data rate in the same physical facility. The copier is still in the same physical place generating static, the same metal studs in the wall are radiating noise and static from other equipment in other rooms, the punch-down blocks in the closet next to the elevator motor are still pleased to provide you the finest in ambient electrical interference, the RJ-45 connectors are still able to properly vibrate and jiggle in the loose connection adapters for your workstation, and the longer unshielded runs still have a serious decibel-dropoff because 100 meters is the *maximum* allowed run, not the preferred one.

Yes, life on UTP is full and bountiful—full of noise, to be sure.

Noise and Unshielded Twisted Pair

A 10-ms burst of static on UTP when carrying data at 9600 bps can be caught and corrected before the user knows anything has happened, usually with parity checking or some other simple error-checking sequence. The same burst of static at 10 Mbps destroys a substantial number of packets and causes serious overhead on the systems on both ends of the connection. The same burst of static at 100 Mbps causes the equivalent of *War and Peace* to take a dive: this is unacceptable, performance-wise. Different types of equipment may signal the data in new and unique ways, to help take advantage of the capabilities of the medium (such as Manchester encoding, 4b/5b, threat-parameter encoding, and signal semaphores), and this may help reduce some of the grief that noise will cause. None of them, however, eliminates noise, which means that at higher signaling rates, the same burst of noise will cause more grief than at a lower signaling rate. And this does not begin to address the decibel-dropoff problems with UTP and the other issues mentioned before. Noise alone is a killer.

Radiation Emissions and the Law

Emissions are a legal problem, not a technical one. Why? Laws can be modified by agreements that require absolutely nothing more than the right political pressure or sufficient votes in the law-making body to make the modification happen. Technical problems can be solved, but there is no vote or nontechnical way to magically make the modification to the technology involved. Sure, we all would like to avoid getting a fresh, involuntary tan after using our network equipment or retaining that healthy glow-in-the-dark look after two hours in the telephone closet. That's part of the emission control issue involved (yes, I am being flip, but it's what I do).

The FCC sets the tolerable emission rates for equipment in the United States. Vendors have to comply or get in deep kimshi with the government. Basically, there is a myriad of conformance requirements, emission-wise, but they boil down to the venerable Class A and Class B equipment conformance requirements. Network equipment typically has conformed to Class A, but more and more equipment is being required to conform to Class B, because of where the equipment is located and who is using it. Also, since there is a definite march to use equipment in the home and other areas that require Class B conformance, the requirement on the vendors to get network equipment to Class B emission conformance is becoming a biggie. In February 1992, some new conformance regulations kicked in that aggressively enforce the Class B distinction and require many products currently nonclassified or classified as Class A to become Class B-compliant or not be sold. Although some of the regulations are based on technical issues, most are legalities and, therefore, political in nature. For example, there is no technical reason why very high data rates cannot be achieved on UTP (as long as UTP is clean). The limitation may be political and have nothing to do with technology.

What's this have to do with UTP? Plenty. At the 100-Mbps FDDI rate, a much higher signaling rate is required than the 20 to 30 MHz that is currently used in the Manchester-encoded Ethernet/802.3 environment of today. If the 4b/5b encoding technique of FDDI were used, straight up, on UTP right now, 125 MHz would be required to support a 100-Mbps data rate. Although the overall issues involved in measurement of the Class B conformance are complex, by and large anything over about 30-MHz signaling will begin to exceed the conformance requirement—getting the vendor or the user in deep with the FCC.

Some companies have gotten clever and come up with various signaling techniques to allow 100 Mbps on UTP without requiring super-high signaling rates and therefore help to reduce emissions. One company has developed a technology called "wave shaping" that allows FDDI speed over UTP and is "within range" of the Class B conformance requirement (it isn't compliant yet, so don't get in a rush). Others have started to push for a 24-gauge data-grade UTP wiring standard (this is *not* the current UTP everyone knows and loves) for FDDI speed over UTP. In other words, the technology may be available in the future for FDDI speeds over UTP, but the legal problems still exist and there is still our friend: noise.

What Happens the Next Time Around?

One other, and less considered, reason to cast the hairy eyeball at UTP is simple: What is going to happen next? Sure, 100 Mbps is great, but what happens next? 1 Gbps? 100 Gbps? One thing in the computer business that is a fact is that you can never be too small or too fast. The result is that the network of

100 Mbps will not be fast enough in the future. If we are pushing the limits of UTP to get 100 Mbps to work properly, what happens when 1 Gbps is required in the near future? UTP will definitely be out of the question as a cabling plant then. Most companies that look at only the next step in technology are not really working on a long-term solution; they are only trying to put out the next fire. True, long-term vision and planning has to look at what's happening next, after the next hurdle, and get in-house systems and technology aligned to meet the challenge of not only the next hurdle, but the one after that as well.

STP Is Still Your Friend

Shielded twisted pair has been around for some time and is a known commodity. It has its problems, such as capacitance buildup as the cable gets longer, but since the pairs are individually shielded (in *real* STP cabling), the hazards of crosstalk and noise problems are dramatically reduced. Don't kid yourself: STP can be interfered with as well by noise and interference sources, some the same as those that wouldst clobber thy UTP network. It is much better shielded, however, and can withstand more noise abuse than UTP and allow higher data rates with the same clever signaling that would allow UTP to work at higher rates.

One test I saw recently showed 3 Gbps running over twisted pair, shielded or unshielded. The STP cable, however, had a substantial amount fewer errors due to interference than did the UTP cable. In fact, the UTP error rate was so high that it could not be used in a production network. Sure, there are still configuration rules and requirements, and it is not trivial to put in either network plant, but the STP cable stood up to the challenge of reliable (that's the key word) higher data rates better than its UTP cousin. There comes a point when any type of twisted pair cable's signaling capabilities will be shot in the rear due to the medium type, but STP helps push a little more out of the medium.

Therefore, if twisted pair is a medium that you require for your building, then consideration of STP is probably a better long-term solution for you than UTP. If you have UTP, you have some growth capability for a while, but eventually you will need to replace it with something else. Yes, I agree that with STP you will eventually need to replace it as well, but it will be somewhat longer and that is in your favor. The longer a cable plant can last, the clearer the next medium-of-choice will be. It'll probably be wireless, but that is a different problem.

100-Mbps Wireless?

While we're here, the same test on UTP and STP data-vs.-noise and errors I was witness to was also done on a commercially supplied 10-Mbps wireless network in the 18-GHz range (if you cannot figure out that the wireless network used in the test comes from a rather large microprocessor and communications manufacturer based in Illinois, you have been avoiding your trade journals too long again). Interestingly enough, the wireless network had fewer errors and better throughput than either the UTP or STP network, not to mention 1/100th the cabling hassle. Therefore, sometimes the choice of medium in the future will be wireless for less hassle and good performance at the same time. Some vendors are already hard at work on getting 100 Mbps over wireless facilities and are reaching a modicum of success doing so. So, will we see 100 Mbps over the airwaves? Of course. I, however, am holding out for 100 Gbps over the airwaves, and that is what some vendors are predicting before the year 2000 (for testing only).

Of note is a network technology from Israel called JOLT. This 100-Mbps spread-spectrum wireless FDDI "clone" is available at this writing and shows that the trend, even for very high speed networks (today) is toward the usage of wireless networks for interconnection.

FDDI over Thinwire (RG-58) Coaxial Cable

Some sites that are using thinwire (RG-58) Ethernet/802.3 network cabling plants have the opportunity to use the thinwire plant as another alternative to UTP or STP cabling at 100 Mbps. In June 1991, DEC announced support for thinwire as the FDDI cabling plant with the use of their FDDIController-700 range for various systems. Basically, the BNC "T" is removed and the cable is connected to two ports on the back of the FDDIController. A special version of the DEC Concentrator-500 is used as the backbone-to-thinwire connection point (where the backbone is a classical optic FDDI DAS network drop). The effect is that of a ring, logically, but the cabling plant is physically point-to-point daisy-chained between stations. It sounds weird, but it seems to work all right in the two sites I saw running tests.

What this translates to is that the user and installer of thinwire Ethernet/802.3 can convert to a proprietary (DEC-manufactured) FDDI-compatible solution (if using DEC systems that support the FDDIController-700 series) without recabling the building. If DEC were to come up with an adapter that looked like fiber ST connectors to the workstation and BNC connections to the cable, other types of systems could easily be connected into the thinwire plant and communicate as FDDI nodes. Whether they (DEC) will or won't come up with such a device is unknown, but it makes a lot of sense if they are serious about supporting thinwire as an alternate medium for FDDI. Thinwire has its configuration problems as well as any other network, but noise and FCC compliance problems are reduced dramatically with such a solution.

Plastic Fiber

Plastic fiber is an alternative whose time has not yet come. Sure, there are some vendors out there with some plastic fiber solutions, but these are new and market acceptance hasn't happened yet. Personally, I think that when a physical cable is needed in the near future (3 to 10 years), plastic may be the logical choice. It's cheap, plentiful, and easy to install (compared to copper and glass fiber). It has limitations, but these are tolerable and workable. The problems with plastic fiber right now can be summed up as timing (new), lack of supported products, and standards (none). When these get rectified, plastic fiber will be acceptable.

Wireless still has them all beat. A year ago, I worked on a wireless network that cost me about $1400 a connection. One, which I put in about three weeks ago using Motorola's Altair solution, ran me about $600 a connection. With my current estimate of about $850 a connection for twisted pair, wireless has become an attractive solution for cabling new and existing buildings. Two things have contributed to this trend: (1) Motorola dropped its prices on the components recently, and (2) wireless means wireless between work clusters and using thinwire or something else between nodes in the work clusters to reduce the number of wireless "repeaters" required. With this approach, the network goes in within hours instead of days, moves when the group moves, meets FCC compliance, and averts noise problems (by and large). It will take a while for this type of "cable" plant to catch on, but that is mostly due to accusations of witchcraft and voodoo and other disparaging things leveled at the technology by competitive vendors and naive network managers.

The Number of Network Connections Is on the Rise

One last problem with media choice for future FDDI-like networks has to do with the number of network connections in a workplace. There seems to be this belief in the industry that one network connection per office is plenty. Wrong, buffalo breath! Have you ever noticed how many actual physical AC sockets are in your office? Is it a fact that you have more items to plug in than you have sockets in your office? Why is that? Bad architectural planning. Before the early 1980s, architects never considered that the office of today would require eight to ten sockets per office just to plug in all the nonsense we need to do business. We have compensated for the problems by overloading the electrical circuits with AC power strips and power poles for our cubicles, but this "Band-Aid" is not a well-considered solution.

Networks are starting to force the same situation. Too often we place one network connection point in an office only to find that soon we need four to five connection points, due to the systems becoming distributed. Five years ago, everything was one big happy node. Now we have the printer, terminal, disk, and other components as separate nodes on the network. In other words, simply because we have upgraded and installed new technologies, an office now requires more than one connection. That's assuming, of course, one worker per office. What happens when a node on the network is the monitor, the mouse, the keyboard, the scanner, the modem? Laughing? Keep it up. That's basically what the Apple Desktop Bus (ADB) does in the Macintosh environment (the keyboard, mouse, and other devices are separate, daisy-chained nodes on a desktop network). Want proof? Try hooking up two keyboards to the same ADB and watch what happens. It's a great way to train new users.

Designing a network for FDDI—any network plant—will require multiple network connections at the same time in the same workplace. Failure to accept this will cause serious expansion grief.

How Many Pairs of STP for Networking?

So, what cable to put in? STP. How many pairs? I recommend 16 pairs, minimum, but that is because I believe in color-coding pairs in the closet. (Ever try to figure out which pair is Ethernet and which pair is RS-232 in a punch-down block? Color is your friend.) I also believe that there will be more than one network technology to the same workplace at the same time. How are they divided up? As follows:

- 4 pairs—Ethernet/802.3
- 4 pairs—EIA-232 or other serial connection
- 4 pairs—CDDI (FDDI over twisted pair)
- 4 pairs—ISDN or other service, such as voice (business service)

Of course, you may substitute Ethernet/802.3 for token ring/802.5 and ISDN for other networking types. Personally, I would probably be happier with broadband plastic fiber to the office, but that is cost-prohibitive today. I would be marginally happy with 12 pairs because there is little expansion, but I know that, like using a power strip, I can add ports in the office using off-the-shelf expansion devices (STP "hublets" that allow four RJ-45 connections over 10BASET, muxes for RS-232, SAS devices for CDDI, and so on). I also know that, over the very long term, fiber and wireless is the name of the game.

Not everyone will agree with my suggestions, but that is what opinion is all about. If we all agreed, life would be very boring and there would not be the "network technology of the week" award for the latest way to confuse and amaze us huddled masses. I do know that having slogged through countless problems on networks around the world in various types of environments, I have always had more trouble with UTP networks than with any other type. I also know I want my networks to last and grow with minimal hassle, and STP is a way to help that along.

For now.

When to FDDI

Before I get accused of network blasphemy, let me start by claiming eternal allegiance to advancements in network science.

That said, I can now proceed.

FDDI is upon us. I have been proclaiming for several years its benefits and advantages to the larger sites of the world, and I still continue to believe that it will be essential to many networks now and in the future. Recently, however, I have been inundated with recommendation requests for fiber and whether now is the time for FDDI. With rare exceptions, the issue is, yes, install glass fiber as backbone network connections where reasonable and feasible. And, yes, FDDI is appropriate for very large data-rate applications such as magnetic resonance imaging.

But . . .

By and large, many of the applications and companies in the world do not need FDDI today. They will need it, of course, with time, but not just yet. More important, the cost of FDDI is still quite high, and it's impractical for most companies to pay the amounts demanded for service speed that they do not need.

How Do You Know If You Need FDDI?

That said, the question becomes: How do I know if I need FDDI?

Most vendors will tell you that you need it now. Then again, they're trying to sell you something as well. In truth, it makes good sense to put in the proper fiber for FDDI if your company is in the process of installing any fiber at all. This does not mean that you need FDDI speed, but you do not want your fiber plant to become obsolete too early, either. Most companies will need FDDI, initially, as a backbone network to interconnect Ethernet/802.3 and token ring/802.5 networks. Eventually, as new application technologies such as interactive video (between workstations, initially), embedded audio (in word processing documents, databases, and such), and other high-speed, network-oriented technologies become the norm, the need for network transmission speeds will increase dramatically and very quickly. My guess is that this is about two to three years out for most companies. That means plan now, install the right kind of fiber, and wait it out.

You will know that you are ready for FDDI when these things happen:

■ The Ethernet/802.3 or token ring/802.5 networks start exhibiting average load rates that exceed 30–50% of available load capability.

- Controller buffering and transmission rates exceed available resources.
- Nodes start to connect to more than an average of five to eight other systems (this is the average today, but it will increase with X Window terminals and the like).
- The cost of FDDI becomes reasonable enough that whether to install one of today's LAN technologies or FDDI becomes muddled (that is, the cost of the technologies are comparable).
- FDDI-to-other-LAN bridges become plentiful, and comparison shopping is possible.
- FDDI becomes embedded in purchased systems (some vendors will embed FDDI as the internal computer bus or as the connection bus between peripherals and CPUs).
- Your site becomes X Window terminal-happy (this will happen in the next couple of years as the cost of the terminals comes down).
- Data distribution between systems becomes the norm and not the exception.

There are many other tip-offs to the need for FDDI, but these will get you started.

Some FDDI Findings vs. Ethernet/802.3 Networks

I have an Ethernet/802.3 network in my house (I have one in the office too, but my house network is larger and better suited for testing). I am up to 26 nodes now, and I tend to beat it up pretty hard from time to time. Even at a 60% load, which is not the norm at 99% of the sites I visit, Ethernet/802.3 still does the job for me. Due to a contract I have right now to develop a high-speed network technology for a large customer, I installed an FDDI to interconnect two Ethernet/802.3 segments on my personal network. Here are some unscientific preliminary findings:

1. Ethernet backbones are no faster than FDDI backbones in my application (it is a distributed database and remote video-access application). My data is compressed enough to not tax an Ethernet (12% of cable load), so it is not any faster going over FDDI.
2. In some applications, such as diskless workstations accessing systems over a bridge, applications degraded due to bridge buffering problems. The degradation between FDDI and Ethernet versus Ethernet and Ethernet was about the same.
3. Controllers remain the single worst bottleneck.
4. I have been told by vendors that my findings are inaccurate. I find that hard to believe considering that I did the measurements and I did the comparisons with my tools and other tools on the market and I know I tested

them correctly, so how can *my* findings on *my* applications be inaccurate? To make sure, I had my findings checked for the way that I use the tools, and guess what? I was right for what I am doing.

5. The cost per actual transferred megabyte of data is much higher for FDDI, today, due to component cost and my not using the total bandwidth. Then again, I expected that and also expected that I would not use the entire bandwidth. Unfortunately, I could not buy half an FDDI.

6. Upgrading to a faster network technology also means upgrading the connected CPUs (network protocols are compute-bound, and faster transmission technology means faster transfers, more packets arriving more quickly, and so on). The single best improvement in overall data rate happened when the CPUs were upgraded to take advantage of additional network capabilities.

There are many other issues and measurements, but the bottom line is that I tax my network much more heavily than most customers of mine ever will. Further, I will admit to a little cheating: I have already installed quite a few FDDI networks at various places and not all of them have seen the performance improvements or throughput they were hoping for (I warned them, too). The worse thing is that I can't even use an FDDI properly (load-wise) in my application—and I know how to use one properly. So, the need for FDDI as a speedy network technology has not yet arrived. We also need to come up with better software architectures and protocols that can take advantage of what FDDI can do before we will see serious improvement.

Sure, some vendors are going to tell us all how wonderful FDDI is. No argument. As usual, we will see the multicolored "Gee, ain't it neat" ads in every trade publication and PBS special that exists. Many managers are going to see these ads, believe them, make buying decisions based on them, and get really infuriated when things don't work as advertised.

Sound familiar? I call it "Round 2 of x rounds."

These are the same people who try to get us to do data-over-voice on inadequate PBX configurations, risk whole networks on active hub repeaters simply because they are the latest hot product (there are good places for them), glass fiber to the terminal (which is grossly expensive on a per-connection basis), and so forth. Don't believe all the hoopla and hype—remember that selling is a science and it has been perfected for centuries. Computer science has only been around for less than one century.

So, install the right kind of fiber, use it for interconnections between your favorite LAN, and don't get too antsy to install FDDI. It's neat—a great technology—and will provide the path you will need in the future. In the meantime, try to use what you have to the fullest.

Good luck.

Summary

FDDI is an important new LAN/MAN technology. It provides a high-speed, re-dundant cabling environment for networks requiring a fast, highly available network environment. It is pricey, however, and it will be a while before it is cost-effective at the desktop level. In the meantime, it serves as a very useful backbone network technology or a system-internal interconnect technology. As networks evolve over the next few years, FDDI will be a central focus for LANs and should be a part of any well-conceived network scheme.

Protocol Identifiers for IEEE 802.3 and Ethernet V2.0   *A*

06-00	XEROX NS IDP		10-0A	Berkeley Trailer 10 Block
06-60	DLOG Olching, Germany		10-0B	Berkeley Trailer 11 Block
06-61	DLOG Olching, Germany		10-0C	Berkeley Trailer 12 Block
			10-0D	Berkeley Trailer 13 Block
08-00	TCP/IP Internet Protocol		10-0E	Berkeley Trailer 14 Block
08-01	X.75 Internet		10-0F	Berkeley Trailer 15 Block
08-02	NBS Internet			
08-03	ECMA Internet		16-00	VALID System Protocol
08-04	CHAOSnet			
08-05	X.25 Level 3		42-42	PCS Basic Block Protocol
08-06	TCP/IP Address Resolution			
08-07	Xerox NS Compatibility		52-08	BBN Simnet
08-1C	Symbolics Private			
08-88	Xyplex Terminal Server		60-00	DEC Experimental
08-89	Xyplex Parameter Server		60-01	DEC MOP Dump/Load
08-8A	Xyplex Reserved		60-02	DEC MOP Remote Console
			60-03	DEC Phase IV DNA Routing
09-00	Unger-Bass Network Debugger		60-04	DEC Local Area Transport
			60-05	DEC Diagnostics Protocol
0A-00	IEEE 802.3 PUP		60-06	DEC Customer Protocol
0A-01	IEEE 802.3 PUP Address		60-07	DEC LAVC–SCA
	Translation		60-08	DEC Amber
			60-09	DEC DSM/MUMPS
0B-AD	Banyan/Vines StreetTalk		60-10	3Com Reserved
			60-11	3Com Reserved
10-00	Berkeley Trailer Negotiation		60-12	3Com Reserved
10-01	Berkeley Trailer 1 Block		60-13	3Com Reserved
10-02	Berkeley Trailer 2 Block		60-14	3Com Reserved
10-03	Berkeley Trailer 3 Block			
10-04	Berkeley Trailer 4 Block		70-00	Ungermann-Bass Download
10-05	Berkeley Trailer 5 Block		70-01	Ungermann-Bass NIU Boot
10-06	Berkeley Trailer 6 Block		70-02	Ungermann-Bass NIU Translation
10-07	Berkeley Trailer 7 Block		70-05	Ungermann-Bass NIU Management
10-08	Berkeley Trailer 8 Block		70-07	OS/9 Microwave
10-09	Berkeley Trailer 9 Block		70-20	LRT Reserved

70-21	LRT Reserved		80-66	University of Massachusetts at
70-22	LRT Reserved			Amherst
70-23	LRT Reserved		80-67	Veeco Integrated Automation
70-24	LRT Reserved		80-68	General Dynamics
70-25	LRT Reserved		80-69	AT&T
70-26	LRT Reserved		80-6A	AutoPhon
70-27	LRT Reserved		80-6C	ComDesign
70-28	LRT Reserved		80-6D	Compugraphics Corporation
70-29	LRT Reserved		80-6E	Landmark Graphics Corporation
70-30	Proteon		80-6F	Landmark Graphics Corporation
70-34	Cabletron		80-70	Landmark Graphics Corporation
			80-71	Landmark Graphics Corporation
80-03	Cronus VLN		80-72	Landmark Graphics Corporation
80-04	Cronus Direct		80-73	Landmark Graphics Corporation
80-05	Hewlett-Packard Probe		80-74	Landmark Graphics Corporation
80-06	Nestar		80-75	Landmark Graphics Corporation
80-08	AT&T		80-76	Landmark Graphics Corporation
80-10	Excelan		80-77	Landmark Graphics Corporation
80-13	Silicon Graphics Diagnostics		80-7A	Matra
80-14	Silicon Graphics Net Games		80-7B	Dansk Data Elektronik
80-15	Silicon Graphics		80-7C	Merit Internodal
80-16	Silicon Graphics NameServer		80-7D	Vitalink Bridge Management
80-19	Apollo DOMAIN		80-7E	Vitalink Bridge Management
80-2E	TymShare		80-7F	Vitalink Bridge Management
80-2F	Tigan		80-80	Vitalink TransLAN III
80-35	Stanford University Reverse ARP		80-81	Counterpoint Computers
80-36	Aeonic Systems		80-82	Counterpoint Computers
80-38	DEC LANBridge Management		80-83	Counterpoint Computers
80-39	DEC DSM/DTP		80-88	Xyplex
80-3A	DEC Argonaut Console		80-89	Xyplex
80-3B	DEC VAX ELAN		80-8A	Xyplex
80-3C	DECnet DNA Naming Service		80-9B	EtherTalk (AppleTalk)
80-3D	DEC CSMA/CD Encryption		80-9C	Datability
80-3E	DECnet DNA Time Service		80-9D	Datability
80-3F	DEC LAN Traffic Monitor		80-9E	Datability
80-40	DEC NetBIOS Emulator		80-9F	Spider LAN Monitor
80-41	DEC Local Area System Transport		80-A3	Nixdorf Computers
80-42	DEC Unassigned		80-A4	Siemens Gammasonics Inc.
80-44	Planning Research Corporation		80-A5	Siemens Gammasonics Inc.
80-46	AT&T		80-A6	Siemens Gammasonics Inc.
80-47	AT&T		80-A7	Siemens Gammasonics Inc.
80-49	ExperData		80-A8	Siemens Gammasonics Inc.
80-5B	Stanford V Kernel Exp.		80-A9	Siemens Gammasonics Inc.
80-5C	Stanford V Kernel Prod.		80-AA	Siemens Gammasonics Inc.
80-5D	Evans & Sutherland		80-AB	Siemens Gammasonics Inc.
80-60	Little Machines		80-AC	Siemens Gammasonics Inc.
80-62	Counterpoint Computers		80-AD	Siemens Gammasonics Inc.
80-65	University of Massachusetts at		80-AE	Siemens Gammasonics Inc.
	Amherst		80-AF	Siemens Gammasonics Inc.

80-B0	Siemens Gammasonics Inc.	80-F4	AppleTalk (Kinetics)
80-B1	Siemens Gammasonics Inc.	80-F5	AppleTalk (Kinetics)
80-B2	Siemens Gammasonics Inc.	80-F7	Apollo Computers
80-B3	Siemens Gammasonics Inc.	80-FF	Wellfleet Communications
80-C0	DCA Data Exchange Cluster		
80-C1	DCA Data Exchange Cluster	81-00	Wellfleet Communications
80-C2	DCA Data Exchange Cluster	81-01	Wellfleet Communications
80-C3	DCA Data Exchange Cluster	81-02	Wellfleet Communications
80-C4	Banyan Systems	81-03	Wellfleet Communications
80-C5	Banyan Systems	81-07	Symbolics Private
80-C6	Pacer Software	81-08	Symbolics Private
80-C7	Applitek Corporation	81-09	Symbolics Private
80-C8	Intergraph Corporation	81-30	Waterloo Microsystems
80-C9	Intergraph Corporation	81-31	VG Laboratory Systems
80-CA	Intergraph Corporation	81-32	Bridge Communications
80-CB	Intergraph Corporation	81-33	Bridge Communications
80-CC	Intergraph Corporation	81-34	Bridge Communications
80-CD	Harris Corporation	81-35	Bridge Communications
80-CE	Harris Corporation	81-36	Bridge Communications
80-CF	Taylor Instrument	81-37	Novell
80-D0	Taylor Instrument	81-38	Novell
80-D1	Taylor Instrument	81-39	KTI San Jose
80-D2	Taylor Instrument	81-3A	KTI San Jose
80-D3	Rosemont Corporation	81-3B	KTI San Jose
80-D4	Rosemont Corporation	81-3C	KTI San Jose
80-D5	IBM SNA Services	81-3D	KTI San Jose
80-DD	Varian Associates	81-48	Logicraft
80-DE	Integrated Solutions TRFS	81-49	Network Computing Devices
80-DF	Integrated Solutions	81-4A	Alpha Micro
80-E0	Allen-Bradley	81-4C	SNMP
80-E1	Allen-Bradley	81-4D	BIIN
80-E2	Allen-Bradley	81-4E	BIIN
80-E3	Allen-Bradley	81-4F	Network Professor Management
80-E4	Datability	81-50	Rational Corporation
80-E5	Datability	81-51	Qualcomm
80-E6	Datability	81-52	Qualcomm
80-E7	Datability	81-53	Qualcomm
80-E8	Datability	81-5C	Computer Protocol Pty Ltd.
80-E9	Datability	81-5D	Computer Protocol Pty Ltd.
80-EA	Datability	81-5E	Computer Protocol Pty Ltd.
80-EB	Datability	81-64	Charles River Data Systems
80-EC	Datability	81-65	Charles River Data Systems
80-ED	Datability	81-66	Charles River Data Systems
80-EE	Datability	81-7D	Protocol Engines
80-EF	Datability	81-7E	Protocol Engines
80-F0	Datability	81-7F	Protocol Engines
80-F2	Retix	81-80	Protocol Engines
80-F3	AppleTalk Address Resolution Protocol	81-81	Protocol Engines
		81-82	Protocol Engines

81-83	Protocol Engines	81-DA	Artisoft
81-84	Protocol Engines	81-DB	Artisoft
81-85	Protocol Engines	81-DC	Artisoft
81-86	Protocol Engines	81-DD	Artisoft
81-87	Protocol Engines	81-E6	Polygon
81-88	Protocol Engines	81-E7	Polygon
81-89	Protocol Engines	81-E8	Polygon
81-8A	Protocol Engines	81-E9	Polygon
81-8B	Protocol Engines	81-EA	Polygon
81-8C	Protocol Engines	81-EB	Polygon
81-8D	Motorola Computer X	81-EC	Polygon
81-9A	Qualcomm	81-ED	Polygon
81-9B	Qualcomm	81-EE	Polygon
81-9C	Qualcomm	81-EF	Polygon
81-9D	Qualcomm	81-F0	COMSAT Laboratories
81-9E	Qualcomm	81-F1	COMSAT Laboratories
81-9F	Qualcomm	81-F2	COMSAT Laboratories
81-A0	Qualcomm	81-F3	Science Applications International
81-A1	Qualcomm	81-F4	Science Applications International
81-A2	Qualcomm	81-F5	Science Applications International
81-A3	Qualcomm	81-F6	VG Analytical Ltd.
81-A4	ARAI Bunkichi	81-F7	VG Analytical Ltd.
81-A5	RAD Network Devices	81-F8	VG Analytical Ltd.
81-A6	RAD Network Devices		
81-A7	RAD Network Devices	82-03	Quantum Software Systems
81-A8	RAD Network Devices	82-04	Quantum Software Systems
81-A9	RAD Network Devices	82-05	Quantum Software Systems
81-AA	RAD Network Devices	82-21	Ascom Banking Systems
81-AB	RAD Network Devices	82-22	Ascom Banking Systems
81-AC	RAD Network Devices	82-3E	Advanced Encryption Systems
81-AD	RAD Network Devices	82-3F	Advanced Encryption Systems
81-AE	RAD Network Devices	82-40	Advanced Encryption Systems
81-B7	Xyplex	82-7F	Athena Programming
81-B8	Xyplex	82-80	Athena Programming
81-B9	Xyplex	82-81	Athena Programming
81-CC	Apricot Computers	82-82	Athena Programming
81-CD	Apricot Computers	82-8A	Network-1 Remote Activation
81-CE	Apricot Computers	82-8B	Network-1 Network Loader
81-CF	Apricot Computers	82-8C	Network-1 Reserved #14
81-D0	Apricot Computers	82-8D	Network-1 Reserved #13
81-D1	Apricot Computers	82-8E	Network-1 Reserved #12
81-D2	Apricot Computers	82-8F	Network-1 Reserved #11
81-D3	Apricot Computers	82-90	Network-1 Reserved #10
81-D4	Apricot Computers	82-91	Network-1 Reserved #9
81-D5	Apricot Computers	82-92	Network-1 Reserved #8
81-D6	Artisoft	82-93	Network-1 Reserved #7
81-D7	Artisoft	82-94	Network-1 Reserved #6
81-D8	Artisoft	82-95	Network-1 Reserved #5
81-D9	Artisoft	82-96	Network-1 Reserved #4

82-97	Network-1 Reserved #3		FF-02	ISC-Bunker Ramo
82-98	Network-1 Reserved #2		FF-03	ISC-Bunker Ramo
82-99	Network-1 Reserved #1		FF-04	ISC-Bunker Ramo
			FF-05	ISC-Bunker Ramo
90-00	Loopback Protocol		FF-06	ISC-Bunker Ramo
90-01	3Com XNS Bridge Management		FF-07	ISC-Bunker Ramo
90-02	3Com Bridge TCP/IP System Management		FF-08	ISC-Bunker Ramo
			FF-09	ISC-Bunker Ramo
90-03	3Com Bridge Network Management		FF-0A	ISC-Bunker Ramo
			FF-0B	ISC-Bunker Ramo
AA-AA	EtherTalk Phase II		FF-0C	ISC-Bunker Ramo
			FF-0D	ISC-Bunker Ramo
AF-AF	LogiCraft PC/286 Server		FF-0E	ISC-Bunker Ramo
			FF-0F	ISC-Bunker Ramo
FF-00	BBN Vital-LANBridge Cache			
FF-01	ISC-Bunker Ramo			

Hardware Vendor Prefixes for IEEE 802.3 and Ethernet V2.0   B

00-00-0C	Cisco	00-00-D8	3Com, Novell–PS/2
00-00-0F	NeXT	00-00-DD	Gould
00-00-10	Sytek	00-00-DE	Unigraph
00-00-1D	Cabletron	00-00-E2	Acer Counterpoint
00-00-20	DIAB (Data Industrier AB)	00-00-EF	Alantec
00-00-22	Visual Technology	00-00-FD	High Level Hardware (Orion, U.K.)
00-00-2A	TRW		
00-00-5A	S & Koch	00-01-02	BBN–BBN Internal Usage (Not Registered)
00-00-5E	U.S. Department of Defense		
00-00-65	Network General	00-08-52	Technically Elite Concepts
00-00-6B	MIPS	00-17-00	Kabel
00-00-77	MIPS	00-80-2D	Xylogics (Including New "Encore" Annexes)
00-00-7A	Ardent		
00-00-89	Cayman Systems–Gatorbox	00-80-8C	Frontier Software Development
00-00-93	Proteon	00-AA-00	Intel
00-00-9F	Ameristar Technology	00-DD-00	Ungermann-Bass
00-00-A2	Wellfleet	00-DD-01	Ungermann-Bass
00-00-A3	Network Application Technology		
00-00-A6	Network General (Internal Assignment, Not for Products)	02-04-06	BBN–BBN Internal Usage (Not Registered)
		02-07-01	MICOM/Interlan, UNIBUS or QBUS Machines, Apollo
00-00-A7	NCD–X-Terminals	02-60-86	Satelcom MegaPac (U.K.)
00-00-A9	Network Systems	02-60-8C	3Com, EBM PC; Imagen; Valid; Cisco
00-00-AA	Xerox–Xerox Machines		
00-00-B3	CIMLinc	02-CF-1F	CMC, Masscomp; Silicon Graphics; Prime EXL
00-00-B7	Dove–Fastnet		
00-00-BC	Allen-Bradley		
00-00-C0	Western Digital	08-00-02	3Com (Formerly Bridge)
00-00-C6	HP Intelligent Networks Operation (Formerly Eon Systems)	08-00-03	Advanced Computer Communications
		08-00-05	Symbolics–Symbolics LISP Machines
00-00-C8	Altos		
00-00-C9	Emulex–Terminal Servers	08-00-08	BBN
00-00-D7	Dartmouth College (NED Router)	08-00-09	Hewlett-Packard

08-00-0A	Nestar Systems	08-00-4E	BICC
08-00-0B	Unisys	08-00-56	Stanford University
08-00-11	Excelan, BBN Butterfly, Masscomp, Silicon Graphics	08-00-58	DECsystem-20
		08-00-5A	IBM
08-00-17	NSC	08-00-67	Comdesign
08-00-1A	Data General	08-00-68	Ridge
08-00-1B	Data General	08-00-69	Silicon Graphics
08-00-1E	Apollo	08-00-6E	Excelan
08-00-20	Sun–Sun Machines	08-00-75	DDE (Danish Data Elektronik A/S)
08-00-22	NBI		
08-00-25	CDC	08-00-7C	Vitalink–TransLAN III
08-00-26	Norsk Data (Nord)	08-00-80	XIOS
08-00-27	PCS Computer Systems GmbH	08-00-86	Imagen/QMS
08-00-28	TI–Explorer	08-00-87	Xyplex
08-00-2B	DIGITAL	08-00-89	Kenetics–AppleTalk-Ethernet interface
08-00-2E	Metaphor		
08-00-2F	Prime Computer–50-Series LHC300	08-00-8B	Pyramid
		08-00-8D	XyVision–XyVision Machines
08-00-36	Intergraph–CAE Stations	08-00-90	Retix Inc.
08-00-37	Fujitsu–Xerox		
08-00-38	Bull	48-44-53	HDS
08-00-39	Spider Systems		
08-00-3E	Motorola–SIMNET Machines	AA-00-00	DIGITAL
08-00-41	DCA Digital Comm. Assoc.	AA-00-01	DIGITAL
08-00-45	Xylogics	AA-00-02	DIGITAL
08-00-46	Sony	AA-00-03	DIGITAL–Global Physical Address
08-00-47	Sequent		
08-00-49	Univation	AA-00-04	DIGITAL–Logical Address for DECNET
08-00-4C	Encore		

Note: The author does not necessarily endorse or warrant any of the vendors listed. This list is included so that the reader may easily find products and services necessary in the configuration, management, troubleshooting, and support of Ethernet/802.3 networks.

Accounting Software

Computer Associates
711 Stewart Avenue
Garden City, NY 11530
800-531-5236

Core Software
26303 Oak Ridge Drive
Spring, TX 77380
713-298-1492

Cougar Mountain Software
2609 Kootenai
P.O. Box 6886
Boise, ID 83606
800-388-3038

DacEasy
17950 Preston Road, Suite 800
Dallas, TX 75252
800-877-8088

Danyl
1509 Glen Avenue
Moorestown, NJ 08052
800-732-6868

Datamar Systems
8568 Miramar Place
San Diego, CA 92107
800-223-9963

Dragonslayer Systems
2275 Swallowhill Road, Building 800
Pittsburgh, PA 15220
800-447-2522

Dynamic Software
109 South Main Street
Greer, SC 29650
803-877-1122

Expandable Software
10080 North Wolfe Road
Cupertino, CA 95014
408-253-7715

Great Plains Software
1701 38th Street, SW
Fargo, ND 58103
800-456-0025

IBM Desktop Software
3301 Windy Ridge Parkway
Marietta, GA 30067
800-426-7699

Macola
333 East Center Street
Marion, OH 43302
800-468-0834

Microx
9444 Old Katy Road
Houston, TX 77055
800-833-4990

Open Systems
7626 Golden Triangle Drive
Eden Prairie, MN 55344
800-328-2276

RealWorld
292 Loudon Road
Concord, NH 03301
800-678-6336

Solomon Software
1218 Commerce Parkway
Findlay, OH 45839
800-879-2767

Tofias, Fleishman, Shapiro, and Company
205 Broadway
Cambridge, MA 02139
617-547-5900

Asynchronous Communications Servers

3Com
5400 Bayfront Plaza
Santa Clara, CA 95052
800-638-3266

Concept Development Systems
P.O. Drawer 1988
Dennesaw, GA 30144
404-424-6240

Cross Communications
1881 Ninth Street, Suite 212
Boulder, CO 80302
303-444-7799

Crystal Point
22122 20th Avenue, SE, Suite 148
Bothell, WA 98021
206-487-3656

Cubix
2800 Lockheed Way
Carson City, NV 89706
800-829-0550

David Systems
701 East Evelyn Avenue
Sunnyvale, CA 94086
800-762-7848

Emulex
3545 Harbor Boulevard
Costa Mesa, CA 92626
800-368-5393

Gateway Communications
2941 Alton Avenue
Irvine, CA 92714
800-367-6555

IBM
Old Orchard Road
Armonk, NY 10504
800-426-2468
800-426-3333

Intercomputer Communications
8230 Montgomery Road
Cincinnati, OH 45236
513-745-0327

J & L Information Systems
9238 Deering Avenue
Chatsworth, CA 91311
818-709-1778

Lanmaster
1401 North 14th Street
Temple, TX 76501
817-771-2124

Microtest
3519 East Shea Boulevard, Suite 134
Phoenix, AZ 85028
800-526-9675

Multi-Tech Systems
2205 Woodale Drive
Mounds View, MN 55112
800-328-9717

Network Products
1440 West Colorado Boulevard
Pasadena, CA 91105
800-638-7765

Novell
122 East 1700 South
Provo, UT 84606
800-638-9273

Penril DataComm Networks
1300 Quince Orchard Boulevard
Gaithersburg, MD 20878
800-473-6745

Photoring
440 Portafino Court, Suite 112
Pomona, CA 91766
714-620-5370

Shiva
One Cambridge Center
Cambridge, MA 02112
800-458-3550

Softronics
5085 List Drive
Colorado Springs, CO 80919
800-225-8590

Star Gate Technologies
29300 Aurora Road
Solon, OH 44139
800-782-7428

Telebit
1315 Chesapeake Terrace
Sunnyvale, CA 94089
800-835-3248

Triton Technologies
200 Middlesex Turnpike
Iselin, NJ 08830
908-855-9440

Ungermann-Bass
3900 Freedom Circle
Santa Clara, CA 95054
800-873-6381

Bridges

3Com
5400 Bayfront Plaza
Santa Clara, CA 95052
800-638-3266

Accton Technology
46750 Fremont Boulevard, Building 104
Fremont, CA 94538
800-926-9288

Advanced Computer Communications
720 Santa Barbara Street
Santa Barbara, CA 93101
800-444-7854

Alantec
47800 Westinghouse Drive
Fremont, CA 94539
800-727-1050

Allied Telesis
575 East Middlefield Road
Mountain View, CA 94043
800-424-4284

Andrew
2771 Plaza Del Amo
Torrance, CA 90503
800-733-0331

Applitek
100 Brickstone Square
Andover, MA 01810
508-475-4050

Artel Communications
22 Kane Industrial Drive
Hudson, MA 01749
800-225-0228

AT&T
One Speedwell Avenue
Morristown, NJ 07960
800-247-1212

BICC Communications
103 Millbury Street
Auburn, MA 01501
800-447-6526

Cabletron Systems
35 Industrial Way
P.O. Box 5005
Rochester, NH 03867
603-332-4616

Caliber Tek
353 Vintage Park Drive
Foster City, CA 94404
415-570-4233

Canoga-Perkins
21012 Lassen Street
Chatsworth, CA 91311
818-718-6300

Chipcom
118 Turnpike Road
Southborough, MA 01772
800-228-9930

Cisco Systems
1525 O'Brien Drive
Menlo Park, CA 94025
800-553-6387

Clearpoint Research
35 Parkwood Drive
Hopkinton, MA 01748
800-253-2778

Codex/Motorola
20 Cabot Boulevard
Mansfield, MA 02048
800-426-1212

CrossComm
133 East Main Street
P.O. Box 699
Marlborough, MA 01752
508-481-4060

David Systems
701 East Evelyn Avenue
Sunnyvale, CA 94086
800-762-7848

Develcon Electronics
515 Consumers Road, Suite 500
Willowdale, Ontario M2J 4Z2
800-667-9333

Digital Equipment Corporation
146 Main Street
Maynard, MA 01754
800-343-4040

DuPont Electro-Optic Products
P.O. Box 13625
Research Triangle Park, NC 27709
800-888-5261

FiberCom
3353 Orange Avenue, NE
Roanoke, VA 24012
800-423-1183

Fibermux
9310 Topanga Canyon Boulevard
Chatsworth, CA 91311
818-709-6000

Fibronics
One Communications Way
Hyannis, MA 12601
800-327-9526

General DataComm
1475 Straits Turnpike
Middlebury, CT 06762
203-574-1118

Graybar Electric
34 North Meramec
Clayton, MO 63105
314-727-3900

Hewlett-Packard
19310 Pruneridge
Cupertino, CA 95014
800-752-0900

Hughes LAN Systems
1225 Charleston Road
Mountain View, CA 94043
415-966-7300

IBM
Old Orchard Road
Armonk, NY 10504
800-426-2468
800-426-3333

In-Net
15150 Avenue of Science, Suite 100
San Diego, CA 92128
800-283-3334

Intellicom
20415 Nordhoff Street
Chatsworth, CA 91311
818-407-3900

Kalpana
125 Nicholson Lane
San Jose, CA 95134
800-488-0775

LAN-Link
744 Goddard Avenue
St. Louis, MO 63005
314-537-9800

Lancast/Casat Technology
10 Northern Boulevard, Unit 5
Amherst, NH 03031
800-752-2768

Lannet Data Communications
7711 Center Avenue, Suite 600
Huntington Beach, CA 92647
800-969-4123

LanWan Technologies
1566 La Pradera Drive
Campbell, CA 95008
408-374-8190

Madge Networks
42 Airport Parkway
San Jose, CA 95110
800-876-2343

Memotec Data
40 High Street
North Andover, MA 01845
508-681-0600

Microcom
500 River Ridge Drive
Norwood, MA 02062
800-822-8224

Netronix
1372 North McDowell Boulevard
Petaluma, CA 94954
800-282-2535

Network-1
P.O. Box 8370
Long Island City, NY 11101
718-932-7599

Network Application Technology
1686 Dell Avenue
Campbell, CA 95008
800-543-8887

Network Equipment Technologies
800 Saginaw Drive
Redwood City, CA 04963
800-234-4638

Network Systems
7600 Boone Avenue North
Minneapolis, MN 55428
612-424-4888

Newbridge Networks
593 Herndon Parkway
Herndon, VA 22070
800-332-1080

Olicom
1002 North Central Expressway, Suite 289
Richardson, TX 75080
214-680-8131

Optical Data Systems
1101 East Arapahoe
Richardson, TX 75081
214-234-6400

Penril DataComm Networks
1300 Quince Orchard Boulevard
Gaithersburg, MD 20878
800-473-6745

Performance Technology
7800 IH 10 West, Suite 800
San Antonio, TX 78230
210-349-2000

Persoft
465 Science Drive
Madison, WI 53711
800-368-5283

Plexcom
65 Moreland Road
Simi Valley, CA 93065
805-522-3333

PureData
180 West Beaver Creek Road
Richmond Hill, Ontario L4B 1B4
416-731-6444

Racal Interlan
155 Swanson Road
Boxborough, MA 01719
800-526-8255

RAD Network Devices
7711 Center Avenue, Suite 600
Huntington Beach, CA 92647
800-969-4723

Retix
2644 30th Street
Santa Monica, CA 90405
800-225-2333

SynOptics Communications
4401 Great America Parkway
P.O. Box 51815
Santa Clara, CA 95052
800-776-6895

TCL
41829 Albrae Street
Fremont, CA 94538
415-657-3800

Technically Elite Concepts
2615 Pacific Coast Highway, Suite 322
Hermosa Beach, CA 90254
310-379-2505

Timeplex
400 Chestnut Ridge Road
Woodcliff Lake, NJ 07675
800-755-8526

Ungermann-Bass
3900 Freedom Circle
Santa Clara, CA 95054
800-873-6381

Vitalink Communications
6607 Kaiser Drive
Fremont, CA 94555
800-443-5740

Xyplex
330 Codmin Hill Road
Boxborough, MA 01709
508-264-9900

Cable

3M Private Networks
6801 Riverplace Boulevard
Austin, TX 78769
800-745-7459

AMP
P.O. Box 3608, M/S 210-26
Harrisburg, PA 17105
800-522-6752

Apple Computer
20525 Mariani Avenue
Cupertino, CA 95014
800-776-2333

Belden Wire and Cable/Cooper Industries
P.O. Box 1980
Richmond, IN 47375
800-235-3361

Belkin Components
1303 Walnut Parkway
Compton, CA 90220
800-223-5546

BICC Communications
103 Millbury Street
Auburn, MA 01501
800-447-6526

BJM Electronics
2589 Richmond Terrace
Staten Island, NY 10303
800-342-5256

C Enterprises
3110-110 Via Vera Cruz
San Marcos, CA 92069
800-334-3815

Cable Techniques
7933 Silverton Avenue, Suite 716
San Diego, CA 92126
619-695-3533

Chromatic Technologies
31 Hayward Street
Franklin, MA 02038
800-473-1203

Comm/Scope, Network Cable Division
3642 Highway 60
East Claremont, NC 28610
800-982-1708

Communication Cable
P.O. Box 600
Wayne, PA 19087
215-644-1900

Compu-Link Cable Assemblies
13100 56th Street, Suite 705
Clearwater, FL 34620
800-231-6685

Danbru Wire and Cable
11630 Coley River Circle
Fountain Valley, CA 92708
800-432-6278

Data Set Cable
748 Danbury Road
Ridgefield, CT 06877
800-344-9684

DNA Networks
351 Phoenixville Pike
Malvern, PA 19355
800-999-3622

Eagle Technology
1160 Ridder Park Drive
San Jose, CA 95131
408-452-2267

FOCS
93 Grand Street
Worcester, MA 01610
508-757-0611

Fotec
529 Main Street
P.O. Box 246
Boston, MA 02129
800-537-8254

Graybar Electric
34 North Meramec
Clayton, MO 63105
314-727-3900

Illinois Computer Cable
1404 Sherman Road
Romeoville, IL 60441
800-326-2320

Link Computer
560 South Melrose Street
Placentia, CA 92670
714-993-0800

Lynn Products
1601 Loch Ness Place
Torrance, CA 90501
800-634-5093

Madison Cable
125 Goddard Memorial Drive
Worcester, MA 01603
508-752-7320

MBA Technique
Number 239-4 Kin Hwa Street
Taipei, Taiwan R.O.C.
8862-341-1260

Mitsubishi International
520 Madison Avenue
New York, NY 10022
212-605-2392

Mod-Tap
285 Ayer Road
P.O. Box 706
Harvard, MA 01451
508-662-5630

Mohawk Wire and Cable
9 Mohawk Drive
Leominster, MA 01453
800-422-9961

NEK Cable
110 Orville Drive
Bohemia, NY 11716
800-645-1715

Optical Cable
P.O. Box 11967
Roanoke, VA 24022
800-622-7711

Optical Fiber Technologies
2 Liberty Way
Westford, MA 01886
800-937-6384

Remee Products
186 North Main Street
Florida, NY 10921
800-431-3864

Royal Cable
155 34th Street
Brooklyn, NY 11232
718-499-6853

SBD Cable Products
4744 Baltimore Avenue
Hyattsville, MD 20781
301-864-9200

Shaxon Industries
4950 East Hunter Avenue
Anaheim, CA 92807
800-345-8295

Siecor
489 Siecor Park
P.O. Box 489
Hickory, NC 28603
800-634-9064

Siemon
76 Westbury Park Road
P.O. Box 400
Watertown, CT 06795
203-274-2523

South Hills Datacomm
760 Beechnut Drive
Pittsburgh, PA 15205
800-245-6215

SSI The Shop
Drawer Z
Manor, TX 78653
512-990-2233

TCL
41829 Albrae Street
Fremont, CA 94538
415-657-3800

Thomas-Conrad
1908-R Dramer Lane
Austin, TX 78758
800-332-8683

Unicom Electric
11980 Telegraph Road, Suite 103
Santa Fe Springs, CA 90670
800-346-6668

Cable-Testing Equipment

3Com
5400 Bayfront Plaza
Santa Clara, CA 95052
800-638-3266

Beckman Industrial
3883 Ruffin Road
San Diego, CA 92123
800-854-2708

BICC Communications
103 Millbury Street
Auburn, MA 01501
800-447-6526

BJM Electronics
2589 Richmond Terrace
Staten Island, NY 10303
800-342-5256

Calan
1776 Independence Drive
Dingmans Ferry, PA 18328
717-828-2456

Digitech Industries
66 Grove Street
Ridgefield, CT 06877
203-438-4184

EXFO E.O. Engineering
352 St. Sacrement Avenue
Quebec City, Quebec G1N 3Y2
800-284-8509

Fotec
529 Main Street
P.O. Box 246
Boston, MA 02129
800-537-8254

Graybar Electric
34 North Meramec
Clayton, MO 63105
314-727-3900

Hewlett-Packard
19310 Pruneridge
Cupertino, CA 95014
800-752-0900

Hewlett-Packard, Colorado Telecom Division
5070 Centennial Boulevard
Colorado Springs, CO 80919
719-531-4414

Laser Precision
109 North Genessee Street
Utica, NY 13502
315-797-4449

Microtest
3519 East Shea Boulevard, Suite 134
Phoenix, AZ 85028
800-526-9675

Mod-Tap
285 Ayer Road
P.O. Box 706
Harvard, MA 01451
508-662-5630

Netcom Systems
21828 Lassen Street, Unit F
Chatsworth, CA 91311
818-700-0111

Network Communications Corporation
10120 West 76th Street
Eden Prairie, MN 55344-9814
612-944-8559

Noyes Fiber Systems
Belmont Business Park
P.O. Box 398
Laconia, NH 03247
603-528-2025

PureData
180 West Beaver Creek Road
Richmond Hill, Ontario L4B 1B4
416-731-6444

Riser-Bond Instruments
5101 North 57th Street
Lincoln, NE 68507
800-688-8377

Siecor
489 Siecor Park
P.O. Box 489
Hickory, NC 28603
800-634-9064

Siemon
76 Westbury Park Road
P.O. Box 400
Watertown, CT 06795
203-274-2523

Spider Systems
12 New England Executive Park
Burlington, MA 01803
800-447-7807

Standard Microsystems
35 Marcus Boulevard
Hauppauge, NY 11788
516-273-3100

Star-Tek
71 Lynan Street
Northborough, MA 01532
800-225-8528

TCL
41829 Albrae Street
Fremont, CA 94538
415-657-3800

Tektronix
P.O. Box 1197
Redmond, OR 97756
800-833-9200

Thomas and Betts
1001 Frontier Road
Bridgewater, NJ 98897
908-685-1600

Wilcom Products
P.O. Box 508
Laconia, NH 03247
800-222-1898

Database Front Ends

Advanced Business Microsystems
15615 Alton Parkway, Suite 300
Irvine, CA 92718
800-999-1809

Arche Technologies
48881 Dato Road
Fremont,CA 94539
800-422-4674

Borland
1800 Green Hills Road
Scotts Valley, CA 95067
408-438-8400

Channel Computing
63 Main Street
Newmarket, NH 03857
800-289-0053

Concentric Data Systems
110 Turnpike Road
Westborough, MA 01581
800-325-9035

DataEase
7 Cambridge Drive
Trumbull, CT 06611
800-243-3374

Gupta Technologies
1040 Marsh Road
Menlo Park, CA 94025
800-876-3267

Imara Research
111 Peter Street, Suite 804
Toronto, Ontario M5V 2HI
416-581-1740

Information Builders
1250 Broadway
New York, NY 10001
800-969-4636

MDBS
P.O. Box 6089
Lafayette, IN 47903
317-447-1122

Novell
122 East 1700 South
Provo, UT 84606
800-638-9273

Oracle
20 Davis Drive
Belmont, CA 94002
800-633-0598

Progress Software
5 Oak Park
Bedford, MA 01730
617-275-4595

Database Software

Answer Software
20045 Stevens Creek Boulevard
Cupertino, CA 95014
408-253-7515

Data Access
14000 Southwest 119th Avenue
Miami, FL 33186
300-451-3539

DataEase
7 Cambridge Drive
Trumbull, CT 06611
800-243-3374

Emis Software
901 Northeast Loop 410, Suite 526
San Antonio, TX 78209
800-658-1000

Empress Software
6401 Golden Triangle Drive
Greenbelt, MD 20770
301-220-1919

ESP Computer Systems
625 North 19th Avenue
East Newton, IA 50208
800-245-6934

Fox Software
134 West South Boundary
Perrysburg, OH 43551
800-836-3692

Gupta Technologies
1040 Marsh Road
Menlo Park, CA 94025
800-876-3267

Information Builders
1250 Broadway
New York, NY 10001
800-969-4636

MDBS
P.O. Box 6089
Lafayette, IN 47903
317-447-1122

Microsoft
One Microsoft Way
Redmond, WA 98052
800-227-6444

Novell
122 East 1700 South
Provo, UT 84606
800-638-9273

Oracle
20 Davis Drive
Belmont, CA 94002
800-633-0598

Progress Software
5 Oak Park
Bedford, MA 01730
617-275-4595

QNE
136 Granite Hill Court
Langhorne, PA 19047
800-333-0448

Revelation Technologies
2 Park Avenue
New York, NY 10016
800-262-4747

The Small Computer Company
41 Saw Mill River Road
Hawthorne, NY 10532
800-847-4740

Unlimited Processing
8647 Bay Pine Road, Suite 208
Jacksonville, FL 32256
800-874-8555

Diskless Workstations

3Com
5400 Bayfront Plaza
Santa Clara, CA 95052
800-638-3266

Accton Technology
46750 Fremont Boulevard, Building 104
Fremont, CA 94538
800-926-9288

Acer America
401 Charcot Avenue
San Jose, CA 95131
800-733-2237

Alloy Computer Products
165 Forest Street
Marlborough, MA 01752
800-800-2556

American Research
1101 Monterey Pass Road
Monterey Park, CA 91754
213-269-1174

Caliber Tek
353 Vintage Park Drive
Foster City, CA 94404
415-570-4233

CNet Technology
2199 Zanker Road
San Jose, CA 95131
800-486-2638

Compaq Computer
P.O. Box 692000
Houston, TX 77069
800-231-0900

Compex
4055 East La Palma, Suite C
Anaheim, CA 92807
714-630-7302

Cubix
2800 Lockheed Way
Carson City, NV 89706
800-829-0550

Datamedia
20 Trafalgar Square
Nashua, NH 03063
800-362-4636

Lanmaster
1401 North 14th Street
Temple, TX 76501
817-771-2124

Link Computer
560 South Melrose Street
Placentia, CA 92670
714-993-0800

NCR
1334 South Patterson Boulevard
Dayton, OH 45479
513-445-5000

The Network Connection
1324 Union Hill Road
Alpharetta, GA 30201
800-327-4853

Samsung Information Systems
3655 North First Street
San Jose, CA 95134
800-624-8999

Top Microsystems
3022 Scott Boulevard
Santa Clara, CA 95054
800-437-8721

Unisys
P.O. Box 500
Blue Bell, PA 19424
215-986-4011

U-tron
47381 Bayside Parkway
Fremont, CA 94538
415-656-3600

Disk Subsystems

Ciprico
2955 Xenium Lane
Plymouth, MN 55441
612-559-2934

Consan
14625 Martin Drive
Eden Prairie, MN 55344
800-229-3475

Core
7171 North Federal Highway
Boca Raton, FL 33487
407-997-6055

Cubix
2800 Lockheed Way
Carson City, NV 89706
800-829-0550

Fujitsu America
3055 Orchard Drive
San Jose, CA 95134
800-626-4686

Lagacy Storage Systems
200 Butterfield Drive, Unit B
Ashland, MA 01721
508-881-6442

Maximum Strategy
2185 Old Oakland Road
San Jose, CA 95131
800-465-8895

Mega Drive Systems
489 South Robertson
Beverly Hills, CA 90212
800-322-4744

MicroNet Technology
20 Mason Street
Irvine, CA 92718
714-837-6033

Morton Management
12079 Tech Road
Silver Spring, MD 20904
800-548-5744

NCR
1334 South Patterson Boulevard
Dayton, OH 45479
513-445-5000

Perisol Technology
3350 Scott Boulevard, Building 1201
Santa Clara, CA 95054
800-447-8226

Priam Systems
1140 Ringwood
San Jose, CA 95131
408-954-8680

Sanyo/Icon
764 East Timpanogos Parkway
Orem, UT 84057
800-872-7266

Storage Dimensions
2145 Hamilton Avenue
San Jose, CA 95125
800-879-0300

Document Managers

ACS Telecom
25825 Eshelman Avenue
Lomita, CA 90717
800-325-0425

Aim Systems
1130-D Burnett Avenue
Concord, CA 94520
415-682-7922

Circle Development
5986 Knight Arnold Road
Memphis, TN 38115
800-676-0333

Compaq Computer
P.O. Box 692000
Houston, TX 77069
800-231-0900

Danyl
1509 Glen Avenue
Moorestown, NJ 08052
800-732-6868

Gazelle Systems
305 North 500 West
Provo, UT 84601
800-786-3278

Greengage Development
1250 Oakmead Parkway, Suite 210
Sunnyvale, CA 94088
408-773-0366

Interpreter
11455 West 48th Avenue
Wheat Ridge, CO 80033
800-232-4687

PC Docs
124 Marriott Drive, Suite 203
Tallahassee, FL 32301
904-942-3627

R+R Associates
39 Carwall Avenue
Mount Vernon, NY 10552
914-668-4057

Saros
10900 Northeast Eighth Street, Suite 700
Bellevue, WA 98004
800-827-2767

SoftSolutions Technology
3801 South Stewart Avenue, Suite 115
Orem, UT 84058
801-226-6000

Unlimited Processing
8647 Bay Pine Road, Suite 208
Jacksonville, FL 32256
800-874-8555

ViewStar
5820 Shellmound Street, Suite 600
Emeryville, CA 94608
415-841-8565

Electronic Mail

3Com
5400 Bayfront Plaza
Santa Clara, CA 95052
800-638-3266

3rd Planet Software
9819 National Boulevard, Suite 2
Los Angeles, CA 90034
213-841-2260

Banyan Systems
120 Flanders Road
Westborough, MA 01581
508-898-1000

CE Software
1801 Industrial Circle West
Des Moines, IA 50265
800-523-7638

Citadel Systems
P.O. Box 7219
The Woodlands, TX 77387
800-962-0701

Connex Systems
341 Courtland Drive
Rockford, MI 49351
800-748-0212

Cross Communications
1881 Ninth Street, Suite 212
Boulder, CO 80302
303-444-7799

Crystal Point
22122 20th Avenue, SE, Suite 148
Bothell, WA 98021
206-487-3656

Data Access
14000 Southwest 119th Avenue
Miami, FL 33186
300-451-3539

Datapoint
8400 Datapoint Drive
San Antonio, TX 78229
800-733-1500

DaVinci Systems
4200 Six Forks Road, Suite 200
Raleigh, NC 27609
800-328-4624

Daystrom Data Products
405 Tarrytown Road, Suite 414
White Plains, NY 10607
914-896-6564

Enable Software/Higgins Group
1150 Marina Village Parkway, Suite 101
Alameda, CA 94501
800-854-2807

Futurus
3131 North I-10 Service Road, Suite 401
Metairie, LA 70002
800-327-8296

Interactive Systems
1901 North Naper Boulevard
Naperville, IL 60563
800-524-8649

Microsoft
One Microsoft Way
Redmond, WA 98052
800-227-6444

Network Associates
360 Chase Street
Gary, IN 46404
219-882-3282

Photoring
440 Portafino Court, Suite 112
Pomona, CA 91766
714-620-5370

Sitka
950 Marina Village Parkway
Alameda, CA 94501
800-445-8677

Sun Microsystems
2550 Garcia Avenue
Mountain View, CA 94043
800-872-4786

TeLeVell
3175 De La Cruz
Santa Clara, CA 95054
408-748-0111

Touch Communications
250 East Hacienda Avenue
Campbell, CA 95008
408-374-2500

Transend
884 Portola Road
Portola Valley, CA 94028
415-851-3402

Walker Richer and Quinn
2815 Eastlake Avenue East
Seattle, WA 98102
800-872-2829

Electronic Mail Gateways

Banyan Systems
120 Flanders Road
Westborough, MA 01581
508-898-1000

Datapoint
8400 Datapoint Drive
San Antonio, TX 78229
800-733-1500

Enable Software/Higgins Group
1150 Marina Village Parkway, Suite 101
Alameda, CA 94501
800-854-2807

Innosoft
250 West First Street, Suite 240
Claremont, CA 91711
714-624-7907

Interactive Systems
1901 North Naper Boulevard
Naperville, IL 60563
800-524-8649

Management Systems Designers
131 Park Street, NE
Vienna, VA 22180
800-489-0431

Retix
2644 30th Street
Santa Monica, CA 90405
800-225-2333

Touch Communications
250 East Hacienda Avenue
Campbell, CA 95008
408-374-2500

Unified Communications
3001 Metro Drive, Suite 500
Minneapolis, MN 55425
800-272-1710

Walker Richer and Quinn
2815 Eastlake Avenue East
Seattle, WA 98102
800-872-2829

Ethernet Cards

3Com
5400 Bayfront Plaza
Santa Clara, CA 95052
800-638-3266

Accton Technology
46750 Fremont Boulevard, Building 104
Fremont, CA 94538
800-926-9288

Acer America
401 Charcot Avenue
San Jose, CA 95131
800-733-2237

Addtron Technology
46560 Fremont Boulevard, Suite 303
Fremont, CA 94538
415-770-0120

Advanced Digital
5432 Production Drive
Huntington Beach, CA 92649
714-891-4004

AIDI Systems
2121 Ringwood Avenue
San Jose, CA 95131
800-228-0530

Allied Telesis
575 East Middlefield Road
Mountain View, CA 94043
800-424-4284

American Research
1101 Monterey Pass Road
Monterey Park, CA 91754
213-269-1174

Apple Computer
20525 Mariani Avenue
Cupertino, CA 95014
800-776-2333

Artisoft
575 East River Road
Tucson, AZ 85704
602-293-6363

Asante Technologies
404 Tasman Drive
Tucson, AZ 85704
800-837-2617

BICC Communications
103 Millbury Street
Auburn, MA 01501
800-447-6526

Cabletron Systems
35 Industrial Way
P.O. Box 5005
Rochester, NH 03867
603-332-4616

Cayman Systems
26 Landsdowne Street
Cambridge, MA 02139
800-473-4776

CNet Technology
2199 Zanker Road
San Jose, CA 95131
800-486-2638

Codenoll Technology
1086 North Broadway
Yonkers, NY 10701
914-965-9811

Compatible Systems
P.O. Box 17220
Boulder, CO 80308
800-356-0283

Compex
4055 East La Palma, Suite C
Anaheim, CA 92807
714-630-7302

Congent Data Technologies
175 West Street
P.O. Box 926
Friday Harbor, WA 98250
206-378-2929

David Systems
701 East Evelyn Avenue
Sunnyvale, CA 94086
800-762-7848

Dayna Communications
50 South Main Street, 5th Floor
Salt Lake City, UT 84144
801-359-9135

DCA
1000 Alderman Drive
Alpharetta, GA 30202
800-348-3221

DFI
2544 Port Street West
Sacramento, CA 95691
916-373-1234

D-Link Systems
5 Musick
Irvine, CA 92718
714-455-1688

DNA Networks
351 Phoenixville Pike
Malvern, PA 19355
800-999-3622

Dove Computer
1200 North 23rd Street
Wilmington, NC 28405
800-622-7627

Eagle Technology
1160 Ridder Park Drive
San Jose, CA 95131
408-452-2267

Exos Products
207 South Peyton Street
Alexandria, VA 22134
800-255-5967

Farallon Computing
2000 Powell Street, Suite 600
Emeryville, CA 94608
415-596-9020

Fibermux
9310 Topanga Canyon Boulevard
Chatsworth, CA 91311
818-709-6000

Frontier Technologies
10201 North Port Washington Road, 13 West
Mequon, WI 53092
414-241-4555

Gateway Communications
2941 Alton Avenue
Irvine, CA 92714
800-367-6555

Graybar Electric
34 North Meramec
Clayton, MO 63105
314-727-3900

Hayes Microcomputer Products
P.O. Box 105203
Atlanta, GA 30348
404-840-9200

Hewlett-Packard
19310 Pruneridge
Cupertino, CA 95014
800-752-0900

Hong Technologies
P.O. Box 1268
Mountain View, CA 94042
415-964-0100

Hughes LAN Systems
1225 Charleston Road
Mountain View, CA 94043
415-966-7300

IMC Networks
1342 Bell Avenue, Unit 3-E
Tustin, CA 92680
800-624-1070

Intellicom
20415 Nordhoff Street
Chatsworth, CA 91311
818-407-3900

Invisible Software
1142 Chess Drive, Suite D
Foster City, CA 94404
415-570-5967

IQ Technologies
22032 23rd Drive, SE
Bothell, WA 98021
800-752-6526

Kodiak Technology
1338 Ridder Park Drive
San Jose, CA 95131
408-441-6900

Lancast/Casat Technology
10 Northern Boulevard, Unit 5
Amherst, NH 03031
800-752-2768

Lanmaster
1401 North 14th Street
Temple, TX 76501
817-771-2124

Lannet Data Communications
7711 Center Avenue, Suite 600
Huntington Beach, CA 92647
800-969-4123

Lantana Technology
4393 Viewridge Avenue
San Diego, CA 92123
619-565-6400

Link Computer
560 South Melrose Street
Placentia, CA 92670
714-993-0800

MBA Technique
Number 239-4 Kin Hwa Street
Taipei, Taiwan R.O.C.
8862-341-1260

Megahertz
4505 South Wasatch Boulevard
Salt Lake City, UT 84124
714-837-6033

Multi-Tech Systems
2205 Woodale Drive
Mounds View, MN 55112
800-328-9717

Mylex
34551 Ardenwood Boulevard
Fremont, CA 94555
800-776-9539

National Semiconductor
2900 Semiconductor Drive, M/S 25-155
Santa Clara, CA 95052
800-538-8510

NDC Communications
2860 Zanker Road, Suite 1118
San Jose, CA 95134
408-428-9108

Network Interface
15019 West 95th Street
Lenexa, KS 66215
800-343-2853

NetWorth
8101 Ridgepoint Drive, Suite 107
Irving, TX 75063
214-869-1331

Nuvotech
2015 Bridgeway
Sausalito, CA 94965
800-468-8683

Optical Data Systems
1101 East Arapahoe
Richardson, TX 75081
214-234-6400

Photoring
440 Portafino Court, Suite 112
Pomona, CA 91766
714-620-5370

Plexcom
65 Moreland Road
Simi Valley, CA 93065
805-522-3333

PureData
180 West Beaver Creek Road
Richmond Hill, Ontario L4B 1B4
416-731-6444

Racal Interlan
155 Swanson Road
Boxborough, MA 01719
800-526-8255

SBE
2400 Bisso Lane
Concord, CA 94520
800-347-2666

Schneider and Koch
124 University Avenue, Suite 350
Palo Alto, CA 94301
800-752-3334

Spider Communications
8255 Mountain Sights, Suite 305
Montreal, Quebec H4P 2B5
514-739-7432

Standard Microsystems
35 Marcus Boulevard
Hauppauge, NY 11788
516-273-3100

Standard Microsystems
8105 Irvine Center Drive
Irvine, CA 92718
714-932-5000

Sun Microsystems
2550 Garcia Avenue
Mountain View, CA 94043
800-872-4786

TCL
41829 Albrae Street
Fremont, CA 94538
415-657-3800

Thomas-Conrad
1908-R Dramer Lane
Austin, TX 78758
800-332-8683

Tiara Computer Systems
1091 Shoreline Boulevard
Mountain View, CA 94043
800-638-4272

Top Microsystems
3022 Scott Boulevard
Santa Clara, CA 95054
800-437-8721

Transition Engineering
7448 West 78th Street
Edina, MN 55439
800-325-2725

Tri-Data Systems
3270 Scott Boulevard
Santa Clara, CA 95054
800-874-3282

Ungermann-Bass
3900 Freedom Circle
Santa Clara, CA 95054
800-873-6381

Unisys
P.O. Box 500
Blue Bell, PA 19424
215-986-4011

United NetWorks
2178 Paragon Drive
San Jose, CA 95131
800-825-5864

Fault Tolerance

Antares Electronics
One Antares Drive, Suite 400
Nepean, Ontario K2E 8C4
800-267-4261

Datapoint
8400 Datapoint Drive
San Antonio, TX 78229
800-733-1500

Nonstop Networks
20 Waterside
New York, NY 10010
212-481-8488

Ontrack Computer Systems
6321 Bury Drive, Suites 15–19
Eden Prairie, MN 55346
800-752-1333

Sanyo/Icon
764 East Timpanogos Parkway
Orem, UT 84057
800-872-7266

Stratus Computer
55 Fairbanks Boulevard
Marlborough, MA 01752
508-490-6447

Trellis
85 Main Street
Hopkinton, MA 01748
508-435-3066

Vortex Systems
800 Vinial Street
Pittsburgh, PA 15212
412-322-7820

Fax Servers

Alcom
2464 Embarcadero Way
Palo Alto, CA 94303
415-493-3800

All The Fax
917 Northern Boulevard
Great Neck, NY 11021
800-289-3329

American Research
1101 Monterey Pass Road
Monterey Park, CA 91754
213-269-1174

Antares Electronics
One Antares Drive, Suite 400
Nepean, Ontario K2E 8C4
800-267-4261

Biscom
85 Rangeway Road
Billerica, MA 01821
800-477-2472

Brooktrout Technology
144 Gould Street
Needham, MA 02192
617-449-4100

Castelle
3255-3 Scott Boulevard
Santa Clara, CA 95054
800-473-4776

The Complete PC
1983 Concourse Drive
San Jose, CA 95131
800-229-1753

Danyl
1509 Glen Avenue
Moorestown, NJ 08052
800-732-6868

Datapoint
8400 Datapoint Drive
San Antonio, TX 78229
800-733-1500

GammaLink
133 Caspian Court
Sunnyvale, CA 94089
408-744-1430

Innosoft
250 West First Street, Suite 240
Claremont, CA 91711
714-624-7907

The Network Connection
1324 Union Hill Road
Alpharetta, GA 30201
800-327-4853

Optus Software
100 Davidson Avenue
Somerset, NJ 08873
800-962-7422

Pacific Image Communications
1111 South Arroyo, Suite 430
Pasadena, CA 91105
818-441-0104

Share Communications
The Tower Building, Suite 1000
1809 Seventh Avenue
Seattle, WA 98101
206-328-4817

SofNet
775 Franklin Road, Suite 101
Marietta, GA 30067
404-499-0007

T4 Systems
3 Innwood Circle, Suite 116
Little Rock, AR 72211
501-227-6637

Trellis
85 Main Street
Hopkinton, MA 01748
508-435-3066

FDDI Cards

Codenoll Technology
1086 North Broadway
Yonkers, NY 10701
914-965-9811

Digital Technology
2300 Edwin C. Moses Boulevard
Dayton, OH 45408
800-852-1252

Photoring
440 Portafino Court, Suite 112
Pomona, CA 91766
714-620-5370

SBE
2400 Bisso Lane
Concord, CA 94520
800-347-2666

Schneider and Koch
124 University Avenue, Suite 350
Palo Alto, CA 94301
800-752-3334

Silicon Graphics
2011 North Shoreline Boulevard
Mountain View, CA 94039
800-326-1020

Sun Microsystems
2550 Garcia Avenue
Mountain View, CA 94043
800-872-4786

Fiber Optic Networks

Andrew
2771 Plaza Del Amo
Torrance, CA 90503
800-733-0331

Artel Communications
22 Kane Industrial Drive
Hudson, MA 01749
800-225-0228

Chipcom
118 Turnpike Road
Southborough, MA 01772
800-228-9930

Codenoll Technology
1086 North Broadway
Yonkers, NY 10701
914-965-9811

Data Switch
One Enterprise Drive
Shelton, CT 06484
800-328-3279

DuPont Electro-Optic Products
P.O. Box 13625
Research Triangle Park, NC 27709
800-888-5261

FiberCom
3353 Orange Avenue, NE
Roanoke, VA 24012
800-423-1183

Fibermux
9310 Topanga Canyon Boulevard
Chatsworth, CA 91311
818-709-6000

Fibronics
One Communications Way
Hyannis, MA 12601
800-327-9526

In-Net
15150 Avenue of Science, Suite 100
San Diego, CA 92128
800-283-3334

Lannet Data Communications
7711 Center Avenue, Suite 600
Huntington Beach, CA 92647
800-969-4123

Mitsubishi International
520 Madison Avenue
New York, NY 10022
212-605-2392

Network Systems
7600 Boone Avenue North
Minneapolis, MN 55428
612-424-4888

Opcom
1215 West Crosby Road
Carrollton, TX 75006
214-323-7061

Optical Data Systems
1101 East Arapahoe
Richardson, TX 75081
214-234-6400

Raylan
120 Independence Drive
Menlo Park, CA 94025
800-472-9526

Reliable Electric
11333 Addison Street
Franklin Park, IL 60131
708-455-8010

Ship Star
36 Woodhill Drive, Suite 19
Newark, DE 19711
302-738-7782

TCL
41829 Albrae Street
Fremont, CA 94538
415-657-3800

Thomas-Conrad
1908-R Dramer Lane
Austin, TX 78758
800-332-8683

File Servers

3Com
5400 Bayfront Plaza
Santa Clara, CA 95052
800-638-3266

Acer America
401 Charcot Avenue
San Jose, CA 95131
800-733-2237

Advanced Digital
5432 Production Drive
Huntington Beach, CA 92649
714-891-4004

Advanced Logic Research
9401 Jeronimo
Irvine, CA 92718
800-444-4257

Arche Technologies
48881 Dato Road
Fremont, CA 94539
800-422-4674

AST Research
16215 Alton Parkway
P.O. Box 19658
Irvine, CA 92713
800-876-4278

Auspex Systems
2952 Bunker Hill Lane
Santa Clara, CA 95054
408-492-0909

Caliber Tek
353 Vintage Park Drive
Foster City, CA 94404
415-570-4233

CNet Technology
2199 Zanker Road
San Jose, CA 95131
800-486-2638

Compaq Computer
P.O. Box 692000
Houston, TX 77069
800-231-0900

Compex
4055 East La Palma, Suite C
Anaheim, CA 92807
714-630-7302

Core
7171 North Federal Highway
Boca Raton, FL 33487
407-997-6055

Cubix
2800 Lockheed Way
Carson City, NV 89706
800-829-0550

Datapoint
8400 Datapoint Drive
San Antonio, TX 78229
800-733-1500

Lanmaster
1401 North 14th Street
Temple, TX 76501
817-771-2124

Morton Management
12079 Tech Road
Silver Spring, MD 20904
800-548-5744

NetFrame Systems
1545 Barber Lane
Milpitas, CA 95035
800-852-3726

The Network Connection
1324 Union Hill Road
Alpharetta, GA 30201
800-327-4853

Parallan Computer
201 Ravendale Drive
Mountain View, CA 94043
415-960-0288

Silicon Graphics
2011 North Shoreline Boulevard
Mountain View, CA 94039
800-326-1020

Systems Integration Associates
222 East Pearson, Suite 502
Chicago, IL 60611
312-440-1275

Top Microsystems
3022 Scott Boulevard
Santa Clara, CA 95054
800-437-8721

Unisys
P.O. Box 500
Blue Bell, PA 19424
215-986-4011

Help Desk Software

Advanced Digital Information Corporation
14737 Northeast 87th Street
Redmond, WA 98073
800-336-1233

Brightwork Development
766 Shrewsbury Avenue, Jerral Center West
Tinton Falls, NJ 07724
800-552-9876

Magic Solutions
180 Franklin Turnpike, Second Floor
Mahwah, NJ 07430
201-529-5533

Image Processing

Computing Management Center
370 South Crenshaw Boulevard, Suite E-106
Torrance, CA 90503
213-212-5064

Saros
10900 Northeast Eighth Street, Suite 700
Bellevue, WA 98004
800-827-2767

ViewStar
5820 Shellmound Street, Suite 600
Emeryville, CA 94608
415-841-8565

Wang Laboratories
One Industrial Avenue
Lowell, MA 01851
800-225-0654

Inventory Software

Aperture Technologies
100 Summit Lake Drive
Valhalla, NY 10595
800-346-6828

Brightwork Development
766 Shrewsbury Avenue, Jerral Center West
Tinton Falls, NJ 07724
800-552-9876

Frye Computer Systems
19 Temple Place
Boston, MA 02111
800-234-3793

Horizons Technology
3990 Ruffin Road
San Diego, CA 92123
619-292-8320

Magee Enterprise
P.O. Box 1587
Norcross, GA 30091
404-446-6611

Pharos Technologies
4243 Hunt Road
Cincinnati, OH 45242
800-548-8871

TouchStone Software
2130 Main Street, Suite 250
Huntington Beach, CA 92648
800-531-0450

Triticom
P.O. Box 11536
St. Paul, MN 55111
612-937-0772

LocalTalk Cards

Apple Computer
20525 Mariani Avenue
Cupertino, CA 95014
800-776-2333

Dayna Communications
50 South Main Street, Fifth Floor
Salt Lake City, UT 84144
801-359-9135

DayStar Digital
5556 Atlanta Highway
Flowery Branch, GA 30542
800-962-2077

Farallon Computing
2000 Powell Street, Suite 600
Emeryville, CA 94608
415-596-9020

Fibermux
9310 Topanga Canyon Boulevard
Chatsworth, CA 91311
818-709-6000

Nuvotech
2015 Bridgeway
Sausalito, CA 94965
800-468-8683

Sitka
950 Marina Village Parkway
Alameda, CA 94501
800-445-8677

Ungermann-Bass
3900 Freedom Circle
Santa Clara, CA 95054
800-873-6381

Mainframe Gateways

Phaser Systems
651 Gateway Boulevard South
San Francisco, CA 94080
800-234-5799

Menu Software

3rd Planet Software
9819 National Boulevard, Suite 2
Los Angeles, CA 90034
213-841-2260

Antares Electronics
One Antares Drive, Suite 400
Nepean, Ontario K2E 8C4
800-267-4261

Automated Design Systems
375 Northridge Road, Suite 270
Atlanta, GA 30350
800-366-2552

Bonsai Technologies
P.O. Box 6296
Rochester, MN 55903
507-252-1585

Byte/Wide Software
P.O. Box 1778
De Land, FL 32721
904-738-4923

Circle Development
5986 Knight Arnold Road
Memphis, TN 38115
800-676-0333

Command Software Systems
1061 East Indiantown Road, Suite 510
Jupiter, FL 33477
800-423-9147

Daystrom Data Products
405 Tarrytown Road, Suite 414
White Plains, NY 10607
914-896-6564

Intel, LAN Enhancements
C03-07, 5200 Northeast Elam Young Parkway
Hillsboro, OR 97124
800-525-3019

Magee Enterprise
P.O. Box 1587
Norcross, GA 30091
404-446-6611

NETinc
P.O. Box 271105
Houston, TX 77277
713-974-1810

Quarterdeck Office Systems
150 Pico Boulevard
Santa Monica, CA 90405
213-392-9851

Saber Software
P.O. Box 9088
Dallas, TX 75209
800-338-8754

Sessionware
2444 Moorpark Avenue, Suite 300
San Jose, CA 95218
408-292-9951

Trellis
85 Main Street
Hopkinton, MA 01748
508-435-3066

Multimedia Networks

Applitek
100 Brickstone Square
Andover, MA 01810
508-475-4050

Commtex
1655 Crofton Boulevard
Crofton, MD 21114

Datapoint
8400 Datapoint Drive
San Antonio, TX 78229
800-733-1500

Lancast/Casat Technology
10 Northern Boulevard, Unit 5
Amherst, NH 03031
800-752-2768

Opcom
1215 West Crosby Road
Carrollton, TX 75006
214-323-7061

TriLAN Systems
2900 Dukane Drive
St. Charles, IL 60174
708-584-2300

Viewsonics
6454 East Rogers Circle
Boca Raton, FL 33487
800-645-7600

Network Design Software

Cable Technology Group
55 Chapel Street
Newton, MA 02160
617-969-8552

Caci
3344 North Torrey Pines Court
La Jolla, CA 92037
619-457-9681

Comdisco
919 East Hillsdale Boulevard, Suite 300
Foster City, CA 94404
415-574-4800

Digital Equipment Corporation
146 Main Street
Maynard, MA 01754
800-343-4040

Internetix
8903 Presidential Parkway, Suite 210
Upper Marlboro, MD 20772
800-562-7292

Isicad
1920 West Corporate Way
Anaheim, CA 92803
800-634-1223

Network-1
P.O. Box 8370
Long Island City, NY 11101
718-932-7599

Network and Communication Technology
24 Wampum Road
Park Ridge, NJ 07656
201-307-9000

Trilogy Development Group
350 Cambridge Avenue, Suite 200
Palo Alto, CA 94306
415-321-5481

Triticom
P.O. Box 11536
St. Paul, MN 55111
612-937-0772

Network Management—Hardware

Andrew
2771 Plaza Del Amo
Torrance, CA 90503
800-733-0331

Chipcom
118 Turnpike Road
Southborough, MA 01772
800-228-9930

Data Switch
One Enterprise Drive
Shelton, CT 06484
800-328-3279

Digital Equipment Corporation
146 Main Street
Maynard, MA 01754
800-343-4040

Jensen Tools
7815 South 46th Street
Phoenix, AZ 85044
602-968-6231

Lannet Data Communications
7711 Center Avenue, Suite 600
Huntington Beach, CA 92647
800-969-4123

Network Application Technology
1686 Dell Avenue
Campbell, CA 95008
800-543-8887

Network Communications Corporation
10120 West 76th Street
Eden Prairie, MN 55344-9814
612-944-8559

Network Equipment Technologies
800 Saginaw Drive
Redwood City, CA 04963
800-234-4638

Network Interface
15019 West 95th Street
Lenexa, KS 66215
800-343-2853

NetWorth
8101 Ridgepoint Drive, Suite 107
Irving, TX 75063
214-869-1331

Novell Network Analysis Products Division
2180 Fortune Drive
San Jose, CA 95131
800-243-8526

Oneac
27944 North Bradley Road
Libertyville, IL 60048
800-327-8801

Optical Data Systems
1101 East Arapahoe
Richardson, TX 75081
214-234-6400

Plexcom
65 Moreland Road
Simi Valley, CA 93065
805-522-3333

Racal Interlan
155 Swanson Road
Boxborough, MA 01719
800-526-8255

RAD Network Devices
7711 Center Avenue, Suite 600
Huntington Beach, CA 92647
800-969-4723

Retix
2644 30th Street
Santa Monica, CA 90405
800-225-2333

Star-Tek
71 Lynan Street
Northborough, MA 01532
800-225-8528

SynOptics Communications
4401 Great America Parkway
P.O. Box 51815
Santa Clara, CA 95052
800-776-6895

TCL
41829 Albrae Street
Fremont, CA 94538
415-657-3800

Thomas and Betts
1001 Frontier Road
Bridgewater, NJ 98897
908-685-1600

Tutankhamon Electronics
1800 Ardith Drive
Pleasant Hill, CA 94523
415-682-6510

Wellfleet Communications
15 Crosby Drive
Bedford, MA 01730
617-275-2400

Network Management—Software

Advanced Computer Communications
720 Santa Barbara Street
Santa Barbara, CA 93101
800-444-7854

AG Group
2540 Comino Diablo, Suite 202
Walnut Creek, CA 94596
415-937-7900

AIDI Systems
2121 Ringwood Avenue
San Jose, CA 95131
800-228-0530

Alantec
47800 Westinghouse Drive
Fremont, CA 94539
800-727-1050

Andrew
2771 Plaza Del Amo
Torrance, CA 90503
800-733-0331

Applitek
100 Brickstone Square
Andover, MA 01810
508-475-4050

AT&T
One Speedwell Avenue
Morristown, NJ 07960
800-247-1212

BICC Communications
103 Millbury Street
Auburn, MA 01501
800-447-6526

Bytex
120 Turnpike Road
Southborough, MA 01772
508-480-0840

Cabletron Systems
35 Industrial Way
P.O. Box 5005
Rochester, NH 03867
603-332-4616

Chi/Cor Information Management
300 South Wacker Drive
Chicago, IL 60606
800-448-8777

Chipcom
118 Turnpike Road
Southborough, MA 01772
800-228-9930

Cisco Systems
1525 O'Brien Drive
Menlo Park, CA 94025
800-553-6387

Clearpoint Research
35 Parkwood Drive
Hopkinton, MA 01748
800-253-2778

Codenoll Technology
1086 North Broadway
Yonkers, NY 10701
914-965-9811

Codex/Motorola
20 Cabot Boulevard
Mansfield, MA 02048
800-426-1212

Data Switch
One Enterprise Drive
Shelton, CT 06484
800-328-3279

David Systems
701 East Evelyn Avenue
Sunnyvale, CA 94086
800-762-7848

Digilog/CXR
1370 Welsh Road
Montgomeryville, PA 18936
800-344-4564

Digital Equipment Corporation
146 Main Street
Maynard, MA 01754
800-343-4040

Dolphin Software
4405 International Boulevard, Suite B-108
Norcross, GA 30093
404-279-7050

DuPont Electro-Optic Products
P.O. Box 13625
Research Triangle Park, NC 27709
800-888-5261

Farallon Computing
2000 Powell Street, Suite 600
Emeryville, CA 94608
415-596-9020

FiberCom
3353 Orange Avenue, NE
Roanoke, VA 24012
800-423-1183

Fibermux
9310 Topanga Canyon Boulevard
Chatsworth, CA 91311
818-709-6000

FTP Software
338 Main Street
Wakefield, MA 01880
617-246-0900

General Technology
415 Pineda Court
Melbourne, FL 32940
800-274-2733

Halley Systems
1590 Oakland Road
San Jose, CA 95131
408-441-2139

Hewlett-Packard
19310 Pruneridge
Cupertino, CA 95014
800-752-0900

Hughes LAN Systems
1225 Charleston Road
Mountain View, CA 94043
415-966-7300

IBM
Old Orchard Road
Armonk, NY 10504
800-426-2468
800-426-3333

In-Net
15150 Avenue of Science, Suite 100
San Diego, CA 92128
800-283-3334

Lannet Data Communications
7711 Center Avenue, Suite 600
Huntington Beach, CA 92647
800-969-4123

Luxcom
3249 Laurelview Court
Fremont, CA 94538
415-770-3300

Madge Networks
42 Airport Parkway
San Jose, CA 95110
800-876-2343

Microcom
500 River Ridge Drive
Norwood, MA 02062
800-822-8224

Micro Technology
5065 East Hunter Avenue
Anaheim, CA 92807
800-999-9684

Network-1
P.O. Box 8370
Long Island City, NY 11101
800-638-9751

Network Application Technology
1686 Dell Avenue
Campbell, CA 95008
800-543-8887

Network Communications Corporation
10120 West 76th Street
Eden Prairie, MN 55344-9814
612-944-8559

Network Equipment Technologies
800 Saginaw Drive
Redwood City, CA 04963
800-234-4638

Network General
4200 Bohannon Drive
Menlo Park, CA 04925
800-395-3151

Network Interface
15019 West 95th Street
Lenexa, KS 66215
800-343-2853

Network Systems
7600 Boone Avenue North
Minneapolis, MN 55428
612-424-4888

NetWorth
8101 Ridgepoint Drive, Suite 107
Irving, TX 75063
214-869-1331

Newbridge Networks
593 Herndon Parkway
Herndon, VA 22070
800-332-1080

Novell Network Analysis Products Division
2180 Fortune Drive
San Jose, CA 95131
800-243-8526

Optical Data Systems
1101 East Arapahoe
Richardson, TX 75081
214-234-6400

Plexcom
65 Moreland Road
Simi Valley, CA 93065
805-522-3333

Proteon
Two Technology Drive
Westborough, MA 01581
508-898-2800

ProTools
14976 Northwest Greenbrier Parkway
Beaverton, OR 97006
800-743-4335

PureData
180 West Beaver Creek Road
Richmond Hill, Ontario L4B 1B4
416-731-6444

Racal Interlan
155 Swanson Road
Boxborough, MA 01719
800-526-8255

RAD Data Communications
8 Hanechoshet Street
Tel Aviv, Israel 69710
972-3-494511

RAD Network Devices
7711 Center Avenue, Suite 600
Huntington Beach, CA 92647
800-969-4723

Software Marketing Group
108 Third Street, Suite 201
Des Moines, IA 50309
800-395-0209

Standard Microsystems
35 Marcus Boulevard
Hauppauge, NY 11788
516-273-3100

Sun Microsystems
2550 Garcia Avenue
Mountain View, CA 94043
800-872-4786

Synertics
85 Tangeway Road
North Billerica, MA 01862
508-670-9009

SynOptics Communications
4401 Great America Parkway
P.O. Box 51815
Santa Clara, CA 95052
800-776-6895

Technology Dynamics
430 10th Street, Suite S-008
Atlanta, GA 30318
800-226-0428

Thomas and Betts
1001 Frontier Road
Bridgewater, NJ 98897
908-685-1600

Thomas-Conrad
1908-R Dramer Lane
Austin, TX 78758
800-332-8683

Timeplex
400 Chestnut Ridge Road
Woodcliff Lake, NJ 07675
800-755-8526

Tribe Computer Works
1195 Park Avenue
Emeryville, CA 94608
415-547-3874

Vitalink Communications
6607 Kaiser Drive
Fremont, CA 94555
800-443-5740

Network Operating Systems

3Com
5400 Bayfront Plaza
Santa Clara, CA 95052
800-638-3266

Accton Technology
46750 Fremont Boulevard, Building 104
Fremont, CA 94538
800-926-9288

American Research
1101 Monterey Pass Road
Monterey Park, CA 91754
213-269-1174

Apple Computer
20525 Mariani Avenue
Cupertino, CA 95014
800-776-2333

Artisoft
575 East River Road
Tucson, AZ 85704
602-293-6363

Atlantix
4800 North Federal Highway, Suite 01-B
Boca Raton, FL 33431
407-362-9700

AT&T
One Speedwell Avenue
Morristown, NJ 07960
800-247-1212

Banyan Systems
120 Flanders Road
Westborough, MA 01581
508-898-1000

Compex
4055 East La Palma, Suite C
Anaheim, CA 92807
714-630-7302

Datapoint
8400 Datapoint Drive
San Antonio, TX 78229
800-733-1500

DCA
1000 Alderman Drive
Alpharetta, GA 30202
800-348-3221

Digital Equipment Corporation
146 Main Street
Maynard, MA 01754
800-343-4040

Digital Research
70 Garden Court
Monterey, CA 93942
408-649-3896

D-Link Systems
5 Musick
Irvine, CA 92718
714-455-1688

DNA Networks
351 Phoenixville Pike
Malvern, PA 19355
800-999-3622

Eagle Technology
1160 Ridder Park Drive
San Jose, CA 95131
408-452-2267

Farallon Computing
2000 Powell Street, Suite 600
Emeryville, CA 94608
415-596-9020

Fresh Technology Group
1478 North Tech Boulevard, Suite 101
Gilbert, AZ 85234
602-497-4200

Grapevine LAN Products
8519 154th Avenue, NE
Redmond, WA 98052
206-869-2506

IBM
Old Orchard Road
Armonk, NY 10504
800-426-2468
800-426-3333

IGC
3081 Holcomb Bridge Road, Suite C-1
Norcross, GA 30071
800-866-5597

Invisible Software
1142 Chess Drive, Suite D
Foster City, CA 94404
415-570-5967

Microsoft
One Microsoft Way
Redmond, WA 98052
800-227-6444

Miramar Systems
201 North Salspuedes Street, Suite 204
Santa Barbara, CA 93103
805-966-2432

NCR
1334 South Patterson Boulevard
Dayton, OH 45479
513-445-5000

Novell
122 East 1700 South
Provo, UT 84606
800-638-9273

Photoring
440 Portafino Court, Suite 112
Pomona, CA 91766
714-620-5370

Sitka
950 Marina Village Parkway
Alameda, CA 94501
800-445-8677

Sun Microsystems
2550 Garcia Avenue
Mountain View, CA 94043
800-872-4786

Ungermann-Bass
3900 Freedom Circle
Santa Clara, CA 95054
800-873-6381

U.S. Sage/MainLAN Networks
1215 North Highway 427, Suite 135
Longwood, FL 32750
800-999-6770

Webcorp
3000 Bridgeway
Sausalito, CA 94965
415-331-1449

NOS Gateways

Congent Data Technologies
175 West Street
P.O. Box 926
Friday Harbor, WA 98250
206-378-2929

Miramar Systems
201 North Salspuedes Street, Suite 204
Santa Barbara, CA 93103
805-966-2432

Phaser Systems
651 Gateway Boulevard South
San Francisco, CA 94080
800-234-5799

Spry
1319 Dexter Avenue North
Seattle, WA 98109
206-286-1412

Trellis
85 Main Street
Hopkinton, MA 01748
508-435-3066

Optical Disk Servers

Consan
14625 Martin Drive
Eden Prairie, MN 55344
800-229-3475

Meridian Data
5615 Scotts Valley Drive
Scotts Valley, CA 95066
408-438-3100

MicroNet Technology
20 Mason Street
Irvine, CA 92718
714-837-6033

Morton Management
12079 Tech Road
Silver Spring, MD 20904
800-548-5744

NCR
1334 South Patterson Boulevard
Dayton, OH 45479
513-445-5000

The Network Connection
1324 Union Hill Road
Alpharetta, GA 30201
800-327-4853

Online Computer Systems
20251 Century Boulevard
Germantown, MD 20874
800-922-9204

Optical Software Solutions
1001 Galaxy Way, Suite 310
Concord, CA 94520
415-825-3441

Perisol Technology
3350 Scott Boulevard, Building 1201
Santa Clara, CA 95054
800-447-8226

Storage Dimensions
2145 Hamilton Avenue
San Jose, CA 95125
800-879-0300

Trellis
85 Main Street
Hopkinton, MA 01748
508-435-3066

Wang Laboratories
One Industrial Avenue
Lowell, MA 01851
800-225-0654

OSI Software

Digital Equipment Corporation
146 Main Street
Maynard, MA 01754
800-343-4040

Frontier Technologies
10201 North Port Washington Road, 13 West
Mequon, WI 53092
414-241-4555

Interactive Systems
1901 North Naper Boulevard
Naperville, IL 60563
800-524-8649

Network-1
P.O. Box 8370
Long Island City, NY 11101
718-932-7599

Novell
122 East 1700 South
Provo, UT 84606
800-638-9273

Retix
2644 30th Street
Santa Monica, CA 90405
800-225-2333

Sun Microsystems
2550 Garcia Avenue
Mountain View, CA 94043
800-872-4786

Touch Communications
250 East Hacienda Avenue
Campbell, CA 95008
408-374-2500

Unified Communications
3001 Metro Drive, Suite 500
Minneapolis, MN 55425
800-272-1710

Print Servers

3rd Planet Software
9819 National Boulevard, Suite 2
Los Angeles, CA 90034
213-841-2260

Apple Computer
20525 Mariani Avenue
Cupertino, CA 95014
800-776-2333

ASP Computer Products
1026 West Maude Avenue, Suite 305
Sunnyvale, CA 94086
800-445-6190

Automated Design Systems
375 Northridge Road, Suite 270
Atlanta, GA 30350
800-366-2552

Barr Systems
4131 Northwest 28th Lane
Gainesville, FL 32606
800-227-7797

Brightwork Development
766 Shrewsbury Avenue, Jerral Center West
Tinton Falls, NJ 07724
800-552-9876

Castelle
3255-3 Scott Boulevard
Santa Clara, CA 95054
800-473-4776

Connexperts
8333 Douglas Avenue, Suite 700
Dallas, TX 75225
800-433-5373

Datapoint
8400 Datapoint Drive
San Antonio, TX 78229
800-733-1500

Digital Equipment Corporation
146 Main Street
Maynard, MA 01754
800-343-4040

Digital Products
108 Water Street
Watertown, MA 02172
800-243-2333

D-Link Systems
5 Musick
Irvine, CA 92718
714-455-1688

Emulex
3545 Harbor Boulevard
Costa Mesa, CA 92626
800-368-5393

Frontier Technologies
10201 North Port Washington Road, 13 West
Mequon, WI 53092
414-241-4555

FTP Software
338 Main Street
Wakefield, MA 01880
617-246-0900

Insight Development
220 Powell Street, Suite 500
Emeryville, CA 94608
800-825-4115

Intel, LAN Enhancements
C03-07, 5200 Northeast Elam Young Parkway
Hillsboro, OR 97124
800-525-3019

LANQuest
1251 Parkmoor Avenue
San Jose, CA 95126
800-487-7779

Microplex Systems
265 East First Avenue
Vancouver, British Columbia V5T 1A7
604-875-1461

Rose Electronics
10850 Wilcrest, Suite 900
Houston, TX 77099
800-333-9343

Ultinet Development
P.O. Box 34016
Los Angeles, CA 90034
213-204-0111
Wang Laboratories
One Industrial Avenue
Lowell, MA 01851
800-225-0654

Project Management Software

Applied Business Technology
361 Broadway, Second Floor
New York, NY 10013
212-219-8945

Chronos Software
55 Deharo Street, Suite 240
San Francisco, CA 94107
800-777-7907

Computer Aided Management
1318 Redwood Way, Suite 210
Petaluma, CA 94954
800-635-5621

Microsystems Software
600 Worcester Road
Framingham, MA 01701
508-626-8511

Pathfinder
11 Allison Drive
P.O. Box 5027
Cherry Hill, NJ 08034
609-424-7100

Poc-It Management Services
429 Santa Monica Boulevard, Suite 460
Santa Monica, CA 90401
213-393-4552

PowerCore
One Diversatech Drive
Manteno, IL 60955
800-237-4754

Primavera Systems
Two Bala Plaza
Bala-Cynwyd, PA 19004
800-423-0245

Strategic Software Planning
101 Main Street
Cambridge, MA 02142
800-783-1504

Protocol Analyzers

AG Group
2540 Comino Diablo, Suite 202
Walnut Creek, CA 94596
415-937-7900

Azure Technologies
38 Pond Street
Franklin, MA 02038
800-233-3800

Concord Communications
753 Forest Street
Marlborough, MA 01752
508-481-9772

Digilog/CXR
1370 Welsh Road
Montgomeryville, PA 18936
800-344-4564

Digital Technology
2300 Edwin C. Moses Boulevard
Dayton, OH 45408
800-852-1252

FTP Software
338 Main Street
Wakefield, MA 01880
617-246-0900

Hewlett-Packard, Colorado Telecom Division
5070 Centennial Boulevard
Colorado Springs, CO 80919
719-531-4414

Hewlett-Packard, INO
1501 Page Mill Road
Palo Alto, CA 93404
415-857-8897

IBM
Old Orchard Road
Armonk, NY 10504
800-426-2468
800-426-3333

International Data Sciences
501 Jefferson Boulevard
Warwick, RI 02886
800-437-3282

Matrix Computer Systems
One Tara Boulevard
Nashua, NH 03062
603-888-7000

Neon Software
1009 Oak Hill Road, Suite 203
Lafayette, CA 94549
415-283-0771

Network Communications Corporation
10120 West 76th Street
Eden Prairie, MN 55344-9814
612-944-8559

Network General
4200 Bohannon Drive
Menlo Park, CA 04925
800-395-3151

Novell Network Analysis Products Division
2180 Fortune Drive
San Jose, CA 95131
800-243-8526

ProTools
14976 Northwest Greenbrier Parkway
Beaverton, OR 97006
800-743-4335

Silicon Graphics
2011 North Shoreline Boulevard
Mountain View, CA 94039
800-326-1020

Spider Systems
12 New England Executive Park
Burlington, MA 01803
800-447-7807

SynOptics Communications
4401 Great America Parkway
P.O. Box 51815
Santa Clara, CA 95052
800-776-6895

Tekelec
26580 West Agoura Road
Calabasas, CA 91302
800-835-3532

Tektronix/LP Com
270 Santa Ana Court
Sunnyvale, CA 94086
408-789-8008

Triticom
P.O. Box 11536
St. Paul, MN 55111
612-937-0772

Ungermann-Bass
3900 Freedom Circle
Santa Clara, CA 95054
800-873-6381

Wandel and Goltermann
2200 Gateway Centre Boulevard
Morrisville, NC 27560
800-346-6332

Remote-Access Software

3Com
5400 Bayfront Plaza
Santa Clara, CA 95052
800-638-3266

3rd Planet Software
9819 National Boulevard, Suite 2
Los Angeles, CA 90034
213-841-2260

Antares Electronics
One Antares Drive, Suite 400
Nepean, Ontario K2E 8C4
800-267-4261

Avalan Technology
116 Hopping Brook Park
Holliston, MA 01746
800-441-2281

Barr Systems
4131 Northwest 28th Lane
Gainesville, FL 32606
800-227-7797

Brightwork Development
766 Shrewsbury Avenue, Jerral Center West
Tinton Falls, NJ 07724
800-552-9876

Century Software
5284 South 320 West, Suite C-134
Salt Lake City, UT 84107
801-268-3088

Concept Development Systems
P.O. Drawer 1988
Dennesaw, GA 30144
404-424-6240

Cross Communications
1881 Ninth Street, Suite 212
Boulder, CO 80302
303-444-7799

Digital Equipment Corporation
146 Main Street
Maynard, MA 01754
800-343-4040

DMA
1776 East Jericho Turnpike
Huntington, NY 11743
516-462-0440

Emis Software
901 Northeast Loop 410, Suite 526
San Antonio, TX 78209
800-658-1000

Excelltech
300 West Third Street
Yankton, SD 57078
800-284-8509

Farallon Computing
2000 Powell Street, Suite 600
Emeryville, CA 94608
415-596-9020

Fresh Technology Group
1478 North Tech Boulevard, Suite 101
Gilbert, AZ 85234
602-497-4200

IBM
Old Orchard Road
Armonk, NY 10504
800-426-2468
800-426-3333

Intel, LAN Enhancements
C03-07, 5200 Northeast Elam Young Parkway
Hillsboro, OR 97124
800-525-3019

Invisible Software
1142 Chess Drive, Suite D
Foster City, CA 94404
415-570-5967

Knozall Systems
375 East Elliot Road, Suite 10
Chandler, AZ 85225
800-545-0006

Lanmaster
1401 North 14th Street
Temple, TX 76501
817-771-2124

Le Tech Software
P.O. Box 2582
Iowa City, IA 52244
319-354-6804

Microcom
500 River Ridge Drive
Norwood, MA 02062
800-822-8224

Micro Net
2356 Parkside
Boise, ID 83712
208-384-9137

Network-1
P.O. Box 8370
Long Island City, NY 11101
800-638-9751

Norton-Lambert
P.O. Box 4085
Santa Barbara, CA 93140
805-964-6767

Novell
122 East 1700 South
Provo, UT 84606
800-638-9273

Server Technology
2332-B Walsh Avenue
Santa Clara, CA 95051
800-835-1515

Triton Technologies
200 Middlesex Turnpike
Iselin, NJ 08830
908-855-9440

Routers

3Com
5400 Bayfront Plaza
Santa Clara, CA 95052
800-638-3266

Advanced Computer Communications
720 Santa Barbara Street
Santa Barbara, CA 93101
800-444-7854

Amnet
1881 Worcester Road
Framingham, MA 01701
508-876-6306

Apple Computer
20525 Mariani Avenue
Cupertino, CA 95014
800-776-2333

APT Communications
96–7 Drive Perry Road
Ijamsville, MD 21754
800-842-0626

AT&T
One Speedwell Avenue
Morristown, NJ 07960
800-247-1212

Aydin Corporation
700 Dresher Road
Horsham, PA 19044
215-657-8600

Cayman Systems
26 Landsdowne Street
Cambridge, MA 02139
800-473-4776

Chipcom
118 Turnpike Road
Southborough, MA 01772
800-228-9930

Cisco Systems
1525 O'Brien Drive
Menlo Park, CA 94025
800-553-6387

Compatible Systems
P.O. Box 17220
Boulder, CO 80308
800-356-0283

CrossComm
133 East Main Street
P.O. Box 699
Marlborough, MA 01752
508-481-4060

Datapoint
8400 Datapoint Drive
San Antonio, TX 78229
800-733-1500

Data Switch
One Enterprise Drive
Shelton, CT 06484
800-328-3279

David Systems
701 East Evelyn Avenue
Sunnyvale, CA 94086
800-762-7848

Dayna Communications
50 South Main Street, Fifth Floor
Salt Lake City, UT 84144
801-359-9135

Digital Equipment Corporation
146 Main Street
Maynard, MA 01754
800-343-4040

Eicon Technology
2196 32nd Avenue
Montreal, Quebec H8T 3H7
514-631-2592

Farallon Computing
2000 Powell Street, Suite 600
Emeryville, CA 94608
415-596-9020

Fibronics
One Communications Way
Hyannis, MA 12601
800-327-9526

Frontier Technologies
10201 North Port Washington Road, 13 West
Mequon, WI 53092
414-241-4555

Gateway Communications
2941 Alton Avenue
Irvine, CA 92714
800-367-6555

Gupta Technologies
1040 Marsh Road
Menlo Park, CA 94025
800-876-3267

Hewlett-Packard
19310 Pruneridge
Cupertino, CA 95014
800-752-0900

LAN-Link
744 Goddard Avenue
St. Louis, MO 63005
314-537-9800

LanWan Technologies
1566 La Pradera Drive
Campbell, CA 95008
408-374-8190

NEC America
10 Rio Robles
San Jose, CA 95134
800-222-4632

Network Equipment Technologies
800 Saginaw Drive
Redwood City, CA 04963
800-234-4638

Network Systems
7600 Boone Avenue North
Minneapolis, MN 55428
612-424-4888

Newbridge Networks
593 Herndon Parkway
Herndon, VA 22070
800-332-1080

Newport Systems Solutions
4019 Westerly Place
Newport Beach, CA 92660
800-368-6533

Niwot Networks
5595 Arapahoe, Suite G
Boulder, CO 80303
303-444-7765

Novell
122 East 1700 South
Provo, UT 84606
800-638-9273

Nuvotech
2015 Bridgeway
Sausalito, CA 94965
800-468-8683

OpenConnect Systems
2033 Chennauylt Drive
Dallas, TX 75006
214-490-4090

Penril DataComm Networks
1300 Quince Orchard Boulevard
Gaithersburg, MD 20878
800-473-6745

Plexcom
65 Moreland Road
Simi Valley, CA 93065
805-522-3333

Proteon
Two Technology Drive
Westborough, MA 01581
508-898-2800

RAD Network Devices
7711 Center Avenue, Suite 600
Huntington Beach, CA 92647
800-969-4723

Retix
2644 30th Street
Santa Monica, CA 90405
800-225-2333

Schneider and Koch
124 University Avenue, Suite 350
Palo Alto, CA 94301
800-752-3334

Shiva
One Cambridge Center
Cambridge, MA 02112
800-458-3550

Sun Microsystems
2550 Garcia Avenue
Mountain View, CA 94043
800-872-4786

SynOptics Communications
4401 Great America Parkway
P.O. Box 51815
Santa Clara, CA 95052
800-776-6895

Systems Strategies
One Penn Plaza, Suite 4311
New York, NY 10119
212-279-8400

Telebit
1315 Chesapeake Terrace
Sunnyvale, CA 94089
800-835-3248

Timeplex
400 Chestnut Ridge Road
Woodcliff Lake, NJ 07675
800-755-8526

Tri-Data Systems
3270 Scott Boulevard
Santa Clara, CA 95054
800-874-3282

Ungermann-Bass
3900 Freedom Circle
Santa Clara, CA 95054
800-873-6381

Unisync
1380 West Ninth Street
Upland, CA 91786-5723
909-985-5088

Vitalink Communications
6607 Kaiser Drive
Fremont, CA 94555
800-443-5740

Wellfleet Communications
15 Crosby Drive
Bedford, MA 01730
617-275-2400

Xyplex
330 Codmin Hill Road
Boxborough, MA 01709
508-264-9900

Security

Automated Design Systems
375 Northridge Road, Suite 270
Atlanta, GA 30350
800-366-2552

Banyan Systems
120 Flanders Road
Westborough, MA 01581
508-898-1000

Baseline Software
P.O. Box 1219
Sausalito, CA 94966
800-523-2702

Blue Lance
1700 West Loop South, Suite 700
Houston, TX 77027
713-680-1187

Brightwork Development
766 Shrewsbury Avenue, Jerral Center West
Tinton Falls, NJ 07724
800-552-9876

Centel Federal Systems
11400 Commerce Park Drive
Reston, VA 22091
800-843-1132

Chi/Cor Information Management
300 South Wacker Drive
Chicago, IL 60606
800-448-8777

Citadel Systems
P.O. Box 7219
The Woodlands, TX 77387
800-962-0701

Command Software Systems
1061 East Indiantown Road, Suite 510
Jupiter, FL 33477
800-423-9147

Crystal Point
22122 20th Avenue, SE, Suite 148
Bothell, WA 98021
206-487-3656

Datamedia
20 Trafalgar Square
Nashua, NH 03063
800-362-4636

Digital Equipment Corporation
146 Main Street
Maynard, MA 01754
800-343-4040

IC Engineering
P.O. Box 321
Owings Mills, MD 21117
301-363-8748

Magna
2540 North First Street, Suite 302
San Jose, CA 95131
408-465-2500

Microcom
500 River Ridge Drive
Norwood, MA 02062
800-822-8224

Microtest
3519 East Shea Boulevard, Suite 134
Phoenix, AZ 85028
800-526-9675

NETinc
P.O. Box 271105
Houston, TX 77277
713-974-1810

Network-1
P.O. Box 8370
Long Island City, NY 11101
800-638-9751

Ontrack Computer Systems
6321 Bury Drive, Suites 15–19
Eden Prairie, MN 55346
800-752-1333

Rainbow Technologies
9292 Jeronimo Road
Irvine, CA 92718
800-852-8569

RG Software Systems
6900 East Camelback Road, Suite 630
Scottsdale, AZ 85251
602-423-8000

Trend Micro Devices
2421 West 205th Street, Suite D-100
Torrance, CA 90501
800-228-5651

Server Management Software

3Com
5400 Bayfront Plaza
Santa Clara, CA 95052
800-638-3266

Antares Electronics
One Antares Drive, Suite 400
Nepean, Ontario K2E 8C4
800-267-4261

Banyan Systems
120 Flanders Road
Westborough, MA 01581
508-898-1000

Blue Lance
1700 West Loop South, Suite 700
Houston, TX 77027
713-680-1187

Cheyenne Software
55 Bryant Avenue
Roslyn, NY 11576
800-243-9462

Citadel Systems
P.O. Box 7219
The Woodlands, TX 77387
800-962-0701

Computer Aided Business Solutions
17000 South Golden Road
Golden, CO 80401
303-279-1868

Computer Software Solutions
11676 Nebraska Avenue
Los Angeles, CA 90025
213-473-6300

Daystrom Data Products
405 Tarrytown Road, Suite 414
White Plains, NY 10607
914-896-6564

Elgar
9250 Brown Deer Road
San Diego, CA 92121
800-733-5427

Fresh Technology Group
1478 North Tech Boulevard, Suite 101
Gilbert, AZ 85234
602-497-4200

Frye Computer Systems
19 Temple Place
Boston, MA 02111
800-234-3793

Gateway Communications
2941 Alton Avenue
Irvine, CA 92714
800-367-6555

Intel, LAN Enhancements
C03-07, 5200 Northeast Elam Young Parkway
Hillsboro, OR 97124
800-525-3019

Knozall Systems
375 East Elliot Road, Suite 10
Chandler, AZ 85225
800-545-0006

NETinc
P.O. Box 271105
Houston, TX 77277
713-974-1810

Network Compatibility Group
130 East Wilson Bridge Road, Suite 100
Columbus, OH 43805
614-436-2962

Novell
122 East 1700 South
Provo, UT 84606
800-638-9273

Ontrack Computer Systems
6321 Bury Drive, Suites 15–19
Eden Prairie, MN 55346
800-752-1333

Preferred Systems
15 River Road, Suite 110
Wilton, CT 06897
800-222-7638

Sarbec
12326 Deerbrook
Austin, TX 78750

Server Technology
2332-B Walsh Avenue
Santa Clara, CA 95051
800-835-1515

Standard Microsystems Corporation
8105 Irvine Center Drive
Irvine, CA 92718
714-932-5000

TouchStone Software
2130 Main Street, Suite 250
Huntington Beach, CA 92648
800-531-0450

Trellis
85 Main Street
Hopkinton, MA 01748
508-435-3066

SNA Mainframe Gateways

Apple Computer
20525 Mariani Avenue
Cupertino, CA 95014
800-776-2333

Attachmente
13231 Southeast 36th Street
Bellevue, WA 98006
800-426-6283

Avatar
65 South Street
Hopkinton, MA 01748
800-282-3270

Banyan Systems
120 Flanders Road
Westborough, MA 01581
508-898-1000

Barr Systems
4131 Northwest 28th Lane
Gainesville, FL 32606
800-227-7797

Computer Logics
31200 Carter Street
Cleveland, OH 44139
216-349-8600

Data Interface Systems
8701 North MoPac Expressway, Suite 415
Austin, TX 78759
800-351-4244

Data Switch
One Enterprise Drive
Shelton, CT 06484
800-328-3279

DCA
1000 Alderman Drive
Alpharetta, GA 30202
800-348-3221

Digital Equipment Corporation
146 Main Street
Maynard, MA 01754
800-343-4040

Eicon Technology
2196 32nd Avenue
Montreal, Quebec H8T 3H7
514-631-2592

Gateway Communications
2941 Alton Avenue
Irvine, CA 92714
800-367-6555

Gupta Technologies
1040 Marsh Road
Menlo Park, CA 94025
800-876-3267

IBM
Old Orchard Road
Armonk, NY 10504
800-426-2468
800-426-3333

ICOT
P.O. Box 5143
San Jose, CA 95105
408-433-3300

McData
310 Interlocken Parkway
Broomfield, CO 80021
800-545-5773

Micro Integration
215 Paca Street
Cumberland, MD 21502
800-237-5888

Microsoft
One Microsoft Way
Redmond, WA 98052
800-227-6444

Multi-Tech Systems
2205 Woodale Drive
Mounds View, MN 55112
800-328-9717

National Semiconductor
2900 Semiconductor Drive, M/S 25-155
Santa Clara, CA 95052
800-538-8510

NCR
1334 South Patterson Boulevard
Dayton, OH 45479
513-445-5000

NDC Communications
2860 Zanker Road, Suite 1118
San Jose, CA 95134
408-428-9108

Network Software Associates
31 Technology Drive, Second Floor
Irvine, CA 92718
714-753-0800

Novell
122 East 1700 South
Provo, UT 84606
800-638-9273

OpenConnect Systems
2033 Chennauylt Drive
Dallas, TX 75006
214-490-4090

Rabbit Software
7 Great Valley Parkway
Malvern, PA 19355
800-722-2482

Sun Microsystems
2550 Garcia Avenue
Mountain View, CA 94043
800-872-4786

Tri-Data Systems
3270 Scott Boulevard
Santa Clara, CA 95054
800-874-3282

Software Development

CGI Systems
One Blue Hill Plaza
Pearl River, NY 10965
800-722-1866

Digital Equipment Corporation
146 Main Street
Maynard, MA 01754
800-343-4040

Exim Services
P.O. Box 5417
Clinton, NJ 08809
908-735-7640

Intersolv
3200 Tower Oaks Boulevard
Rockville, MD 20852
800-547-4000

Mortice Kern Systems
35 Keng Street North
Waterloo, Ontario N2J 2W9
800-265-2797

Netwise
2477 55th Street
Boulder, CO 80301
800-733-7722

Network-1
P.O. Box 8370
Long Island City, NY 11101
800-638-9751

Peerlogic
555 Deharo Street, Suite 300
San Francisco, CA 94107
415-626-4545

Saros
10900 Northeast Eighth Street, Suite 700
Bellevue, WA 98004
800-827-2767

SilverWare
3010 LBJ Freeway, Suite 740
Dallas, TX 75234
214-247-0131

Spectrum Concepts
150 Broadway
New York, NY 10038
800-365-9266

Tape-Backup Hardware

Advanced Digital Information Corporation
14737 Northeast 87th Street
Redmond, WA 98073
800-336-1233

Alloy Computer Products
165 Forest Street
Marlborough, MA 01752
800-800-2556

Colorado Memory Systems
800 South Taft Avenue
Loveland, CO 80537
800-346-9881

Compaq Computer
P.O. Box 692000
Houston, TX 77069
800-231-0900

Consan
14625 Martin Drive
Eden Prairie, MN 55344
800-229-3475

Contemporary Cybernetics Group
11846 Rock Landing
Newport News, VA 23606
804-873-9000

Datapoint
8400 Datapoint Drive
San Antonio, TX 78229
800-733-1500

Emerald Systems
12230 World Trade Drive
San Diego, CA 92128
619-673-2161

Emeritus Technologies
2750 North Clovis Avenue, Suite 126
Fresno, CA 93727
800-228-9236

Exabyte
1685 38th Street
Boulder, CO 80301
303-447-7366

Giga Trend
2234 Rutherford Road
Carlsbad, CA 92008
619-931-9122

Irwin Magnetic Systems
2101 Commonwealth Boulevard
Ann Arbor, MI 48105
313-930-9000

Lagacy Storage Systems
200 Butterfield Drive, Unit B
Ashland, MA 01721
508-881-6442

Maynard Electronics
36 Skyline Drive
Lake Mary, FL 32746
800-821-8782

MicroNet Technology
20 Mason Street
Irvine, CA 92718
714-837-6033

Mountain Network Solutions
240 East Hacienda Avenue
Campbell, CA 95008
800-458-0300

Palindrome
850 East Diehi Road
Naperville, IL 60638
708-505-3300

Perisol Technology
3350 Scott Boulevard, Building 1201
Santa Clara, CA 95054
800-447-8226

Sigen
479 Macara Avenue, Suite 803
Sunnyvale, CA 94086
408-737-3904

Sony Computer Peripheral Products
655 River Oaks Parkway
San Jose, CA 95134
408-432-0190

Sysgen
556 Gibraltar Drive
Milpitas, CA 95035
800-821-2151

Tallgrass Technologies
11100 West 82nd Street
Lenexa, KS 66214
800-736-6002

Tecmar
6225 Cochran Road
Solon, OH 44139
800-624-8560

Transitional Technology
5401 East La Palma Avenue
Anaheim, CA 92807
714-693-1133

Unisys
P.O. Box 500
Blue Bell, PA 19424
215-986-4011

Tape-Backup Software

Advanced Digital Information Corporation
14737 Northeast 87th Street
Redmond, WA 98073
800-336-1233

AT&T Bell Laboratories
185 Monmouth Parkway West
Long Branch, NJ 07784
908-870-7234

Cheyenne Software
55 Bryant Avenue
Roslyn, NY 11576
800-243-9462

Colorado Memory Systems
800 South Taft Avenue
Loveland, CO 80537
800-346-9881

Computertime Network
10340 Cote De Liesse
Montreal, Quebec H8T 1A3
800-465-4734

Core
7171 North Federal Highway
Boca Raton, FL 33487
407-997-6055

Datapoint
8400 Datapoint Drive
San Antonio, TX 78229
800-733-1500

Distinct
14082 Loma Rio Drive
Saratoga, CA 95070
408-741-0781

Emeritus Technologies
2750 North Clovis Avenue, Suite 126
Fresno, CA 93727
800-228-9236

Gazelle Systems
305 North 500 West
Provo, UT 84601
800-786-3278

Giga Trend
2234 Rutherford Road
Carlsbad, CA 92008
619-931-9122

Irwin Magnetic Systems
2101 Commonwealth Boulevard
Ann Arbor, MI 48105
313-930-9000

Legato Systems
260 Sheridan Avenue
Palo Alto, CA 94306
415-329-8898

Maynard Electronics
36 Skyline Drive
Lake Mary, FL 32746
800-821-8782

Mountain Network Solutions
240 East Hacienda Avenue
Campbell, CA 95008
800-458-0300

Palindrome
850 East Diehi Road
Naperville, IL 60638
708-505-3300

SitBack Technologies
9290 Bond Street, Suite 104
Overland Park, KS 66214

Sun Microsystems
2550 Garcia Avenue
Mountain View, CA 94043
800-872-4786

Sysgen
556 Gibraltar Drive
Milpitas, CA 95035
800-821-2151

Sytron
1334 Flanders Road
Westborough, MA 01581
508-898-0100

Tallgrass Technologies
11100 West 82nd Street
Lenexa, KS 66214
800-736-6002

Tecmar
6225 Cochran Road
Solon, OH 44139
800-624-8560

Transitional Technology
5401 East La Palma Avenue
Anaheim, CA 92807
714-693-1133

Ultinet Development
P.O. Box 34016
Los Angeles, CA 90034
213-204-0111

Unisys
P.O. Box 500
Blue Bell, PA 19424
215-986-4011

TCP/IP Software

Apple Computer
20525 Mariani Avenue
Cupertino, CA 95014
800-776-2333

Banyan Systems
120 Flanders Road
Westborough, MA 01581
508-898-1000

Beame and Whiteside Software
P.O. Box 8130
Dundas, Ontario L9H 5W9
416-648-6556

Datapoint
8400 Datapoint Drive
San Antonio, TX 78229
800-733-1500

Distinct
14082 Loma Rio Drive
Saratoga, CA 95070
408-741-0781

Fibronics
One Communications Way
Hyannis, MA 12601
800-327-9526

Frontier Technologies
10201 North Port Washington Road, 13 West
Mequon, WI 53092
414-241-4555

FTP Software
338 Main Street
Wakefield, MA 01880
617-246-0900

Hughes LAN Systems
1225 Charleston Road
Mountain View, CA 94043
415-966-7300

IBM
Old Orchard Road
Armonk, NY 10504
800-426-2468
800-426-3333

In-Net
15150 Avenue of Science, Suite 100
San Diego, CA 92128
800-283-3334

Interactive Systems
1901 North Naper Boulevard
Naperville, IL 60563
800-524-8649

Network Research
2380 North Rose Avenue
Oxnard, CA 93030
800-541-9508

Novell
122 East 1700 South
Provo, UT 84606
800-638-9273

OpenConnect Systems
2033 Chennauylt Drive
Dallas, TX 75006
214-490-4090

Racal Interlan
155 Swanson Road
Boxborough, MA 01719
800-526-8255

Sun Microsystems
2550 Garcia Avenue
Mountain View, CA 94043
800-872-4786

TGV
603 Mission Street
Santa Cruz, CA 95060
800-848-3440

Unisys
P.O. Box 500
Blue Bell, PA 19424
215-986-4011

Walker Richer and Quinn
2815 Eastlake Avenue East
Seattle, WA 98102
800-872-2829

Wireless Networks

BICC Communications
103 Millbury Street
Auburn, MA 01501
800-447-6526

California Microwave
985 Almanor Avenue
Sunnyvale, CA 94086
800-772-5465

Motorola
3215 Wilke Road
Arlington Heights, IL 60004
800-233-0877

NCR
1334 South Patterson Boulevard
Dayton, OH 45479
513-445-5000

Photonics
200 East Hacienda Avenue
Campbell, CA 95008
408-370-3033

PureData
180 West Beaver Creek Road
Richmond Hill, Ontario L4B 1B4
416-731-6444

Telesystems SLW
85 Scarsdale Road, Suite 201
Don Mills, Ontario M3B 2R2
416-441-9966

Windata
10 Bearfoot Road
Northborough, MA 01532
508-393-3330

Wiring Hubs

3Com
5400 Bayfront Plaza
Santa Clara, CA 95052
800-638-3266

Accton Technology
46750 Fremont Boulevard, Building 104
Fremont, CA 94538
800-926-9288

Accunetics
190 Blydenburgh Road
Islandia, NY 11722
516-348-1566

ADC Kentrox
P.O. Box 10704
Portland, OR 97210
800-325-0425

Addtron Technology
46560 Fremont Boulevard, Suite 303
Fremont, CA 94538
415-770-0120

AIDI Systems
2121 Ringwood Avenue
San Jose, CA 95131
800-228-0530

Allied Telesis
575 East Middlefield Road
Mountain View, CA 94043
800-424-4284

American Research
1101 Monterey Pass Road
Monterey Park, CA 91754
213-269-1174

AMP
P.O. Box 3608, M/S 210-26
Harrisburg, PA 17105
800-522-6752

Andrew
2771 Plaza Del Amo
Torrance, CA 90503
800-733-0331

Asante Technologies
404 Tasman Drive
Tucson, AZ 85704
800-837-2617

Belkin Components
1303 Walnut Parkway
Compton, CA 90220
800-223-5546

BICC Communications
103 Millbury Street
Auburn, MA 01501
800-447-6526

Cabletron Systems
35 Industrial Way
P.O. Box 5005
Rochester, NH 03867
603-332-4616

Canary Communications
1435 Kill Circle
San Jose, CA 95112
408-453-9201

Chipcom
118 Turnpike Road
Southborough, MA 01772
800-228-9930

CNet Technology
2199 Zanker Road
San Jose, CA 95131
800-486-2638

Codenoll Technology
1086 North Broadway
Yonkers, NY 10701
914-965-9811

Compex
4055 East La Palma, Suite C
Anaheim, CA 92807
714-630-7302

Datapoint
8400 Datapoint Drive
San Antonio, TX 78229
800-733-1500

Data Switch
One Enterprise Drive
Shelton, CT 06484
800-328-3279

David Systems
701 East Evelyn Avenue
Sunnyvale, CA 94086
800-762-7848

Digital Equipment Corporation
146 Main Street
Maynard, MA 01754
800-343-4040

D-Link Systems
5 Musick
Irvine, CA 92718
714-455-1688

DuPont Electro-Optic Products
P.O. Box 13625
Research Triangle Park, NC 27709
800-888-5261

Exos Products
207 South Peyton Street
Alexandria, VA 22134
800-255-5967

Farallon Computing
2000 Powell Street, Suite 600
Emeryville, CA 94608
415-596-9020

Fibermux
9310 Topanga Canyon Boulevard
Chatsworth, CA 91311
818-709-6000

Garrett Communications
3375 Scott Boulevard
Santa Clara, CA 95054
408-980-9752

Gateway Communications
2941 Alton Avenue
Irvine, CA 92714
800-367-6555

General Technology
415 Pineda Court
Melbourne, FL 32940
800-274-2733

Graybar Electric
34 North Meramec
Clayton, MO 63105
314-727-3900

Hewlett-Packard
19310 Pruneridge
Cupertino, CA 95014
800-752-0900

Hong Technologies
P.O. Box 1268
Mountain Veiw, CA 94042
415-964-0100

IBM
Old Orchard Road
Armonk, NY 10504
800-426-2468
800-426-3333

Intellicom
20415 Nordhoff Street
Chatsworth, CA 91311
818-407-3900

Interphase
13800 Seniac
Dallas, TX 75234

Lancast/Casat Technology
10 Northern Boulevard, Unit 5
Amherst, NH 03031
800-752-2768

Lanmaster
1401 North 14th Street
Temple, TX 76501
817-771-2124

Lannet Data Communications
7711 Center Avenue, Suite 600
Huntington Beach, CA 92647
800-969-4123

Link Computer
560 South Melrose Street
Placentia, CA 92670
714-993-0800

L & N Technologies
2899 Agoura Road, Suite 196
Westlake Village, CA 91361
805-494-4191

Luxcom
3249 Laurelview Court
Fremont, CA 94538
415-770-3300

Lynn Products
1601 Loch Ness Place
Torrance, CA 90501
800-634-5093

Madge Networks
42 Airport Parkway
San Jose, CA 95110
800-876-2343

MBA Technque
Number 239-4 Kin Hwa Street
Taipei, Taiwan R.O.C.
8862-341-1260

Mitsubishi Cable America
520 Madison Avenue
New York, NY 10022
212-605-2392

Multi-Tech Systems
2205 Woodale Drive
Mounds View, MN 55112
800-328-9717

Mux Lab
165 Graveline Road
St. Laurent, Quebec H4T 1R3
800-361-1965

NDC Communications
2860 Zanker Road, Suite 1118
San Jose, CA 95134
408-428-9108

Netcom Systems
21828 Lassen Street, Unit F
Chatsworth, CA 91311
818-700-0111

Network Interface
15019 West 95th Street
Lenexa, KS 66215
800-343-2853

Network Systems
7600 Boone Avenue North
Minneapolis, MN 55428
612-424-4888

NetWorth
8101 Ridgepoint Drive, Suite 107
Irving, TX 75063
214-869-1331

Niwot Networks
5595 Arapahoe, Suite G
Boulder, CO 80303
303-444-7765

North Hills
575 Underhill Boulevard
Syosset, NY 11791
800-753-4526

Nuvotech
2015 Bridgeway
Sausalito, CA 94965
800-468-8683

Optical Data Systems
1101 East Arapahoe
Richardson, TX 75081
214-234-6400

Pivotal Technologies
18240 Purdue Drive
Saratoga, CA 95070
800-445-4628

Plexcom
65 Moreland Road
Simi Valley, CA 93065
805-522-3333

Proteon
2 Technology Drive
Westborough, MA 01581
508-898-2800

PureData
180 West Beaver Creek Road
Richmond Hill, Ontario L4B 1B4
416-731-6444

Racal Interlan
155 Swanson Road
Boxborough, MA 01719
800-526-8255

Raylan
120 Independence Drive
Menlo Park, CA 94025
800-472-9526

South Hills Datacomm
760 Beechnut Drive
Pittsburgh, PA 15205
800-245-6215

Standard Microsystems
35 Marcus Boulevard
Hauppauge, NY 11788
516-273-3100

Star-Tek
71 Lynan Street
Northborough, MA 01532
800-225-8528

Synertics
85 Tangeway Road
North Billerica, MA 01862
508-670-9009

SynOptics Communications
4401 Great America Parkway
P.O. Box 51815
Santa Clara, CA 95052
800-776-6895

TCL
41829 Albrae Street
Fremont, CA 94538
415-657-3800

Thomas-Conrad
1908-R Dramer Lane
Austin, TX 78758
800-332-8683

Tiara Computer Systems
1091 Shoreline Boulevard
Mountain View, CA 94043
800-638-4272

Timeplex
400 Chestnut Ridge Road
Woodcliff Lake, NJ 07675
800-755-8526

Transition Engineering
7448 West 78th Street
Edina, MN 55439
800-325-2725

Tribe Computer Works
1195 Park Avenue
Emeryville, CA 94608
415-547-3874

Tutankhamon Electronics
1800 Ardith Drive
Pleasant Hill, CA 94523
415-682-6510

Ungermann-Bass
3900 Freedom Circle
Santa Clara, CA 95054
800-873-6381

Unicom Electric
11980 Telegraph Road, Suite 103
Santa Fe Springs, CA 90670
800-346-6668

Workgroup Software

AT&T
One Speedwell Avenue
Morristown, NJ 07960
800-247-1212

Enable Software/Higgins Group
1150 Marina Village Parkway, Suite 101
Alameda, CA 94501
800-854-2807

Lotus Development
55 Cambridge Parkway
Cambridge, MA 02142
800-343-5414

Novell
122 East 1700 South
Provo, UT 84606
800-638-9273

Sun Microsystems
2550 Garcia Avenue
Mountain View, CA 94043
800-872-4786

X.25 Gateways

3Com
5400 Bayfront Plaza
Santa Clara, CA 95052
800-638-3266

Amnet
1881 Worcester Road
Framingham, MA 01701
508-876-6306

Apple Computer
20525 Mariani Avenue
Cupertino, CA 95014
800-776-2333

Banyan Systems
120 Flanders Road
Westborough, MA 01581
508-898-1000

Datapoint
8400 Datapoint Drive
San Antonio, TX 78229
800-733-1500

David Systems
701 East Evelyn Avenue
Sunnyvale, CA 94086
800-762-7848

Digital Equipment Corporation
146 Main Street
Maynard, MA 01754
800-343-4040

Eicon Technology
2196 32nd Avenue
Montreal, Quebec H8T 3H7
514-631-2592

Frontier Technologies
10201 North Port Washington Road, 13 West
Mequon, WI 53092
414-241-4555

Gateway Communications
2941 Alton Avenue
Irvine, CA 92714
800-367-6555

IBM
Old Orchard Road
Armonk, NY 10504
800-426-2468
800-426-3333

ICOT
P.O. Box 5143
San Jose, CA 95105
408-433-3300

J & L Information Systems
9238 Deering Avenue
Chatsworth, CA 91311
818-709-1778

Network Software Associates
39 Argonaut
Laguna Hills, CA 92656
800-352-3270

Novell
122 East 1700 South
Provo, UT 84606
800-638-9273

Sun Microsystems
2550 Garcia Avenue
Mountain View, CA 94043
800-872-4786

Index

Protocol overhead via broadcast messaging, 167–68
Protocol suites, performance issues and, 59, 172
Protocol translation, 45
Proxy connections, 145, 146

Radiation emissions, 78, 216–17
Radio-oriented networks, 76
Radio signals, 2
Receiving stations, 110
Redundancy in bridges, 98–99, 126
Reflectometer, time domain (TDR), 135–36
Remote procedure calls, 159
Repeaters, 7
    802.3-compliant, 10
    fiber, 188–89, 190
    multiport, 88–89, 97–98, 100
    multiport bridges and, 96–97
    replacing with bridges, 91
Resource utilization, 3
Retooling
    Ethernet/802.3, 74–75
    network planning and, 72–73
Retransmissions, 116, 132, 177–78
    loading and, 131–32
    rules of, 108–9
RG-58A/U (thinwire) cable, 5, 15, 80, 81, 219
RG-8 (thickwire) cable, 4, 15
RJ-45 connector, 6
Routers, switching bridges vs., 120–22
Routing algorithms, 93–94
RSA (Rivest-Shamir-Adelman) Public Key Scheme, 150

SAS, 211
"Score-and-break" technique, 214
SCS, 42
SDLC, 35
Security, 142–62
    on cableless telephone systems, 158–59
    cluster security, 159
    common wire plant infiltration, 161
    computer crime and, 143–44
    of distributed database access, 159–60
    encryption, 148–52
    fax infiltration, 160
    features that cause security problems, 145–46

fiber and, 154–55
misuse of protocols and, 155
multicooperative system security, 161–62
multiprotocol networks and, 49–51
need for, 142
network topology security, 156
new and mysterious protocols or nodes and, 156–57
node interaction and, 155–56
pack-content, 146–47
PBX security, 158
piggybacking, 158
potential solution for, 144–45
promiscuous mode and, 152–54
security packages causing security problems, 160–61
session security, 147–48
"trap door" insertions from network components, 157
virus and worm propagation, 157
wireless local area networks and, 154
Security tools, 94–95
Server(s)
    configuration and management of, 164–65
    location of, 172
Server performance, 163–73
    handling, 171–73
    interrupts and, 165–71
    protocol overhead via broadcast messaging, 167–68
Session disconnects, 116
Session piggybacking, 158
Session security, 147–48
SFD, 11
Shadowed logic, 126
Shielded twisted pair cable (STP), 215, 218
    unshielded twisted pair vs., 77–79
Signaling techniques, 75
Signal Quality Error Enabled, 139–40
Signal quality error (SQE), 10, 114, 137–41
    collision presence test (CPT) for, 139–40
    enabling vs. disabling, 140–41
    transceiver cable, 137–39
    understanding, 137
    vendor inconsistency and, 140
Single-attachment stations (SAS), 211
Sliding-lock connector, 17
Slotted ALOHA, 2
SMP, 165–66

"Trap door" insertions, 157
Triangular irregular networks (TINs), 65
TTP, 209
Tuning of system resources, improper, 130–31
Twisted-pair cables
    FDDI over, 215–18, 221
    installation problems, 80–83
    network planning and, 76–84
    number of pairs of, 83–84
    repairing, 191
    security infiltration of, 161
    shielded (STP), 77–79, 215, 218
    unshielded (UTP), 5, 77–79, 105, 216–18
Twisted-pair concentrators, 23
TYPE field, 12, 13

Unit Control Block (UCB), 156
University of Hawaii, 2, 84
Unshielded twisted pair (UTP) cable, 5,
    216–18
    emissions regulation and, 216–17
    noise and, 105, 216
    shielded twisted pair vs., 77–79
Upgrades, 73

V2.0 Digital-Intel-Xerox (DIX) standard, 140
Vaporware, 28, 30
VAX-11/780, 73
VAX 6300 system, 166
VAX 6320 system, 167–69

VAX 8700 system, 170–71
VAX 8810 system, 170
VAXClusters, 159, 170
VAXStation 4000, 73–74
Vendors
    consortiums, 8
    network design services, 70
Verification, session, 147–48
Version numbers, 73
Virtual terminal protocols, 41–42
Viruses, 25, 157
VMS, 165, 177
VMS VPA, 135

Wave shaping, 217
Wide-area capabilities, 7
Windows NT, 159
Wireless networks, 84–86
    configuration of, 7
    FDDI, 218–19, 220
    security and, 154
Wireless PBXs, 85
Workgroup placement, 88–90, 100–101, 172
Workstations, diskless, 131, 202
Worm propagation, 157

X.25 communications, 150
X.500 directory services, 31
Xerox, 3–4, 8

Trademarks

Altair is a trademark of Motorola.

Apple Interpoll, LocalTalk, and Macintosh are trademarks of Apple Computer.

DEC, DECmcc, DECnet, DECServer, DECUS, DELNI, DEMPR, Enterprise Management Architecture (EMA), OpenVMS, PathWorks, PDP, RBMS, TSM, VAX, VAXCluster, VMS, and VT are trademarks of Digital Equipment Corporation.

DES is a copyrighted term of the American National Standards Institute.

EtherExpress is a trademark of Intel.

Ethernet is a trademark of Xerox Corporation.

EtherPeek is a trademark of A.G. Group.

EtherSwitch is a trademark of Cisco Systems.

EtherTwist, HP 4972A, and LANProbe are trademarks of Hewlett-Packard Corporation.

IBM, IBM-PC, PC Network, PS/2, SNA Netview, Systems Network Architecture (SNA), and VTAM are trademarks of International Business Machines Corporation.

LANalyzer, NetWare, NetWare 386, Novell, and Portable NetWare are trademarks of Novell.

LAN Manager, MS-DOS, MS-NET, and MS-Windows are trademarks of Microsoft Corporation.

Network Event Manager (NEM), Network Mapping Utility (NMU), Network Performance Advisor (NPA), Network Planning Utility (NPU), and Network Security Monitor (NSM) are trademarks of Network-1 Software and Technology, Inc.

Network Professor is a trademark of Technically Elite Concepts.

Sniffer is a trademark of Network General.

X Window is a trademark of the X/Open Consortium.

Other products not listed here may be trademarks of their respective owners.